Junior High Edition

BLEST ARE WE

The Story of Jesus

Series Authors
Rev. Richard N. Fragomeni, Ph.D.
Maureen Gallagher, Ph.D.
Jeannine Goggin, M.P.S.
Michael P. Horan, Ph.D.

Scripture Co-editor and Consultant
Maria Pascuzzi, SSL, S.T.D.

Multicultural Consultant
Angela Erevia, MCDP, M.R.E.

*The Ad Hoc Committee to Oversee the Use of the Catechism,
United States Conference of Catholic Bishops, has found this catechetical
series, copyright 2003, to be in conformity with the
Catechism of the Catholic Church.*

SILVER BURDETT GINN RELIGION
A SCOTT FORESMAN IMPRINT
PARSIPPANY, NJ

BLEST ARE WE

Contributing Writer
Ellen Marconi

Contributing Authors
Get Connected: Greg "Dobie" Moser
We Care: Richard Reichert, M.A.
Unit Organizers and Reviews: Joyce A. Crider
Feasts and Seasons: Janie Gustafson, Ph.D.
Our Catholic Teachings: Richard Reichert, M.A.

Advisory Board
Suzy R. Eyler, M.A.; Patricia M. Feeley, SSJ, M.A.; Edmund F. Gordon; Rev. Daniel Kelly; Joni Kohn O'Brien; Dorothy Sanning; Barry Thornton; Cris V. Villapando, D.Min.

Nihil Obstat
M. Kathleen Flanagan, SC, Ph.D.
Ellen Joyce, SC, Ph.D.
Censors Librorum

Imprimatur
✠ Most Reverend Frank J. Rodimer
Bishop of Paterson
April 19, 2002

Music Advisor
Kathryn M. Lewis

Acknowledgments

Excerpts from *The New American Bible with Revised New Testament* © 1991, 1986, 1970 by the Confraternity of Christian Doctrine, Washington, D.C., used with permission. All rights reserved. All adaptations of Scripture are based on *The New American Bible with Revised New Testament*.

Excerpts from the English translation of the *Rite of Penance* © 1974, International Committee on English in the Liturgy, Inc. (ICEL); excerpts from the English translation of the *Rite of Confirmation*, Second Edition © 1975, ICEL; excerpts from the English translation of the *Rite of Marriage* © 1969, ICEL; excerpts from *Pastoral Care of the Sick: Rites of Anointing and Viaticum* © 1982, ICEL; excerpts from the English translation of the *Rite of Baptism for Children* © 1969, ICEL; excerpts from the English translation of *The Roman Missal*, Second Edition © 1985, ICEL.

Excerpts from the English translation of the *Catechism of the Catholic Church* © 1994, 1997, United States Conference of Catholic Bishops. Libreria Editrice Vaticana. Used with permission. All rights reserved.

Music selections copyrighted and/or administered by GIA Publications are used with permission of GIA Publications, Inc., 7404 S. Mason Avenue, Chicago, IL 60638-9927. Music selections copyrighted and/or administered by World Library Publications are used with permission of World Library Publications, 3825 N. Willow Road, Schiller Park, IL 60176-0703. Please refer to songs for specific copyright dates and information.

Bob Keeler, "Remembering Chrissie." *Catholic Peace Voice*, Fall 1999, p. 8; "Our Mission." Salesians of Don Bosco, www.salesians.org/salesian.htm; "Don Bosco's Thoughts." Mother House of the Salesians in Turin-Valdocco, www.donbosco-torino.it/eng/page8.html; "Black Catholics of the 19th–20th Centuries." Holy Angels Church, www.holyangels.com/SaintGuiseppineJosephineBakhita.htm; "Listening to What Bakhita Says." The National Black Catholic Congress, www.nbccongress.org/facts/josephine.htm; Grant Williams, "Giving Away a Personal Treasury." *The Chronicle of Philanthropy*, Thursday, June 18, 1998, www.philanthropy.com/free/articles/v10/i17/1700101.htm; Matthew Bunson et al., *John Paul II's Book of Saints*. Huntington, IN: Our Sunday Visitor, Inc., 1999, pp. 112, 113; "Eileen Egan, 88, Peace and Justice Activist, Served Disadvantaged." *Catholic New York*, October 12, 2000, p. 45; "Katharine Drexel." The Catholic Community Forum, www.catholic-forum.com/saints/saintk03.htm; "The Church: called to repentance; called to prophesy." Salt of the Earth, http://salt.claretianpubs.org/romero/rindex.html; "Catholic Wisdom: Quotes from Our Saints." Saint Michael Center for the Blessed Virgin Mary, www.smcenter.org/teachings_saints_quotes.htm; Excerpt from *Anne Frank, The Diary of a Young Girl (The Definitive Edition)* © 1991, pp. 72–73, 332. New York, NY: Doubleday, 1995, permission pending; David Zimmerman, "Christian musician Smith finds salvation and success." *USA Today*, October 17, 1996, Spaceports, http://www.usatoday.com/life/enter/music/lem227.htm; "Cesar E. Chavez." Chicana/o Latina/o Net, University of California, Riverside, CA, http://www.sscnet.ucla.edu/chavez/; Paul Gray, "Empire of the Spirit" (Man of the Year). *TIME* Domestic, December 26, 1994, Volume 144, No. 26, Catholic.net, www.catholic.net/RCC/News/Time_Mag/cover.html; Pope John Paul II, "The Church Must Learn to Cope with Computer Culture." Eternal World Television Network, Inc., www.ewtn.com/library/PAPALDOC/JP2COMPU.HTM; *Catholic Digest*, May 2001, p. 33; Jack Canfield et al., *Chicken Soup for the Preteen Soul*. Deerfield Beach, FL: Health Communications, Inc., 2000, pp. 6–7, 8, 9; Adaptation from "In the Spirit of Jesus" from *This Is Our Faith*, Grade 7, by Janaan Manternach et al., pp. 372, 373. Copyright © 1998 Silver Burdett Ginn, Inc. Reprinted by permission of Pearson Education, Inc; "What Is Doctors Without Borders/Médecins Sans Frontières (MSF)?" Doctors Without Borders/Médecins Sans Frontières (MSF), www.doctorswithoutborders.org/about/; John Burger, "Father Judge, a Hero, Died a Hero's Death." *National Catholic Register*, 9/23/01–9/29/02, www.ncregister.com/Register_News/Burger-Judge.htm; Jim Forest, "A Biography of Dorothy Day." The Catholic Worker Movement, www.catholicworker.org/dorothyday/ddbiographytext.cfm?Number=72;"Christian music moves against current to go mainstream." CNN, December 14, 2002, www.cnn.com/2000/SHOWBIZ/Music/12/14/wb.christian/#1; ºDjibril Diallo, "From the Editor-in-Chief." *Choices*, September 2001, p. 2, http://www.undp.org/dpa/choices/; Alberto Bovone, Edward Nowak, "Vatican Decree on the Heroic Virtues of Venerable Padre Pio." The National Centre for Padre Pio, http://www.ncfpp.com/decree1.html; Reverend John C. Flynn, homily at Funeral Mass for Sister Barbara Ann Ford, S.C; "Sarah Hart Bio." Official Sarah Hart Web site, www.madbear.com/sarahhart/biography.html; Mary T. Clark, *An Aquinas Reader*. Garden City, NY: Doubleday & Company, Inc., 1972, p. 534; "Celebrate Humanity—2002: Johann Koss." Official Web site of the Olympic Movement, www.olympic.org/uk/passion/humanity/koss_uk.asp; *The Book of Saints*. Farmingdale, NY: The Regina Press, 1986, pp. 9, 10, 12, 44, 143, 231–232; "Mission Statement." Harry Chapin Foundation, www.harrysfriends.com/hcf/details1.htm; "Salesian Cooperator, Sean Devereux." Salesian Missions, www.salesianmissions.org/salesians/st/sea.htm; "The Story." The Taizé Community, www.taize.fr/en/encomhst.htm; Varla Ventura, *Sheroes: Bold, Brash, and Absolutely Unabashed Superwomen from Susan B. Anthony to Xena*. Berkeley, CA: Conari Press, 1998, pp. 103, 104; Bill Howard, "The New Musical Evangelization." *The Texas Catholic* © 2000, www.francescoproductions.com/articles/texasarticle/TexasCatholic.html; Information on Jeff Johnson provided by and printed with permission of Carmen Johnson.

In appreciation: St. Ann Melkite Catholic Church, West Paterson, NJ; St. Anselm Church, Wayside, NJ; St. Margaret Church, Morristown, NJ; St. Patrick Church, Yorktown Heights, NY

Credits

Design and Electronic Production: Kirchoff/Wohlberg, Inc.

Cover: Gene Plaisted, OSC, The Crosiers

Scripture Art: Tim Ladwig

Photos and Art: v, ix, 6–7, 22, 30, 47, 62, 70, 86–87, 102, 110, 126–127, 136–137, 142, 150, 166, 190–191, 247 Tim Ladwig vi, 242, 249, 250 David Young-Wolff, PhotoEdit ix, x, 72, 113 Scala/Art Resource, NY ix, xi-xiii Elizabeth Wolf, 183 Elizabeth Wolf ix, xvii, Cathy Melloan, PhotoEdit xiv-xvi, xvii Roman Dunets, 6, 46, 88, 96, 126, 144, 182 Roman Dunets 1 Nazareth Village (BR) Elizabeth Wolf, 4 Courtesy Sisters of St. Joseph at Brentwood 4, 20, 44, 60, 124, 164, 180 (T) Rick Stomoski/Carol Lee Stermer 5, 57, 163, 173, 177 Myrleen Ferguson Cate, PhotoEdit/Index Stock 8 Michael O'Neill McGrath, OSFS 9 Don Stevenson, Index Stock Imagery/PictureQuest 10 Benelux Press, b.v./eStock Photography/PictureQuest 12 Printed with permission of Steve Angrisano 12 Salesians of St. John Bosco 13 PhotoDisc 15, 98, 101, 241 Michael Newman, PhotoEdit 16 Canossian Sisters 17 Nancy Freeman 18 Don W. Faucett, Visuals Unlimited 20 Liaison Agency/Getty Images 21, 25, 239 Tony Freeman, PhotoEdit 24 Courtesy, German Resistance Memorial Center 26 Stone Images 27 John Chard, Stone 28 Maria Donahue/Courtesy, Eileen Egan 28 Doug Beasley, Beasley Photography 34 Mark Richards, PhotoEdit 35 Doug Wilson, Corbis 36, 53 John Hovell, KW 41 D. Michael Hostetler, Nazareth Village 43 Annie Griffiths Belt, Corbis 44 Leif Skoogfors, Corbis 45, 114, 146 Jeff Greenberg, Visuals Unlimited 45 Howard Davies, Corbis 48, 61, 64, 68, 92, 100, 108 AP/Wide World 49 Robert Casilla, KW 50 Mary Steinbacher, PhotoEdit 51 Michelle Bridwell, PhotoEdit 52 Archives of the Sisters of the Blessed Sacrament 52 Nancy Gordon, with permission of Mr. John A. Roberts 54, 174 Bill and Peggy Wittman © W.P. Wittman 55, 74, 134, 138, 206, 224, 234, 237, 238 Gene Plaisted, OSC, The Crosiers 56 Retuers NewMedia Inc./Corbis 58 Bohemian Nomad Picturemakers/Corbis 59 Caroline Penn, Corbis 60 Chr. Kaiser, Gutersloher Verlahgshaus 63, 141, ChromoSohm (Photo Researchers, Inc., Unicorn Stock Photos) 63 CLEO Freelance Photography 66 Joe McDonald, Corbis 67 Lucille Khornak, Index Stock Imagery 68 Philip Jon Bailey, Stock Boston 69 Tom and Dee Ann McCarthy, Unicorn Stock Photos 75, 189, 255 Steve Skjold, Skjold Photographs 81, 125 Morton Beebe, S.F./Corbis 84, 164, 180 Rick Stromoski, Carol Lee Stermer 84, 188 Catholic News Service 89 Paul Conklin, PhotoEdit 90 © Panoramic Images, Chicago 92, 228 Nancy Wiechec, Catholic News Service 93 Joe Rimkus, Jr., Catholic News Service 94, 145, 230 Bill Wittman © W.P. Wittman 97, 109, 130, 171 SuperStock 97 G.E., Rainbird Graphics, Inc. 97, 128 Christie's Images/SuperStock 105, 185, 204, 205, 231, 240, 253, 256 James L. Shaffer, PhotoEdit 106 Peter Weimann, Animals Animals/Earth Scenes 106, 222 Michael Di Giorgio 108, 172 Reuters NewMedia Inc/Corbis 112 Drawing and mosaic by Prof. Angelo Marelli, Casa Marelli Studios 115, 243 Corbis (Historical Picture Archive) 121 Rabbula Icon of Glory, Eparchy of Saint Maron of Brooklyn, Msgr. Ronald Beshara, Project Director/St Anthony's Maronite Catholic Church 123, 152 Alan Odie, PhotoEdit 124 Courtesy, Sisters of Charity of St. Vincent de Paul of New York 132 Ben Pearson, Merge Left/Tricia Scott-Sahler 132 Ann Piasecki, Catholic Explorer/Catholic News Service 133 Bill Aron, PhotoEdit 140 John Moss, Black Star 146 Robert van der Hilst, Corbis 148 Maria Davis, Angelina Productions 148 Bettmann/Corbis 149 Audrey Gibson, Visuals Unlimited 154 Gary Russ, Image Bank 161 (Bkgd) Corbis Media (C) Elizabeth Wolf 164 Salesian Missions 165 Michael Pole, Corbis 168 Seton Shrine Center 169 Jim Whitmer 170 Hanan Isachar, A.S.A.P. Ltd. 172 Sabine Leutenegger, Taize Community 172 Wade Jaynes, JesusGlue Ministries Inc., 2000 176 R. Crandall, The Image Works, Inc. 177 Spencer Grant, PhotoEdit 178 Joseph Sohm, ChromoSohm Inc./Corbis 180, 204, 254 A. Ramey, Unicorn Stock Photos 181 Luis Castaneda, Image Bank 184 North Wind Picture Archives 186 Francis/Donna Caldwell, Visuals Unlimited 187 Esther Baran, KW 188 Courtesy St. Cloud Visitor 189 Arvis Stewart, KW 92 Cloy Kent, Sisters of Mercy of the Americas 193 (C) Donna Perrone 194 Jan Stromme, PhotoEdit 195 Nathan Benn, Stock Boston 196 Tom Leonard/KW 201, 217 Charles J. Schisla 203 Philip Bailey, Corbis Stock Market 204 Richmond Times-Dispatch 207 Dennis Degnan, Corbis 208 Icon Courtesy of Holy Transfiguration Monastery 209 Rhoda Sidney, PhotoEdit 211 Howard L. Garrett, Rainbow 212, 220 Bill & Peggy Wittman © W.P. Wittman 214 Arena Chapel,Cappella degli Scrovegni, Padua, Italy/SuperStock 218 Adrian Kupman, SuperStock 220 L'Arche Noah Seath 225 A. Tjagny-Rjadno 225 Linda Wingerter 229 Bill Wittman, Catholic News Service 232 Elio Ciol, Corbis 244 (BR) PhotoEdit 245 Cheryl and Leo Meyer, CLEO 248 Milt & Joan Mann, Cameramann International, Ltd. 252 Pax Christi USA

All Other Photos: Scott Foresman and Pearson Learning

Photo Research: Feldman & Associates, Inc.

Every effort has been made to obtain permission for all photographs found in this book and to make full acknowledgment for their use. Omissions brought to our attention will be corrected in subsequent editions.

Copyright © 2003 Pearson Education, Inc. All rights reserved. Printed in the United States of America. This publication, or parts thereof, may not be reproduced in any form by photographic, electronic, mechanical, or any other method, for any use, including information storage and retrieval, without written permission from the publisher.

ISBN 0-382-36383-3

2 3 4 5 6 7 8 9 10 V011 10 09 08 07 06 05 04 03 02

CONTENTS

Getting Started

Welcome to BLEST ARE WE, a program of religious education created especially for you, your family, and your friends. Each chapter draws on the faith already instilled in you in your home, in your parish community, and in your formal religious education. This book was created to help you grow in awareness of your faith, understanding of the Church's teaching, and participation in the life of your parish community this year.

Get Connected

As you look through your book, you will notice that each chapter begins with Get Connected, a feature to help you get ready to learn and appreciate the content of the chapter. We suggest that you pull this page out of the book to share with your family and friends. Your conversations with them will bring out some ideas about religion and values that will add to what you discuss in your religion group meeting.

The best part about Get Connected is that it covers a variety of topics and activities that you can choose from to get started. If you are like most people, you will find that starting a conversation about religion and values at home or among friends will bring out some very surprising and positive aspects of people's personalities.

✝ The Gospels

This year's course of study centers on the person and the mission of Jesus as they are presented in the four Gospels. Our knowledge about Jesus, his times, his preaching, and his ministry is gathered from what we hear in church, what we have learned in religious education, and what we have read in books. This year, you will have the opportunity to put together a complete picture of Jesus' life and his importance for our lives as Christians and as God's people, the Church.

You are invited to enter into the spirit of the earliest Christian communities as they struggled to develop the message of Jesus for their own families and the world around them. As a result, we hope that you will be better able to understand the Gospel reading at Mass and to apply the message of the Gospel in your own life and community.

A Language of Faith

Catholic Tradition has its origins in 2,000 years of believers considering their relationship with God, the teachings of his Son, Jesus Christ, and the saving action of the Holy Spirit. Throughout that time, the Church has found ways to describe its beliefs to the world and to those growing in faith within the Church. This language of faith is what we call Catholic doctrine, or teaching.

Throughout your religious education, you have been gradually exposed to this language of faith. You are now at a point in your education where you can begin to appreciate Catholic teaching as a whole and gain a fuller understanding of your faith as a Catholic. You are ready for a more detailed presentation of Catholic doctrine.

OUR CATHOLIC TEACHINGS

At the back of your book is a section called *Our Catholic Teachings*. This section is divided into four parts: "What Catholics Believe," "How Catholics Worship," "How Catholics Live," and "How Catholics Pray." *Our Catholic Teachings* can be used in a number of ways. Your catechist may choose to spend some time each week going over one or more parts of the section. You can also use *Our Catholic Teachings* as a reference whenever you have a question about doctrine while reading a particular chapter.

Within the chapters, you will find a special feature to assist you with *Our Catholic Teachings*. In certain places within the chapters, you will see an icon of an arrow with the words *GO TO* inside it. This feature indicates the page in *Our Catholic Teachings* to which you may go for a more complete explanation of specific Catholic teachings covered in the chapters. Throughout your book, you will also see key words,

such as *sacrament* or *virtue*, that are main topics of *Our Catholic Teachings*. Sacraments are covered in the "How Catholics Worship" section of *Our Catholic Teachings*, and virtues are covered in "What Catholics Believe." When such key words appear, turn to the Table of Contents for *Our Catholic Teachings* to find out where to read more about them. Take time to read through *Our Catholic Teachings*, and ask a parent or your catechist about any topics that are new to you.

TAKING THE QUIZ

At the end of *Our Catholic Teachings*, there is a four-page quiz, the "Doctrine Review." Your catechist may ask you to take the quiz to find out the areas in which you may need more information. You may also want to take the quiz on your own and ask your catechist to score it for you, just to see how much you remember from previous religious education.

FAITH FORMATION

Of course, there are many aspects to growing in faith. Do not forget to draw upon the riches of your family's celebrations of faith, your friends' religious imagination, and your own relationship with God. By continuing your life of prayer, you will grow in your understanding of faith, your hopes for justice in our world, and your ability to be a witness to the love of Christ.

Commitment Prayer

Name _____

Parish Church _____

Leader: God's Word, Jesus Christ, came to live among us. This year, we will learn about Jesus, the Son of God, by studying his words and actions in the New Testament. We will study Jesus' life and nourish our faith in his divinity.

All: Holy Spirit, with you as you as our guide, we will open our minds and our hearts so that we may come to know our Lord and Savior.

Leader: In the New Testament, we learn who Jesus is from his followers. We are invited to read and understand the Scriptures and to make them part of our lives through the grace of the Holy Spirit.

All: Holy Spirit, we will seek your inspiration as we study and try to live the Gospel this year.

Leader: Jesus was both Son of Man and Son of God. He was a person who experienced life, just like you and I, yet his death on a cross brought us salvation. The sacrifice of his life showed the depth of God's love for us.

All: Holy Spirit, teach me how to imitate Christ in my life in my words and actions.

Leader: The Church invites us to encounter Christ in the Eucharist. It is in the sacrifice of the Mass that our faith is nourished and we truly become one with Jesus.

All: Holy Spirit, come to us this year. Enable us to faithfully respond to the call to holiness that we receive in the Eucharist. May we always be the disciples we were called to become at Baptism. Help us learn about Jesus and trust in him. May our lives be a testimony to the love of God. Amen.

With You by My Side

David Haas

VERSE 1   When I'm feeling all alone,
and I'm far away from home,
God, I need you to hear me.
When my friends all turn away,
then I ache to hear you say
that you are with me through it all.   *(Refrain)*

You are the light, you're the song that I'm sing - ing;
whom should I fear when you are with me? For
you are my God, and with you there is noth - ing I can't
do, with you by my side.

VERSE 2   When I feel all sick inside,
with no safe place to hide,
God, I need you to listen.
When it seems I can't go on,
then I long to hear the song
reminding me you are my friend.   *(Refrain)*

VERSE 3   And as I go through my life,
I will keep you in my sight
to walk with me and be my strength.
God, I know your plan for me:
to help all those in need,
To you alone I give my life!   *(Refrain)*

JESUS AND HIS TIMES

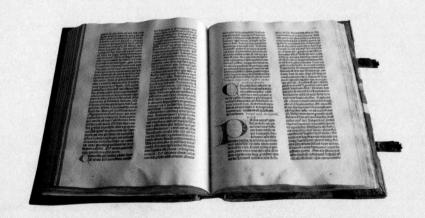

A Look at Jesus

Think about all you've learned about Jesus. What stories about Jesus do you remember the most? What kind of person do you picture Jesus to be? If you had to describe Jesus, what would you say?

Jesus is the Son of God. Jesus is God who became human and showed us the love of God through his words and his caring treatment of others. His miracles testified to his divine power. Jesus is our Savior. His greatest act of love was dying on the cross for our sins.

Much of what we know about Jesus' life has been handed down by the writers of the Gospels and the Tradition of the apostles who knew him. People who followed Jesus addressed him as "Rabbi," because Jesus was a teacher. They also called him a prophet, for he spoke as one who had been sent by God. As Jesus preached and healed people, people began to recognize that he was no ordinary man. But only Jesus' closest disciples believed on some level that Jesus was the *Messiah*, the one God promised to send to save all people from sin. However, even Jesus' apostles did not fully understand his mission until after his death and Resurrection. Only then did they realize that they had witnessed firsthand the life and teachings of the Son of God.

After Jesus' death and Resurrection, the people who met Jesus and witnessed his actions and his teachings were determined to spread the good news that he preached: that God loves us and that he sent his only Son, Jesus Christ, into the world to save us from sin and make us ready for God's kingdom of everlasting happiness and peace.

Most of the details about Jesus come from the New Testament, which was not written in a complete form until about ninety years after Jesus died. It is difficult to know more about Jesus as a person in history, since the New Testament was not written as a biography. Historical or archeological evidence may tell us about the world Jesus lived in, but it does not give us direct knowledge about Jesus as a person. For example, Jesus' name was found in a record of people from the first century whom the Romans had killed, but the specific events leading to his death are not recorded anywhere as they are in the Gospels.

Even without a detailed account of Jesus' life, historians agree that Jesus' life dramatically changed the history of humankind. After Jesus' death and Resurrection, Christianity spread rapidly. Two thousand years have passed since Jesus was alive, and there are now about 2 billion Christians in the world.

This year, you will journey through the New Testament, walking with Jesus and learning more about his life and message of love. Developing a relationship with the risen Christ will help you know and understand how much God loves you.

What Do You Know About Jesus?

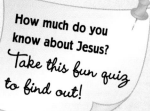

How much do you know about Jesus? Take this fun quiz to find out!

1. According to the Gospels, where did Jesus go after he was baptized?
   (a) the desert
   (b) Jerusalem
   (c) the Temple
   (d) home

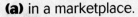

2. The Gospels tell us about the life of
   (a) Matthew.
   (b) Mark.
   (c) Jesus.
   (d) John.

3. What parable did Jesus tell to explain the meaning of the word *neighbor*?
   (a) The Prodigal Son
   (b) The Lost Coin
   (c) The Good Samaritan
   (d) The Lost Sheep

4. Whom did Jesus raise from the dead after four days?
   (a) Elijah
   (b) Lazarus
   (c) Martha
   (d) a Samaritan woman

5. What did people lay on the ground in front of Jesus to honor him as he entered Jerusalem?
   (a) fig leaves
   (b) money
   (c) jewels
   (d) palm branches

6. What do we call the rules of happiness that Jesus taught us?
   (a) the Beatitudes
   (b) the Ten Commandments
   (c) the Law of Love
   (d) the Torah

7. When did Jesus institute the sacrament of the Eucharist?
   (a) after teaching the Lord's Prayer
   (b) on the day he ascended into heaven
   (c) while celebrating a meal with his apostles on the night he was arrested
   (d) on Palm Sunday

8. When Jesus was a child and was lost for three days, Mary and Joseph found him
   (a) in a marketplace.
   (b) in the Temple.
   (c) in the desert.
   (d) in the Jordan River.

9. Before Jesus was crucified, where did he go to spend time in prayer?
   (a) a garden
   (b) mountains
   (c) a lake
   (d) a forest

10. What is the prayer that Jesus taught us?
    (a) the Hail Mary
    (b) the Act of Contrition
    (c) the Nicene Creed
    (d) the Lord's Prayer

11. Which apostle walked on the water with Jesus?
    (a) Thomas
    (b) James
    (c) Peter
    (d) Matthew

Check your score on page xviii!

THE HISTORY OF JESUS

1. JESUS' EARLY LIFE (BEGINNING ABOUT 6 B.C.)

Jesus was born around 6 B.C. According to the Gospels of Matthew and Luke, Jesus' birth took place in Bethlehem, a town outside of Jerusalem in Judea, the southern part of Palestine, or the Holy Land. During Jesus' time, Palestine was part of the Romans' large empire. Jesus was raised in Nazareth, a small village in Galilee (in northern Palestine), by Mary, his mother, and Joseph, a carpenter. During his youth, Jesus was probably an apprentice in his father's trade. With the exception of a story in Luke's Gospel about Jesus and his parents in Jerusalem on the Passover feast, the Gospels say nothing about events in the life of Jesus between his infancy and his public ministry. People who knew Jesus or knew about him shared stories about him through word of mouth after his death and Resurrection. They did not immediately record their stories about Jesus.

2. JESUS' PUBLIC MINISTRY (ABOUT A.D. 27–30)

It was not until Jesus was about thirty years old that he began traveling throughout Israel to preach, spread the message of God's love, and perform healings and miracles. (Each of the four Gospel writers—Matthew, Mark, Luke, and John—explore Jesus' words and actions from this period in detail.) Jewish tradition held that a *messiah*, or anointed one, would come to deliver and unite God's people. Jesus taught that God's kingdom would come not through military victories as some of the Jewish people had expected but through Jesus Christ himself. Jesus chose twelve apostles, or followers, to share in his ministry.

3. JESUS' DEATH AND RESURRECTION (ABOUT A.D. 30)

As Jesus became more widely known, he was seen as a threat to Roman politicians and Jewish religious leaders. Jesus was tried for **blasphemy**. Pontius Pilate, the

A TIMELINE OF NEW TESTAMENT EVENTS

IN THE NEW TESTAMENT

6 B.C.
Jesus is born.

27
Jesus is baptized and begins his ministry.

29
John the Baptizer is beheaded.

30
Jesus dies and rises.

JESUS' EARLY LIFE BEGINNING ABOUT 6 B.C.	JESUS' PUBLIC MINISTRY ABOUT A.D. 27–30	JESUS' DEATH, AND RESURRECTION ABOUT A.D. 30

IN THE WORLD

A.D. 14
Caesar Augustus dies and leaves Tiberius to rule Rome.

26
Pontius Pilate begins to rule as governor.

30
Chinese invent new farming methods.

AND HIS GOOD NEWS

Roman governor, ordered that Jesus be crucified. Jesus' crucifixion took place outside of Jerusalem at Golgotha, known as "the place of the skulls." The events of Jesus' trial, crucifixion, and Resurrection were most likely the first events of Jesus' life to have been written about.

4. FORMATION OF THE EARLY CHURCH (A.D. 30—65)

Paul's Journeys

The Church began at Pentecost, fifty days after Jesus' death. Jesus' disciples, filled with the Holy Spirit, began to spread God's word throughout the land. As their message spread, making believers of Jews and Gentiles (non-Jews), the Romans grew more and more opposed to Christianity. Paul traveled and helped form Christian communities. His journeys began around

A.D. 45. Paul founded churches in twenty cities of the Roman Empire. Several times during his journeys Paul was arrested. Paul wrote letters to the Christian communities to help them follow Jesus' teachings in A.D. 50–60. (In A.D. 65–100, Paul's disciples also wrote some letters in his name.)

5 WRITING OF THE NEW TESTAMENT (A.D. 65—120)

Forty years after Jesus' death and Resurrection, Christians were being martyred, and people who had been around during Jesus' public ministry were beginning to die. Jesus' Second Coming was not going to be as immediate as the early Christians originally thought; stories about Jesus needed to be recorded. The *evangelists,* who proclaimed the word of God through writings, by word of mouth, or by personal testimony, were inspired and guided by the Holy Spirit as they wrote about Jesus in the Gospels. The Gospels were written in A.D. 65–A.D. 100. The New Testament was not completed in full until A.D. 120.

35
Paul converts to Christianity.

30
Christian Church is born.

36
Stephen is first Christian to be martyred.

46–60
Paul goes on missionary journeys and writes letters to Christian communities.

68–70
Dead Sea Scrolls are hidden in caves.

70
Gospel of Mark is written.

75
Gospel of Luke is written.

85
Gospel of Matthew is written.

90–100
Gospel of John is written.

95
Book of Revelation is written.

| FORMATION OF THE EARLY CHURCH A.D. 30–65 | WRITING OF THE NEW TESTAMENT A.D. 65–120 |

37
Caligula rules Rome.

41
Claudius I rules Rome.

54
Nero rules Rome.

64
Fire destroys Rome. Nero persecutes Christians.

70
Romans destroy the Temple in Jerusalem.

80
The coliseum amphitheater in Rome is completed.

79
Mt. Vesuvius erupts and destroys Pompeii, Italy.

105
Paper is invented in China.

Women gathered at wells once a day to collect water. Water was an important part of Jewish rituals, such as washing the feet of guests in one's home.

Scribes were skilled writers who copied Scripture texts onto scrolls of parchment made from sheep or goat skins. Scribes wrote with pens made from reeds, which probably grew on the banks of the Jordan River. In Jesus' time, scribes also helped people in the Jewish community understand God's law in the Scriptures.

Entire villages, as well as friends and family from distant places, were invited to weddings. Festivities lasted a week or more, with much food, wine, and dancing. The couple stood under a canopy symbolizing the home they would share. In John's Gospel, Jesus' first miracle takes place at a wedding in Cana.

The Romans occupied Palestine. The Jewish people disliked paying taxes to the Romans. Most Jews were common people who worked hard for a living. Their main occupations were fishing, farming, and shepherding. Jesus often told stories using examples from their daily lives.

The Sea of Galilee was a popular fishing spot. Fishermen used strong cord nets. The apostles Peter and Andrew were fishing when Jesus called them to follow him.

To make cloth, women used the wool from the goats or sheep kept outside their homes. A spindle, or small rod, was used to spin the wool into yarn. When the yarn was ready, the women used a loom to weave the thread into cloth.

Carpenters used sycamore trees for many of their projects. Carpenters made beams, doors, furniture, and kitchen implements for homes. Jesus probably learned this trade when he was about fifteen years old.

Women baked bread daily. Families ate bread with every meal. To begin supper, the father offered thanks to God and shared pieces of bread with each person.

Farmers harvested olives in autumn by shaking olive trees with a pole. Donkeys pushed a beam connected to a stone to press the olives for oil. Workers placed the crushed olives in a basket and collected the oil that drained. Olive oil was used in lamps, in cooking food, and in making medicine.

PEOPLE WHO WROTE ABOUT JESUS

The New Testament tells us how God fulfilled his promises to the Jews by sending Jesus Christ. The four Gospels in the New Testament are the main source for our knowledge about the life and teachings of our Savior, Jesus Christ. Inspired by the Holy Spirit, the writers of the four Gospels proclaimed the good news of Christ to the world through their writings. As Christians, we *evangelize*, or spread the truth of the Gospels.

Three of the Gospels—Matthew, Mark, and Luke—are called *synoptic* because they give similar accounts of the words and actions of Jesus. In the early Church, these particular Gospels were probably used as a *catechism*, a guide to the Christian faith. In addition to the Gospels, the New Testament also contains *epistles*, or letters. Paul and other disciples wrote letters to Christian communities or the Church to remind people how to follow Jesus.

Here is what we know about the people who wrote about Jesus in the New Testament.

Matthew

Scholars believe that the Gospel writer Matthew was a Jewish Christian who wrote in Antioch, Syria, a major city in the Roman Empire. Matthew wrote to portray Jesus as the promised Messiah. His frequent use of Scripture indicates that he was well educated in Jewish law.

Mark

The Gospel writer we know as "Mark" is believed to have been a Jewish Christian and the first to write about Jesus' life in the form of a Gospel. He was probably a follower of Peter, the first leader of the Church. Possibly writing from Rome, he portrayed Jesus as the suffering Messiah and the Son of God.

Luke

The Gospel of Luke was probably written in a place where the main language was Greek. This writer was probably a Gentile who traveled with Paul on his missionary journeys. Luke portrayed Jesus as the Savior of all people. Luke also wrote the Acts of the Apostles, which was about the early Church.

John

The writer of the fourth Gospel is believed to have been John the Apostle or someone who was close to John or another follower of Jesus. Scholars agree that John's Gospel was the last of the four Gospels to be written. John portrayed Jesus as the eternal Word of God.

Paul

Paul was once called Saul and was a persecutor of Christians. After converting to Christianity, Paul went on three missionary journeys and started churches in Asia Minor and Europe. Paul later wrote letters to these communities.

Look for a first-person account by one of these writers in each unit.

THE PARTS OF THE BIBLE

While God has gradually made himself known to us throughout history, Jesus is God's ultimate *revelation* of himself. The Bible is the story of God's revelation. We show reverence for the Bible because the Holy Spirit inspired those who wrote it. The Holy Spirit guides us as we read and reflect on the meaning of God's revelation.

The Bible is divided into two main parts: the Old Testament, which contains 46 books, and the New Testament, which has 27 books. Jesus' birth, life, and death were revealed by the prophets of the Old Testament. The Old Testament was written first, and it is a valuable part of Sacred Scripture. It prepares us for God's revelation of himself in the person of Jesus. Every time we read the New Testament, we learn more about who Jesus is and how he wants us to live. While we can never fully understand the mystery of God, Jesus helps us grow in faith and love. This is what Christians firmly believe, about 2,000 years after Jesus lived among us.

Both the Old Testament and the New Testament are necessary in our understanding of who God is. Saint Augustine summed up this idea when he said that the "New Testament lies hidden in the Old and the Old Testament is unveiled in the New."

Old Testament

Pentateuch
(first five books of the Bible, about Israel's covenant with God)

Genesis	Numbers
Exodus	Deuteronomy
Leviticus	

(more of the Israelites' story)

Joshua	Ruth
Judges	

Historical Books
(Israel's religious history)

1 Samuel	Nehemiah
2 Samuel	Tobit
1 Kings	Judith
2 Kings	Esther
1 Chronicles	1 Maccabees
2 Chronicles	2 Maccabees
Ezra	

Wisdom Books
(poetry and instruction)

Job	Song of Songs
Psalms	Wisdom
Proverbs	Sirach
Ecclesiastes	

Prophetic Books
(God's word throught the prophets)

Isaiah	Obadiah
Jeremiah	Jonah
Lamentations	Micah
Baruch	Nahum
Ezekiel	Habakkuk
Daniel	Zephaniah
Hosea	Haggai
Joel	Zechariah
Amos	Malachi

New Testament

The Gospels
(life and teachings of Jesus)

Matthew	Luke
Mark	John

Acts of the Apostles
(works of the early Church)

Letters
(letters to early Christians)

Romans	Philippians
1 Corinthians	Colossians
2 Corinthians	1 Thessalonians
Galatians	2 Thessalonians
Ephesians	1 Timothy

2 Timothy	1 Peter
Titus	2 Peter
Philemon	1 John
Hebrews	2 John
James	3 John
	Jude

Book of Revelation
(apocalyptic writing)

A CLOSER LOOK AT THE NEW TESTAMENT

About the Gospel of Matthew

This Gospel is based on Mark's but was for a Jewish audience. It traces Jesus' ancestry to Abraham. It frequently quotes the Old Testament. Since Matthew begins with the *genealogy* of Jesus, his symbol is a human with wings.

About the Gospel of Mark

This is the shortest of the Gospels. It has the most vivid descriptions of Jesus' life. It was written during Christian persecution. Mark's symbol is a lion with wings, a symbol of God's messenger in the desert at the beginning of the Gospel.

About the Gospel of Luke

This Gospel is based on the Gospel of Mark but was for a Greek audience. The symbol for Luke is an ox with wings. This represents the opening of the Gospel, where John the Baptizer's father offers this animal as a sacrifice.

About the Gospel of John

This Gospel was written when most people knew about Jesus' death and Resurrection. It does not include many events found in the synoptic Gospels. John's symbol, an eagle, represents the majesty of his words.

About the Epistles

Paul wrote thirteen of the twenty-one epistles in the New Testament. Written before the Gospels, the epistles offer advice on how to worship and follow Jesus' example.

About the Book of Revelation

Scholars think that a man named John from an island in the Aegean Sea wrote this book to bring hope to Christians facing persecution. John wrote in an apocryphal style, using images with hidden meanings to reveal God's ultimate power over evil.

TYPES OF WRITING

Gospel: an account of the good news of Jesus and of his life, death, and Resurrection.

Parable: a tale that teaches a moral lesson.

Epistle: a written message from one person or group to another.

Genealogy: a listing of ancestors; a family history.

Apocalyptic: describing the ultimate triumph of the kingdom of God.

Answers to "What Do You Know About Jesus?" (page xi)
1) a, 2) c, 3) c, 4) b, 5) d, 6) a, 7) c, 8) b, 9) a, 10) d, 11) c

Scoring:
Give yourself one point for each correct answer.
8–11 points: Super! You are ahead of the game.
5–7 points: Very good!
3–4 points: This is a start. Stay alert for more information about Jesus!
1–2 points: Not to worry—you will learn all about Jesus this year!

The Mystery of the Incarnation

The Gospel accounts of Jesus' birth and early life give us clues to his true identity as the Son of God. These stories also help us understand the holiness to which we are called as God's children.

Joseph went with Mary and Jesus to dwell in Nazareth.

Based on Matthew 2:21, 23

As a youth, Jesus most likely helped Joseph in his carpenter's workshop, as portrayed in this scene from Nazareth Village, a living history museum in Israel. Most houses in Nazareth in Jesus' time probably looked very much like the one shown here.

Come, Emmanuel

Tony Alonso
based on VENI VENI EMMANUEL

VERSE 1

Cantor

Awake now friends, the time is near:
Soon the Lord of life will appear:
Stay awake, prepare God's way:
This is what the Scriptures say:

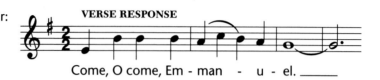

VERSE RESPONSE

Come, O come, Em - man - u - el. _____

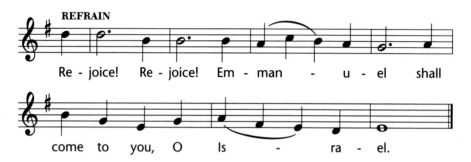

REFRAIN

Re - joice! Re - joice! Em - man - u - el shall

come to you, O Is - ra - el.

VERSE 2

Cantor

Let us see your living face:
Sons and daughters
   of one living race:
Show us mercy, show us love:
Send salvation from above:
(Refrain)

VERSE RESPONSE

Come, O come, Em - man - u - el. _____

VERSE 3

Cantor

God's glory now shall be revealed:
The blind will see,
   the sick be healed:
All will sing together in peace:
All will sit together at the feast:
(Refrain)

VERSE RESPONSE

Come, O come, Em - man - u - el. _____

Get Connected

with family and friends

The Birth of Our Savior

Welcome to a mystery beyond your imagination—the mystery of the Incarnation! In this chapter you will read accounts of the birth of Jesus from the Gospels of Matthew and Luke. You will read how God lovingly revealed himself to all humanity in the Second Person of the Trinity—Jesus Christ.

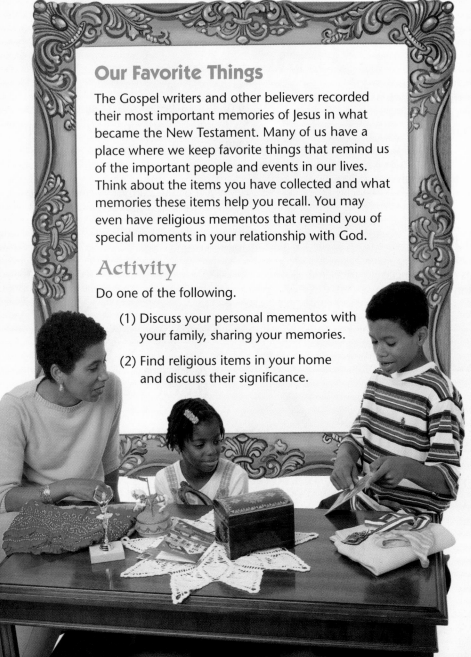

Our Favorite Things

The Gospel writers and other believers recorded their most important memories of Jesus in what became the New Testament. Many of us have a place where we keep favorite things that remind us of the important people and events in our lives. Think about the items you have collected and what memories these items help you recall. You may even have religious mementos that remind you of special moments in your relationship with God.

Activity

Do one of the following.

(1) Discuss your personal mementos with your family, sharing your memories.

(2) Find religious items in your home and discuss their significance.

Check It Out

Little is known about the Magi from the Scriptures. Legend has it that the Magi were kings representing the continents of Arabia, Persia, and India. Melchior offered gold to the Christ child, in honor of his kingship. Gaspar offered the child Jesus incense, to pay homage to his divinity. Balthasar offered myrrh, which prefigured the suffering and death of Jesus. Legend also holds that Saint Thomas the Apostle later visited the Magi and baptized them.

The Roman Basilica of St. Mary Major contains legendary nativity relics: five small sycamore boards thought to be from the crib of Jesus.

Holy Humor!

Catholic Wordplay

incense   holy smoke!

Jonah   the original *Jaws* story

Magi   the most famous three people ever to attend a baby shower

procession   a ceremonial formation at the start of Mass, consisting of altar servers, the celebrant, and late parishioners looking for seats

recessional hymn   a song at the end of Mass that accompanies the procession out of the church, led by parishioners trying to beat the crowd to the parking lot

All-Star Profile

Name: Sister Chrissie Mulready
Born: 1947
Died: 1999
Occupation: social justice coordinator for the Sisters of St. Joseph, issues coordinator for the Inter-Community Center for Justice and Peace
Quote of a Lifetime (about Chrissie): "Even as a great cloud of witnesses gathered for her funeral, Sister Christine Mulready continued making peace, just as she had done in her life."
Claims to Fame: Helped poor Iraqi children with heart defects come to America for medical care. Worked in refugee camps in Bosnia to help the victims of ethnic cleansing. Worked as a Cherish Life Circle member to seek mercy for prison inmates and to abolish the death penalty.
Hobbies: teaching, spending time with friends, storytelling

Wired

Visit Our Web Site
www.blestarewe.com

Web Site Spotlight
www.disciplesnow.org

Check out discussions with others who believe Jesus is worth living for. Find out interesting facts about your faith, and click on links to other sites you won't want to miss!

Something To Do

On Sunday

At Mass this Sunday, think about Jesus' life and his determination to do his Father's will. Then pray for God's help in following Jesus' example.

Through the Week

Be aware of the many opportunities in which God tries to reveal himself to you in people and things around you.

A Prayer for the Week

Lord,
be with our family this week.
Help us share your gifts of peace
and joy with one another.
Grant that we might
recall each day how Jesus
came to save us.
Amen.

1   The Birth of Our Savior

 Listen, O house of David! . . . the Lord himself will give you this sign: the virgin shall be with child, and bear a son, and shall name him Immanuel.

Isaiah 7:13–14

Share

Think about your personality and how it differs from the personalities of your friends. Because we are all unique, each of us communicates in a different way. We determine what to say based on our own experiences and the needs of our listeners. In what ways are our listeners the same or different? Are they young or old? What are their interests? These factors influence how and what we communicate with others. Later, you will discover how this was true for the writers of the Gospels.

Activity

Check the traits that best describe your personality. Then, on the lines below, write about one or more traits that you would like to develop.

X careful   X adventurous   __ compassionate

X quiet   __ funny   X emotional

X observant   __ talkative   X creative

__ assertive   X serious   __ easygoing

I would like to be talkative.

How did the Gospel writers portray Jesus' birth?

Hear & Believe

✠ Scripture The Birth of Jesus

In my Gospel, I wrote about all Jesus taught and did until the day he was taken up. After Jesus rose from the dead, he appeared to his followers many times during forty days and spoke to them about the kingdom of God. He told them to wait for the promise of the Father and said, "You will be my witnesses to the ends of the earth."

Based on Acts 1:1–4

The Gospel writer Luke wrote the above passage about fifty years after Jesus' Resurrection. As Jesus' "witnesses to the ends of the earth," the Gospel writers wrote down what people had been saying about Jesus' life and teachings. Luke included a story about Jesus' birth, as did the Gospel writer Matthew. While Luke began by discussing the birth of John the Baptizer, Matthew began with the genealogy of Jesus. Note the differences in Luke's and Matthew's stories.

Luke: Zechariah and Elizabeth were old and had no children. An angel appeared to Zechariah and announced that he and Elizabeth would have a child named John, who would be great in the sight of the Lord. Elizabeth became pregnant, just as the angel had said.

The angel Gabriel appeared to Mary and told her she would conceive and bear a child, the Son of God. Shortly after, Mary visited her cousin Elizabeth. As they greeted one another, Elizabeth's child leaped within her womb. Filled with the Holy Spirit, Elizabeth recognized Mary as the mother of our Lord. Joseph went from Nazareth in Galilee to the city of Bethlehem to be enrolled with Mary, who was with child. While they were there, Mary gave birth to her firstborn son. She wrapped him in swaddling clothes and laid him in a manger, because there was no room for them in the inn.

An angel appeared to shepherds in nearby fields and said, "A savior has been born for you who is the **Messiah** and the Lord." The shepherds visited the infant Jesus to pay him homage, then returned, praising God and telling everyone about the child.

Based on Luke 1–2

Matthew: The one called the Messiah was born of the house of David. This is how his birth came about. An angel appeared to Joseph in a dream, telling him, "Joseph, son of David, do not be afraid to take Mary into your home. It is through the Holy Spirit that she has conceived a child. She will bear a son, and you are to name him Jesus because he will save his people from their sins." Joseph did as the angel had commanded. Mary gave birth to a son, and he was named Jesus.

Magi from the East saw a new star in the sky that led them to Bethlehem, where they saw the child and Mary, his mother. The Magi prostrated themselves before the child and offered him gifts of gold, frankincense, and myrrh.

Joseph was then told in a dream to flee to Egypt to escape King Herod, who had heard about Jesus and planned a massacre of all the firstborn sons. After Herod died, Joseph went with Mary and Jesus to dwell in Nazareth.

Based on Matthew 1–2

The Message of Jesus' Birth

At first, Jesus' disciples spread God's message by word of mouth, or **oral tradition**. Later they wrote about the mysteries of Jesus' life.

Luke's and Matthew's accounts of the mystery of Jesus' birth differ. Luke wanted to show the Christian community that there were signs from God that his plan to send the Messiah was coming true. He wrote about Elizabeth, who recognized that Mary was to be the mother of the Savior. Luke also wrote about the shepherds, who had little importance in society. Yet an angel appeared to these shepherds to announce the birth of the long-awaited Messiah. This could only mean the Lord had come to help even the lowliest of people.

Matthew wanted to show that Jesus was the fulfillment of the Old Testament. He wrote about the *genealogy* of Jesus—how Jesus had descended from David, Israel's first great king. Matthew also told the story of the Magi, priestly men from the East whose visit to Jesus was a sign of great things to come. The new star in the sky was a sign of the birth of a new ruler. Matthew also included events that had connections to Moses' birth. Matthew wanted the community to recognize that Jesus brought a "new Exodus," freedom from sin forever. He used ancient Israel as his setting, linking Jesus' life to the Old Testament.

The Gospels written by Mark and John do not include accounts of Jesus' birth. Mark chose to begin his Gospel with the preaching of John the Baptizer to emphasize the proclamation of the Good News. John assumed that his readers were already familiar with the story of Jesus' birth, so he concentrated on exploring the reality of the **Incarnation** instead.

The Incarnation

Although Luke's and Matthew's versions of the birth of Jesus differ, their essential message is the same: God lovingly revealed himself to us through Jesus, the Second Person of the Trinity. Without losing his divine nature, God became a man and lived among us. This is called the Incarnation. The Holy Spirit gives us the gift of faith so that we can believe in the mystery of the Incarnation and respond to God's love. With faith, we strive to better understand God's revelation.

Jesus saves us from sin. The very name of Jesus means "God saves." We believe that Jesus is truly the Son of God. All over the world, Christmas pageants and processions retell the story of the birth of Jesus. They sometimes retell the story with events from both Luke's and Matthew's Gospels. What's important is not the exact order of the events, but what Luke and Matthew were trying to tell us about the Incarnation.

Faith Words

Messiah *Messiah* means "God's anointed one" or "savior." A messiah is a person chosen to save people from a particular fate. Jesus is the Messiah, the One promised to deliver all people from sin.

oral tradition Oral tradition is a body of stories that has been passed down by word of mouth. In ancient Israel, before the Gospels were written, people told stories about God and all he did for them.

Incarnation The Incarnation is God's Son becoming man, one like us, Jesus Christ, who is both human and divine.

How can we express God's love to others?

Our Church Teaches

The coming of God's Son was such an astounding event that God willed that everything and everyone would point to the coming of Christ.

By the power of the Holy Spirit, Jesus, the Son of God, became human. Jesus fully possesses a human nature and a divine nature. God and humanity are united in the person of Jesus. Being truly God and truly human like us, Jesus is the *mediator,* someone who acts as a go-between, between God and human beings. The name Jesus means "God saves," and we call Jesus Christ "Lord" because we believe in his total and complete divinity.

Mary, ever a virgin, conceived her Son by the power of the Holy Spirit. She willingly became part of God's divine plan for our salvation. Jesus is Mary's only Son, but her spiritual motherhood extends to all people whom he came to save.

We Believe

The Son of God became human to save us from our sins. The Holy Spirit gives us the gift of faith to help us understand this mystery.

Respond

Mary and the Women of the Bible

The women of the Bible were ordinary women blessed by God to live extraordinary lives. Their testimony of trust and faith in God was and continues to be a source of inspiration to us all as we seek to know God's plan for our lives.

Mary knew about the women of Israel who came before her and were blessed by God. She was aware that in God's plan for salvation, a person could have a very important role. Mary trusted in God and rejoiced in his favor. She shared this wisdom and faith with her cousin Elizabeth. Elizabeth's pregnancy was a sign of God's covenant and a sign of the coming of the Messiah.

Mary accepted God's call freely and responsibly; she was aware of the cost of accepting the call. She knew her life was to be one of loving service to the Father in all ways. Mary's faith led her to give birth to Jesus, watch him grow, witness his ministry, and follow him to his cross and Resurrection. Mary is the Church's model disciple of faith and charity by her complete obedience to the Father's will, to his Son's work for our salvation, and to every prompting of the Holy Spirit. Mary's model of discipleship makes us question our own response to Jesus Incarnate in our lives.

The Windsock Visitation by Brother Michael McGrath

Activities

1. Whether it's the birth of a baby in the family, the winning of a big match, or a special celebration, good news brings people together. Write about a time when good news brought together your family, friends, or team.

What were you celebrating?

_____

Who was part of the celebration?

_____

How did everybody celebrate?

_____

What difference did this good news make to your family, friends, or team?

_____

2. God is truth and love. Think about the wonderful ways in which God is part of your life. How can you, as a faith-filled disciple, bring others to God?

_____

3. *The Messiah* is a famous oratorio composed by George Frideric Handel. The music, which is based on Scripture, is divided into three themes: Advent and the birth of Christ, Jesus' suffering and death, and the Resurrection. Take a moment and creatively express your feelings of wonder about one of these themes. Use the space below for writing verses to a song, drawing a picture, writing a poem, or creating something else.

How can we express our feelings of wonder over the Incarnation?

✝ Prayer Celebration

Halleluia!

The following words are taken from Handel's *The Messiah*. Reflect on the words, then pray them with your religious education group arranged into two sides.

Side 1: For unto us a Child is born, unto us a Son is given.

Side 2: and the government shall be upon his shoulders and his Name shall be called Wonderful, Counsellor, the mighty God, the everlasting Father, the Prince of Peace.

Side 1: For unto us a Child is born, unto us a Son is given.

All: Halleluia, Halleluia, Halleluia, Halleluia!

Side 1: For the Lord God Omnipotent reigneth.

Side 2: The Kingdom of this world is become the Kingdom of our Lord and of his Christ.

Side 1: And he shall reign for ever and ever!

Side 2: And he shall reign for ever and ever!

Side 1: King of Kings

Side 2: and Lord of Lords,

All: Halleluia, Halleluia, Halleluia, Halleluia!

Get Connected

with family and friends

God with Us

New life in God's family begins at Baptism. There is a new garment, an anointing with oil, a pouring of baptismal waters, the lighting of a baptismal candle, and a welcoming into our Christian family. At Baptism, we become members of the Church. Baptism cleanses us from sin and gives us the gift of sharing in God's divine life.

Welcome to the World!

Life is filled with new beginnings. Your baptism was a new beginning for you, your family, and your parish community. Your baptism brought you into the Christian family and into a new relationship with God.

Activity

Do one of the following.

(1) Contact your godparents or other people who were at your baptism, and set up a time to get together. Ask them to tell the story of your baptism in detail. Ask them about their feelings and hopes for you on that day and their feelings and hopes for you now.

(2) Be present at a celebration of Baptism in your parish. Watch family members as they enter the church and are welcomed into God's family. Note the joy and hope that the newly baptized brings to his or her family and to your parish.

Brain Teaser

Unscramble the words associated with Baptism.

tli naledc _____

ewn tnceriao _____

rsngleetiva efil _____

twehi mantegr _____

vehenayl gkndimo _____

teraw _____

Did you know...?

Baptism is the first of three sacraments of initiation. The others are Eucharist and Confirmation. In the Eastern Church these sacraments are celebrated together.

Steve Angrisano Rocks!

Steve Angrisano is an amazing singer, songwriter, and storyteller. Angrisano is a Texas native who uses his music to bring people together to help them determine what is important in life and how they can help others. He uses his music as a way to connect with what is happening in the minds and hearts of young people.

Among Angrisano's many accomplishments has been his growing repertoire of contemporary liturgical music. His CD *Make a Difference*, produced by Oregon Catholic Press (OCP), includes songs that have been used for youth conference liturgies and national youth gatherings.

Angrisano loves teenagers and trains youth ministers. He is also a conference and workshop presenter. He volunteers to help the young people in his parish and also works with teens at a summer work camp that serves those who are poor or in need. Angrisano has dedicated his ministry to the Lord and has touched many lives in the process.

All-Star Profile

Name: Saint John Bosco
Born: 1815
Died: 1888
Family Background: youngest son of a peasant farmer in Italy who died when John was two years old, leaving the family very poor
Occupation: priest, juggler, magician, athlete, musician, fundraiser, educator
Quote of a Lifetime: "Give me souls; take away the rest."
Claims to Fame: Founded the Salesian Society, a worldwide religious order that cares for young people and the poor. Worked with street kids in Italy, involving them in sports, games, and music and later founding schools for them.
Hobbies: magic tricks, music, sports

Wired

Visit Our Web Site
www.blestarewe.com

Web Site Spotlight
www.nfcym.org

Visit the Web site of the National Federation for Catholic Youth Ministry. Get the latest on youth conference events.

Something To Do

On Sunday

When you enter the church, bless yourself slowly with holy water, remembering that your journey of faith began at Baptism.

Through the Week

Make a determined effort to get along peacefully with your family. Since Baptism makes all things new, think about how your family relationships need to change and be renewed.

✝ A Prayer for the Week

Lord, we know that you are there for us. You said that you would love us always and marked us as your own. Help us be there for others and remember your promises. Help us keep our promises to you and share your love. Amen.

Answer Key: lit candle, new creation, everlasting life, white garment, heavenly kingdom, water

2 God with Us

Whoever drinks the water I shall give will never thirst; the water I shall give will become a spring of water welling up to eternal life.

Based on John 4:14

Share

As I carried the cake into the room, I began singing "Happy Birthday." The room was completely dark, but the tiny candles on the cake lit the way to where everyone was gathered. All my aunts, uncles, and cousins were there. They joined me in singing "Happy Birthday" to my dad, and even though we sang off-key, we knew our efforts were appreciated. Then Dad made a wish and blew out all the candles. Aunt Jane turned on the lights, and the festivities continued. Streamers hung from the ceiling, balloons floated around, and Dad began to dish out the cake to everyone. Then came the presents, each of which was opened with great anticipation. Soon after, my cousins and I began sharing stories about our favorite birthday celebrations. I couldn't help but think that it was a great thing to have such a special day on which to celebrate a new year of life.

Activity

In the story above, the candles, cake, balloons, and other items were symbols of the joy of the birthday celebration. List symbols that can represent each word below.

friendship   keychains, parties

family   ~~grandparents day~~ hearts

school   Signs, school colors, features

club or team   banners,

country   ~~4th of July~~ Flags, monument

What symbols can be found in the Rite of Baptism?

13

Worship Celebrating Baptism

Jesus instituted the sacraments as visible signs of his presence and God's action in our lives. We begin our lives as members of the Church when we celebrate the sacrament of Baptism. Just as a birthday is an initiation into a new year of life, Baptism is our initiation into a new community, the Church. Sacramentals, such as holy water, holy oil, a white garment, and a lighted candle, are part of the celebration of Baptism. These sacred objects and the actions and prayers associated with them help awaken us to God's life within us. They help us raise our awareness of what it means to be disciples of Jesus, Christians.

The Holy Water

In the Scriptures, we read how water was used for both physical and spiritual cleansing or purification. In the Old Testament, the Hebrew people found freedom from slavery in Egypt by crossing through the waters of the Red Sea. In the New Testament, water represents a means to **salvation** through Baptism. Water is symbolic of our dying and rising to new life in Christ. In Baptism, the celebrant prays, "The waters of the great flood you made a sign of the waters of baptism that make an end of sin and a new beginning of goodness" (*Rite of Baptism*).

The Holy Oil

In Baptism, the anointing with oil is a sign of our call to carry out the responsibility of being a Christian. It represents the call to be priest, prophet, and king, like Christ. We are empowered through the anointing of Baptism to go forth as God's own disciples. "He now anoints you with the chrism of salvation, so that, united with his people, you may remain for ever a member of Christ who is Priest, Prophet, and King" (*Rite of Baptism*).

The White Garment

The godparents of the newly baptized place a white garment on him or her, symbolizing his or her new life in Christ. The priest or deacon, also known as the celebrant, says, "You have become a new creation and have clothed yourselves in Christ. Receive this baptismal garment and bring it unstained to the judgment seat of our Lord Jesus Christ so that you may have everlasting life" (*Rite of Baptism*).

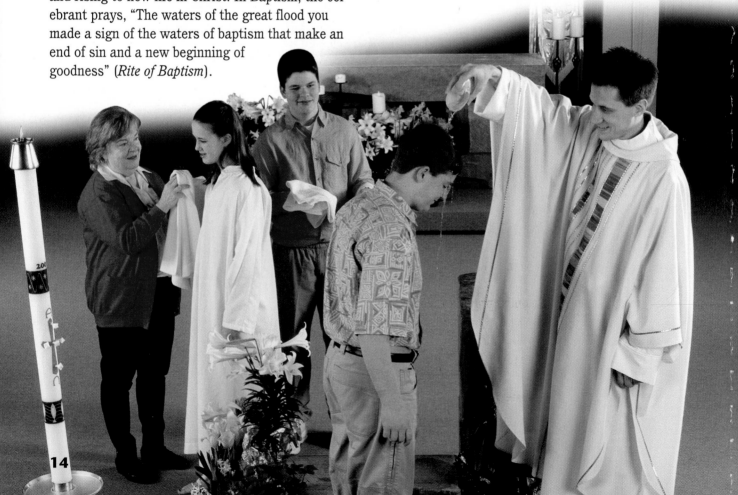

The Lighted Candle

The godparents light a candle with the flame of the Easter candle and present it to the newly baptized. The celebrant prays, "You have been enlightened by Christ. Walk always as children of the light and keep the flame of faith alive in your hearts. When the Lord comes, may you go out to meet him with all the saints in the heavenly kingdom" (*Rite of Baptism*).

The lighted candle is a symbol of the Spirit burning within us. Through our words and actions, we share God's love with others. Following Christ, we are called to be a light of faith to others.

The Gift of Grace

The essential part of the baptismal ritual is when the celebrant immerses the person in water or pours water over his or her head. While doing this, the celebrant says, "I baptize you in the name of the Father, and of the Son, and of the Holy Spirit" (*Rite of Baptism*). In an emergency, anyone can baptize another person by praying these words while pouring water over the person's head. These words and actions symbolize our dying and rising to new life in Christ. Baptism cleanses us from sin and gives us the gift of sharing in God's divine life. We call this gift **baptismal grace**.

In Baptism we become the adoptive children of the Father. We are also filled with the Holy Spirit, making us "temples of the Holy Spirit."

Experiencing Jesus

God reveals himself to us through the sacraments. Jesus has given the Church seven sacraments to draw us into union with him and the Father through the Holy Spirit. Through the sacraments we encounter Christ. Through the grace of the sacraments, we can experience Christ's presence in our daily lives. We can also share a sense of the joy and wonder that was felt by those who experienced Jesus' presence firsthand. In Luke's Gospel the account of Jesus' birth is followed by the story of the presentation of the infant Jesus in the Temple. Simeon, an elderly, righteous Jew, and Anna, a prophetess, were both in the Temple when Mary and Joseph presented Jesus to the Lord. Filled with the Holy Spirit, Simeon immediately recognized Jesus as the Messiah. Anna offered thanks for the gift of Jesus and told others about the amazing experience of meeting the promised Messiah firsthand.

Just as Simeon and Anna praised and worshiped God, we are called to fully participate in the eucharistic liturgy and in the work of Christ and the Church. The eucharistic liturgy celebrates God's love for us through the sacrifice of his Son, Jesus.

 page 233 to read more about Baptism and the other sacraments of initiation.

Faith Words

salvation Salvation is freedom from the pain of sin and assurance of permanent union with God.

baptismal grace Baptismal grace is the gift of sharing in God's divine life that we receive at Baptism, which frees us from sin.

How can we reflect Christ's life in us?

15

Our Church Teaches

Jesus instituted the sacraments in the Church so that we could share in God's divine life. Baptism signifies our birth into a new life in Christ, uniting us with all Christians.

In the Eastern Catholic Church, infants receive Confirmation immediately after Baptism and may receive the Eucharist. In the Roman Catholic Church, infants are baptized at special liturgical celebrations, while older children and adults usually receive all three sacraments at the Easter Vigil. Through Baptism, we share in the priesthood of Christ, meaning that we are called to fully participate in the eucharistic liturgy. The Church also celebrates liturgies in honor of Mary and the saints on specific days. Every time we celebrate the Eucharist, our prayers rise to join the prayers of Mary and the saints and all those who have gone before us.

We Believe

Christ is present in the sacraments. In Baptism we are born to a new life in Christ and are joined to the Church.

Respond

Saint Josephine Bakhita

Saint Josephine Bakhita was born in Sudan, a country in Africa, in 1869. She was kidnapped and sold into slavery when she was just a child. As a slave, she experienced humiliation, torture, and mutilation. Because of the brutality she experienced, she forgot her own name. Bakhita, which means "fortunate," was the name given to her by her kidnappers to tease her because her fate was in their hands.

Eventually, Josephine was taken to Italy to become a nanny. There, she attended a school run by the Daughters of Charity (the Canossian Sisters). Josephine asked the sisters about God and came to know him. After several months of preparation, Josephine celebrated the sacraments of Christian initiation, receiving the name Josephine. Remaining with the sisters, Josephine discerned her call to become a religious sister at age forty-one. She told others, "You teach catechism. I will stay in the chapel and pray for you that you may teach well."

For twenty-five years, Josephine ministered as a cook, seamstress, sacristan, and doorkeeper,

living simply and lovingly. She also cared for war victims during World War I. Her goodness and kind spirit touched many people. Her amiable voice was pleasing to children, comforting to the poor and suffering, and encouraging to those who sought help.

Once asked what she would do if she ever encountered her kidnappers, Josephine said, "I would kneel and kiss their hands. If what happened to me had never taken place, how could I become a Christian and a religious?"

With Josephine's maturity came long, painful years of sickness. Although her health was declining, she continued to be an example of faith and virtue and lived to be seventy-eight. About death, she once said, "When a person loves another very much, she greatly wishes to meet that person. Why, then, should I be afraid of death? Death brings us to God."

Josephine was canonized on October 1, 2000. Today, the Christian Sudanese who continue to suffer from persecution and death honor Josephine as their patron saint.

1. Josephine Bakhita was freed from slavery and captivity, became a Catholic, and died a saint. Record the Christian responses that she made to the challenges that she faced in her lifetime.

Challenge	Christian Response
_____	_____
_____	_____
_____	_____

2. During her twenty-five years in the convent, Josephine Bakhita lived a simple life, performing many humble tasks. List some of the things she did and why they contributed to her becoming a saint.

_____

_____

_____

3. Name some ways in which you have responded to God in your life.

_____

_____

_____

_____

How can we renew our baptismal promises?

Prayer Celebration

Renewal of Baptismal Promises

Leader: Let us renew our promises to turn away from sin and profess our faith in God as Father, Son, and Holy Spirit. Do you reject Satan?

All: I do.

Leader: And all his works?

All: I do.

Leader: And all his empty promises?

All: I do.

Leader: Do you believe in God, the Father almighty, creator of heaven and earth?

All: I do.

Leader: Do you believe in Jesus Christ, his only Son, our Lord,
who was born of the Virgin Mary,
was crucified, died, and was buried,
rose from the dead,
and is now seated at the right hand of the Father?

All: I do.

Leader: Do you believe in the Holy Spirit,
the holy Catholic Church, the communion of saints,
the forgiveness of sins, the resurrection of the body,
and life everlasting?

All: I do.

Rite of Baptism

Leader: God, the all-powerful Father of our Lord Jesus Christ,
has given us a new birth by water and the Holy Spirit,
and forgives all our sins.
May he also keep us faithful to our Lord Jesus Christ for ever and ever.

Easter Vigil Renewal of Baptismal Promises, Roman Missal

All: Amen.

Get Connected

with family and friends

Jesus! Son of God, Son of Man

As a boy, Jesus was found in the Temple, speaking his Father's word. He showed us by his example that our call as disciples takes priority in our lives. As Christians we are called to spend our lives doing good works for others and spreading the Gospel.

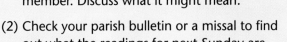

Know Scripture, Know Jesus

You share stories with your friends and take the time to find out what is most important to them. To know Jesus requires that we read about him in the Sacred Scriptures.

Activity

Do one of the following.

(1) Choose one book from the Bible, and read one chapter of it each night with a family member. Discuss what it might mean.

(2) Check your parish bulletin or a missal to find out what the readings for next Sunday are. Choose a time when your family is together to read and discuss the meanings of the readings. Take note of any new meanings you learn about when you hear the readings again at Mass.

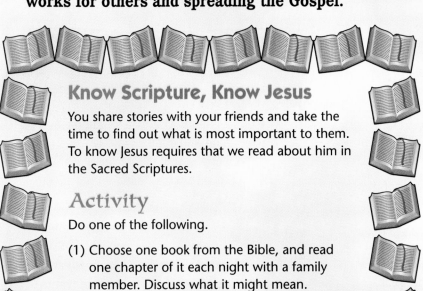

F.A.Q.

Dear Mr. F.A.Q.,

Katie and I are best friends. Elizabeth keeps spreading rumors and tries to turn us against each other. I want to be nice, but she is driving me crazy. How should I handle this?

Signed,
Frustrated in Florida

Dear Frustrated,

How wonderful that Katie is your best friend. That is an example of God's friendship with everyone. Speak with Elizabeth and hear her side of the story. Perhaps she wants to be best friends, too. Talk with Elizabeth to discuss ways to get along. Treat her kindly while not joining in her gossip. Maybe your kindness and good behavior will encourage her to act in the same way as you.

God bless,
Mr. F.A.Q.

Did you know...?

The Ten Commandments are found in two places in the Bible: Exodus 20:1–17 and Deuteronomy 5:6–21. The Ten Commandments are presented as a covenant (a pact) between God and his people.

Holy Humor!

Jokes to Share

You're know you're a Catholic when you watch *Star Wars*, hear "May the force be with you," and want to respond, "And also with you."

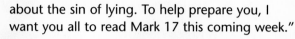

A priest tells the congregation, "For next Sunday's homily, I prepared something about the sin of lying. To help prepare you, I want you all to read Mark 17 this coming week."

The following Sunday, as the priest begins his homily, he asks how many people read Mark 17. Every hand goes up.

The priest smiles.

"Mark has only sixteen chapters," he says. "I will now proceed with my homily on the sin of lying."

All-Star Profile

Name: William E. Simon
Born: 1927
Died: 2000
Occupation: U.S. secretary of the treasury during the presidencies of Nixon and Ford, first administrator of the Federal Energy Office, active member of the U.S. Olympic Committee for more than thirty years, philanthropist and founder of the William E. Simon Foundation
Quote of a Lifetime: ". . . More important than sharing one's material wealth is sharing the wealth of ourselves—our time and energy, our passion and commitment, and, above all, our love."
Claims to Fame: Donated 93 million dollars to help people in need. Authored two best-selling books. Brought communion to dying patients at four hospitals.
Hobbies: supporting the U.S. Olympics, volunteering on committees for the Knights of Malta, New York Hospital, Americares, Catholic Big Brothers, and The Heritage Foundation

Something To Do

On Sunday

Imagine what you would have said and done as one of the people from one of the Scripture Readings at Mass.

Through the Week

Small daily changes make a big difference over time. Spend five minutes in silence each day and ask God what changes he wants you to make in your life.

A Prayer for the Week

Lord, help us to live as your faithful disciples. May your word be written on our hearts so that we will always be faithful to you. Teach us how to be forgiving and to love others as you love us.
Amen.

Wired

Visit Our Web Site
www.blestarewe.com

Web Site Spotlight
www.jesuit.ie/prayer

This site features daily prayers that you can pray, as well as Scripture readings in English, Spanish, Japanese, Portuguese, and other languages.

3 Jesus! Son of God, Son of Man

Whoever sees me sees the one who sent me.

Based on John 14:9

Share

Through Baptism, you are called to be a disciple of Jesus. How can you follow Christ and carry out the mission to share him with others?

There are many opportunities for doing good works—for helping people in your community and beyond. Participate in one of the following activities or an activity of your own choosing.

- Visit patients in a nursing home or veterans' hospital.

- Clean and sort clothes that your family no longer wears and donate them to the St. Vincent de Paul Society or a local Goodwill organization.

- Volunteer to help collect and send food to people in need.

- Contact an agency that supports children suffering from serious illnesses and ask about becoming a pen pal for a seriously ill child.

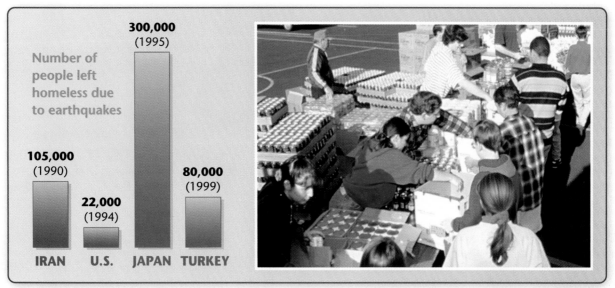

Number of people left homeless due to earthquakes

300,000 (1995)
105,000 (1990)
22,000 (1994)
80,000 (1999)

IRAN   U.S.   JAPAN   TURKEY

Sources: Iran—*Worldbook*; U.S.A.—*Dynamic Isolations Systems Inc.*; Japan and Turkey—*BBC News 6*

Activity

Reflect on your participation in a charitable work or act of kindness. How did you feel doing the work, and what did you learn from your experience?

_____

_____

_____

_____

_____

What does Jesus teach us about his Father's will?

Hear & Believe

✝ Scripture The Boy Jesus in the Temple

When Jesus was twelve years old, he went with Mary and Joseph to the Temple in Jerusalem for the Feast of Passover, as was the custom for Jewish families. When the feast was over and it was time to return home, the boy Jesus remained behind in Jerusalem. Thinking that he was in the caravan, Mary and Joseph journeyed for a day looking for Jesus. Not finding him, they returned to Jerusalem to look for him. After three days they found Jesus in the Temple, sitting with the teachers, and listening to them and asking them questions. All who heard Jesus speak were astounded at his understanding and his answers.

When Mary and Joseph saw him, they were astonished. Mary said to Jesus, "Son, why have you done this to us? Your father and I have been looking for you with great anxiety."

Jesus replied, "Why were you looking for me? Did you not know that I must be in my Father's house?"

But Mary and Joseph did not understand what he said to them. Jesus went with them to Nazareth and was obedient to them. His mother kept all these things in her heart. And Jesus grew in wisdom and age and favor before God and man.

Based on Luke 2:41–52

Honoring God

Mary and Joseph raised Jesus in the Jewish faith. Together, they celebrated important Jewish feasts such as Passover. Despite his young age, Jesus' understanding of his faith reached far beyond his years. This was evident by the insightful answers he gave to the teachers in the Temple. Indeed, Jesus had a close relationship with his Father. This is why his parents found him in his "Father's house" doing his Father's will. Jesus knew he had a mission. Throughout his life, Jesus grew in his faith and was obedient to God's word.

When we reflect on this Scripture story we recognize that we, as Jesus' disciples, have a mission. God invites all of us to participate in and proclaim God's love to the world.

Guided by Our Conscience

How do we discover our specific mission? We discover it through the Holy Spirit, who informs us in our **conscience**. If our conscience tells us something is good to do and we avoid doing it, we are being sinful. We should remind ourselves that we too must "be in our Father's house" in our own way. Our lives and our actions must reflect an ongoing effort to bring about goodness.

When we follow our conscience, we avoid sin. Our conscience helps us judge right from wrong and avoid sin. It helps us know that certain words and actions are right so that we can choose what is good. Knowingly and deliberately choosing to do wrong, even if we think we have "good" reasons for doing so, is a sin.

When we are faced with choices, we must rely upon our conscience to guide us. The sacraments give us the grace we need to make good decisions. We should form our conscience through prayer and self-reflection, and by listening to the guidance of the Church, the Scriptures, and parents or other adults. We must also be open to the guidance of the Holy Spirit.

We must not blame poor choices on ignorance or errors in judgment. We are responsible for choices we freely make and for their consequences. However, there are some situations in which we are not free to make our own choices. For example, fear of personal harm can lead us to make poor decisions. Extreme pressure from others can also limit our ability to choose responsibly. In these cases we have not made our choices freely.

When we choose to love others as Jesus did, we avoid sin. The Church identifies two types of sin: **mortal sin** and **venial sin**. By willfully committing a serious act against God's law or our neighbor, we damage our relationship with God. This is called a mortal sin. A venial sin is a less serious offense that weakens our relationship with God. As Christians, we are called to live a life free from sin that we might live in the fullness of God's love.

As Christians, we embrace others with God's love by showing respect for the human dignity of each person. This includes protecting the reputation of others by not belittling them or spreading false rumors about them. Remember that God gives us freedom of choice. This does not, however, mean that God gives us the right to speak or act in ways that are hurtful or damaging to others. Whenever we are given a choice to make, we are invited—and, as Christians, are expected—to turn to God for help in making the right decision.

Faith Words

conscience A conscience is an ability to know what is right and what is wrong.

mortal sin A mortal sin is a serious act against God's law, done purposely. It separates us from God's grace. It normally requires the sacrament of Reconciliation to be forgiven.

venial sin A venial sin is less serious than a mortal sin. Venial sins weaken our relationship with God and the church community.

How do Jesus and the Church community guide our conscience?

23

Our Church Teaches

Jesus showed us the importance of seeking God, our Father, in everything we do. God's word is a "light for our path," leading us to make the right moral choices. Dignity lies in this freedom of choice. To turn away from God or deny his existence is a sin against the first commandment.

The first commandment also directs us to worship, pray to, and adore God. In the second commandment, we learn that it is wrong to swear by God's name to support a false statement. We honor God by using his name reverently. The second commandment also forbids blasphemy—using offensive language when speaking about God. The story of the boy Jesus in the Temple calls us to share the love of God, our Father, with others. Jesus calls us to spread God's truth. This is our mission as Catholic Christians.

We Believe
We form our conscience by praying to God and practicing our faith. Our conscience guides us in treating others with respect and dignity.

Respond

Blessed Bernard Lichtenburg

Blessed Bernard Lichtenburg was born on December 3, 1875 in East Central Europe. He studied for the priesthood in Austria and became a priest at age twenty-four and went on to study at St. Hedwig's Cathedral in Berlin. Later, he was appointed to serve the cathedral during the time that the Nazis were coming to power.

When word about the rise and agenda of the Nazis began to spread, Bernard was greatly concerned. He felt obligated to become politically involved and to actively protest Nazism and the persecution of Jews. Bernard went directly to the Nazis, pleading for them to act more humanely toward the Jews. The Nazis thought Bernard was simply acting pious or holy, and they did not consider his protests to be a challenge or a threat.

Bernard continued to confront the Nazis about the destruction of Germany and the Catholic faith. He preached to increase awareness of the immoral killing of Jews that was becoming a standard practice in the land. The Nazis warned Bernard not to oppose their actions, but Bernard continued to stand up for his beliefs and invited others to do the same. He distributed a document from Pope Pius XI, titled "With Burning Anxiety," that directly condemned the Nazis' beliefs and practices.

At age sixty-six, Bernard was arrested. He lived in a concentration camp for two years under terrible

conditions. He was then turned over to the Nazi police, or Gestapo, to be "reeducated." This meant that he was threatened with torture unless he surrendered his beliefs and accepted those of the Nazis. Bernard refused. Two years later, on his way to another concentration camp, Bernard died.

What is remarkable is that, despite the Nazis' strong disapproval of Bernard, 4,000 mourners dared to attend his funeral.

Activities

1. Why did Bernard Lichtenburg protest against the Nazis?

_____

_____

_____

2. Why do you think Bernard Lichtenburg is "Blessed"?

_____

_____

This young person makes a difference in the life of a handicapped woman by volunteering his time.

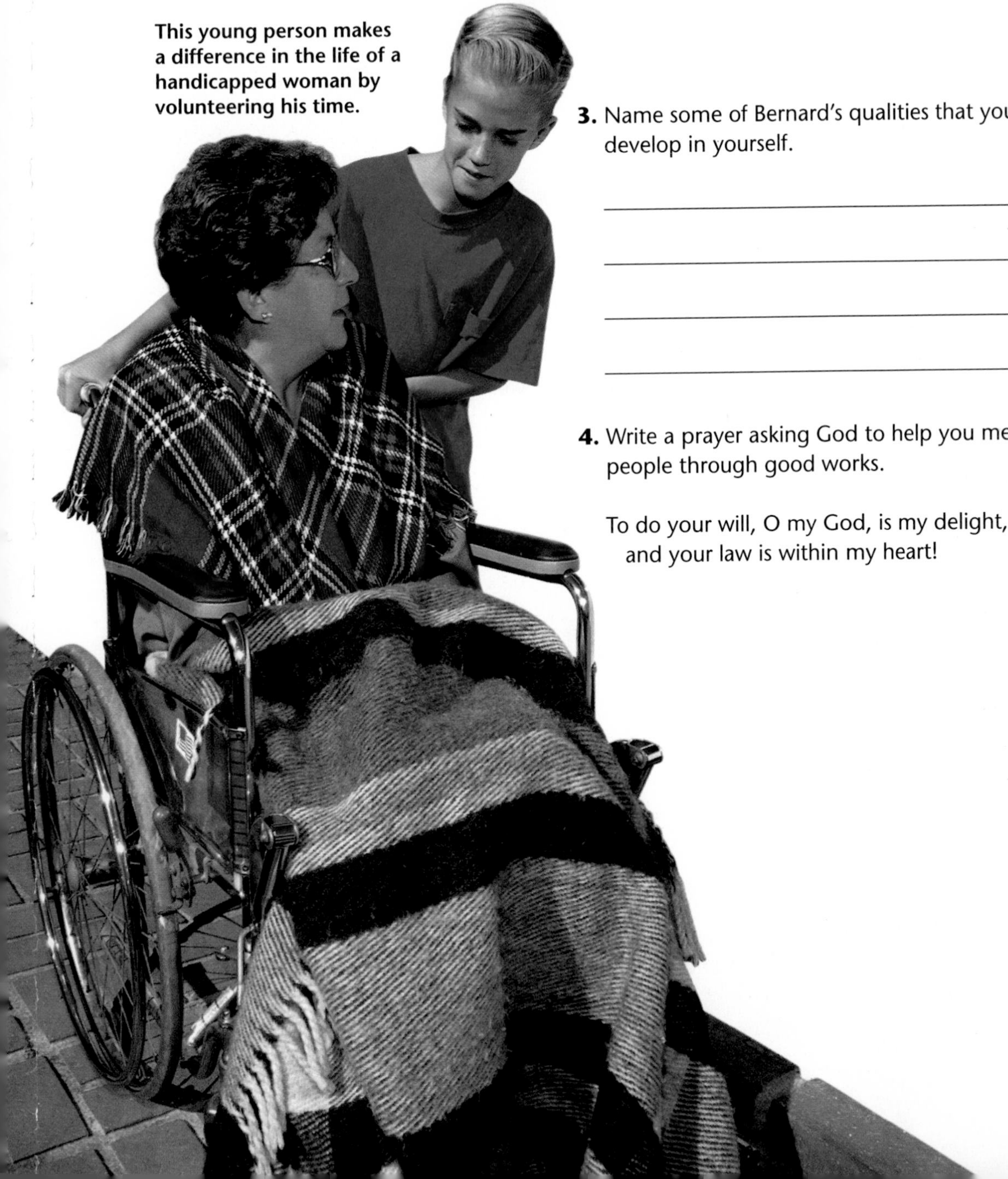

3. Name some of Bernard's qualities that you would like to develop in yourself.

_____

_____

_____

_____

4. Write a prayer asking God to help you meet the needs of people through good works.

To do your will, O my God, is my delight,
   and your law is within my heart!

Psalm 40:9

How can we
affirm our
loving choices?

✝ Prayer Celebration

Loving Choices

Take a moment to reflect on your good works. Imagine having a phone conversation with Jesus about the people you helped through your kind words and actions. Write about your dialogue with Jesus.

Thank you, God, for calling us to be your disciples. Help us grow strong in our faith and live according to your will.

Get Connected

with family and friends

Jesus, One with God in Prayer

When Jesus was tempted in the desert, he was able to resist those temptations through prayer. Prayer is communication with God. Through prayer, the Holy Spirit guides our thoughts, words, and actions.

Turning Fear into Hope

Many women and men of faith have made it through very hard times by turning to God and praying, just as Jesus did. God promises us that our prayers will always be heard and answered, even though we don't know what those answers may be.

Activity

Do one of the following.

(1) In John's Gospel Jesus tells his frightened followers, "It is I. Do not be afraid" (John 6:20). Think about Jesus' words, and remember some times when you felt alone or afraid. How was God with you then? Memorize Jesus' words, and share them with members of your family. Repeat the words throughout the day, and they will give you strength and courage.

(2) If you notice that someone you care about seems to be having a rough time, copy a Scripture passage or write a prayer and leave it for the person to find.

The Password Is

testament

As Catholics, we use the word *testament* when referring to the Old Testament and the New Testament in Sacred Scripture. The word *testament* is from the Latin *testamentum*, derived from the Greek word *diatheke*. This Greek word comes from a Hebrew word meaning "covenant."

Did you know...?

Beginning in the third century, some Christians chose to follow Christ by fleeing to the desert and devoting their lives to silence, prayer, manual labor, and solitude.

A Fire of Love

The desire to sing was a fire **Jeanne Cotter** felt in her belly at a young age. Cotter knew she had to spread love, and for her, music was the way to do it. Cotter grew up to become a talented singer, songwriter, and composer of liturgical music. Storytelling is an important part of Cotter's music. Cotter says that storytelling is an Irish way of making sense out of life, a tradition that was handed on to her to help her create meaning, and maybe even some beauty, out of all that she lives.

She delights audiences throughout Canada and the United States with her original piano performances, inspirational lyrics, and tales about her Irish-Catholic upbringing in southern Minnesota. Her musical style combines soul, pop, and elegant piano. Cotter has produced recordings through her company, Mythic Rain Productions. Her CDs include *Diamonds on the Water, Many Snows,* and *Amber.* Cotter has also written the book *Keyboard Improvisation for the Liturgical Musician.*

All-Star Profile

Name: Eileen M. Egan
Born: 1912
Died: 2000
Family Background: came from Wales to the United States as a teenager
Occupation: Catholic Relief Services worker for more than forty years, peace activist, and co-founder of Pax Christi USA
Quote of a Lifetime: "I think all of us, as an expression of our faith, should be working for peace."
Claims to Fame: Went to countries all over the world to set up relief programs. Asked the bishops at Vatican II to include an anti-war statement in their documents. Wrote for justice and peace and was close friends with Dorothy Day and Mother Teresa.
Hobbies: drama club, literary club

Something To Do

On Sunday

Arrive early for Mass to pray some of the prayers in the missal or liturgy resource book. Look up the readings for the day, and read through them before Mass begins.

Through the Week

Choose an inspirational Scripture verse for each day of the week. Try to recall it three times a day and reflect on how well you have lived it.

Wired

Visit Our Web Site
www.blestarewe.com

Web Site Spotlight
www.webdesk.com/catholic/prayers
Visit this Web site and read prayers that others have written and perhaps contribute one of your own.

A Prayer for the Week

Thank you, Lord, for teaching us to pray and for blessing us with your word. Help us turn to you during our day for guidance and strength. May we live each day knowing that you are ever present in our lives. Amen.

4 Jesus, One with God in Prayer

Ask and it will be given to you; seek and you will find; knock and the door will be opened to you.

Matthew 7:7

Share

When you are close to someone, you trust that person to respect your views and your feelings. Words are not always necessary; you can feel comfortable just being together.

God invites us to be close to him. He calls us to be with him in prayer. He loves and accepts us for who we are. We can turn to God in times of joy and thankfulness as well as in times of sorrow and pain. We can pray for the needs of others as well as our own.

Prayer helps us grow closer to God and to one another. Look at the statistics below to learn what Americans today think about prayer and religion.

Americans who favor prayer in school

Source: The Gallup Poll Organization, 2001

Americans who believe that God answers their prayers

Source: Newsweek, March 31, 1997

Americans who believe that prayer or meditation can help with medical healing

Source: "Many Believe Spirituality Heals," by Lee Bowman, Scripps Howard News Service, 1998

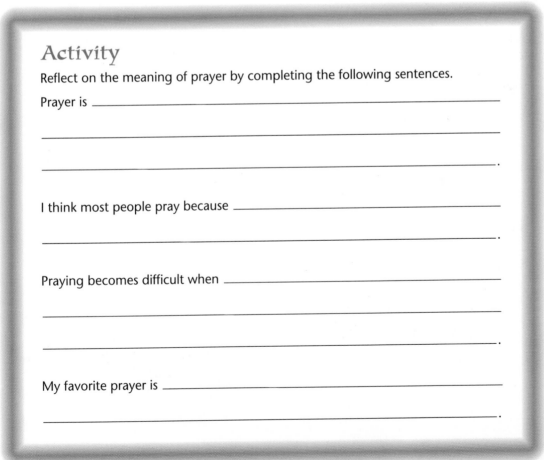

Activity

Reflect on the meaning of prayer by completing the following sentences.

Prayer is _____

_____

_____.

I think most people pray because _____

_____.

Praying becomes difficult when _____

_____

_____.

My favorite prayer is _____

_____.

How does prayer help us resist temptation?

Hear & Believe

Scripture The Temptation of Jesus

After Jesus was baptized, the Holy Spirit led him into the desert, where he was tempted by the devil. For forty days he ate nothing. At the end of this time, he was hungry.

The devil came to Jesus and said, "If you are the Son of God, command this stone to become bread."

Jesus answered him, "It is written, 'One does not live by bread alone.'"

Then the devil tempted Jesus and showed him all the kingdoms of the world in a single instant. He said, "I shall give to you all this power and its glory. All this will be yours if you worship me."

Jesus replied, "It is written: 'You shall worship the Lord, your God, and him alone shall you serve.'"

Then the devil led Jesus to Jerusalem, made him stand on the top of the wall surrounding the Temple, and said to him, "If you are the Son of God, throw yourself down from here, for it is written: 'He will command his angels concerning you, to guard you' and 'With their hands they will support you, lest you dash your foot against a stone.'"

Jesus said to him in reply, "It also says, 'You shall not put the Lord, your God, to the test.'"

When the devil finished tempting Jesus in every way, he departed.

Based on Luke 4:1–13

Overcoming Temptations

In the Gospel of Luke, Jesus is portrayed as someone who always prays when faced with a big decision. In the passage you just read, Jesus went by himself to the desert to pray before beginning his public ministry. But he was not really alone. The Holy Spirit was with Jesus, giving him the strength to overcome **temptation**. Although he may have been weak from hunger, Jesus was strong in his love for God. He responded to every temptation by using words from Scripture. God's word strengthened him to make wise choices.

God's word is also a source of strength for us. God is always present and open to our needs. Like Jesus, we also face temptations and challenges. We are lured by promises of possessions, popularity, or power. Jesus helps us see that God is the source of true happiness. When we are faced with temptation, our prayers to Jesus will help us hear God's word.

The Gift of Prayer

Prayer is a gift that connects us to God. God invites us to pray often so that we grow in his love. As individuals and as a community, we turn to God in prayer with hope. By listening and reflecting on God's presence in our lives, we can become more like Jesus.

There are different forms of prayer within the Church. We are probably most familiar with vocal prayer, in which we speak our prayers to God. Vocal prayer includes traditional prayers, such as the Lord's Prayer, and personal, spontaneous prayers. **Meditation** and **contemplation** are two other ways in which we pray to God. They begin with listening to God, who is always speaking to us in our hearts and minds.

When we meditate, we think about God and how we respond to his presence in our lives. We may read from Scripture, look at a sacred object or image, such as a crucifix, or listen to soft music. We might also reflect on God's teachings and ask him to help us live according to the Gospels. Or we may just quietly listen to what God has to say to us.

Contemplation is a prayer in which we rest in God's presence. Unlike meditation, it does not involve active thinking. We may focus on a word or image at first, but then we free our minds of all thought. We release ourselves to experience God's love in the quiet of our hearts.

Overcoming Difficulties in Praying

Prayer is a powerful way to express our love for God. So why do we have difficulty praying at times? Sometimes we are busy and don't take time to pray. Many activities fill our lives. Busyness can distract us from our relationship with God. Even when we try to talk with God, our prayers can lack warmth and sincerity. By not taking time to have meaningful conversations with God, we can separate ourselves from him.

How can we improve our prayer life and experience the joy of encountering God? We need to commit to spending time with God through prayer to become more immersed in his love. Prayer requires trusting in God. We turn to God not as a last resort but because we trust in his love and goodness. When prayer becomes an integral part of our life, our life itself—all that we say and do—becomes a prayer.

Faith Words

temptation Temptation is an enticement or a pressure to turn away from God through sinful thoughts, words, or actions.

meditation Meditation is a type of prayer in which we are silent and concentrate on listening to God through our feelings, imagination, and thoughts. Meditation is thinking about God's presence in our lives.

contemplation Contemplation is prayer without the need for images, words, or thoughts; it is resting in God's presence.

What is the value of prayer?

Our Church Teaches

Prayer is a loving exchange between God and humanity that has been taking place since God invited the first people into a loving relationship with him. Praying means opening our hearts to God. To participate fully in Christian life, we must pray so that we may grow closer to God. Prayer and Christian life are inseparable.

There are many forms of prayer. We pray with our voices. We pray in meditation and contemplation. We can pray on our own or as a community. Jesus taught us his own prayer to the Father. Through the Holy Spirit, the Church offers us many forms of liturgical prayer.

At times prayer can be difficult. Distractions may interfere with our ability to pray. But to grow spiritually we must try to give more attention to prayer and also trust that God will answer us.

We Believe

Prayer is opening our hearts to God so that we may be filled with his love. God invites each of us to pray often.

Respond

Josh's Prayer

Josh walked into his bedroom and tossed his heavy backpack onto his bed. *If only it were that easy to get rid of my problems,* he thought. His parents had recently separated and Josh was having trouble concentrating in school. In fact, today his teacher had returned his science test with a failing grade. He was tempted to lie about it to his parents. Josh wondered whether his parents, with all their problems, really cared about his grades, anyway. He was also worried about the upcoming tryouts for the soccer team. Josh was afraid he wouldn't make the team.

When Josh confided in his grandmother about his problems, she asked him if he prayed. *Of course I pray,* he thought. He didn't see how that was going to help him now. Josh's grandmother reminded him that God could help him deal with his problems. He could still hear her saying, "Spend some time with God, Josh. Prayer is God's special gift to you."

Josh thought about his grandmother's words as he sat down on his bed. With difficulty at first, he began to relax and let go of his tensions. In the quiet of his room, Josh closed his eyes and began to pray.

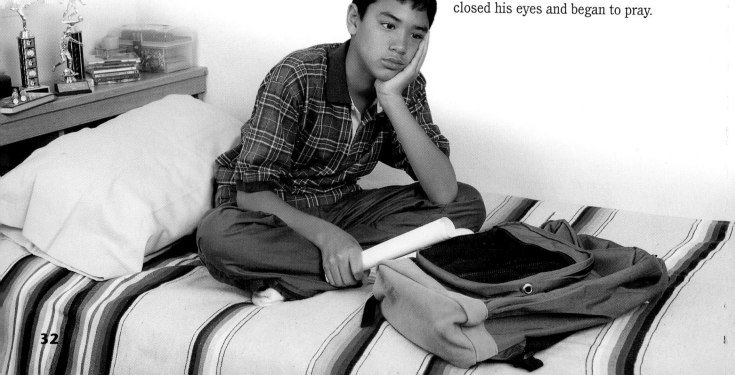

Activities

1. Jesus shows us that prayer helps us to know God's will for us. From Jesus we learn that prayer can bring us strength, hope, and guidance. Check off the statements that reflect your beliefs about prayer.

❏ I believe in the power of prayer.

❏ I want an answer to my prayers immediately.

❏ I only pray to ask God for something I want.

❏ God sometimes answers prayers in unexpected ways.

❏ I am too busy to pray.

❏ I am comfortable praying without words.

❏ I pray with the church community, but am uncomfortable praying by myself.

❏ Prayer is necessary for our faith to grow.

Do the beliefs you checked off help or interfere with your relationship with God?

2. Write a prayer that holds special meaning for you. Then spend a moment in silence, reflecting on God's message in the prayer.

_____

_____

_____

_____

How can we rest in God's presence?

✝ Prayer Celebration

In God's Presence

Jesus turned to God in prayer for strength and guidance. We, too, are invited to share in this intimate exchange with God our Father. Let us take a moment to spend some time with him in meditation.

Let everything around you become quiet. Become quiet within yourself. Put all your thoughts aside and begin to listen. God speaks to us in the silence of our hearts. God is the light in our darkness. His light brings us comfort, reassurance, and love.

(Take a few moments to reflect in silence)

SIDE 1: The LORD is my shepherd; I shall not want.
  In verdant pastures he gives me repose;
  Beside restful waters he leads me;
  he refreshes my soul.
  He guides me in right paths
  for his name's sake.
  Even though I walk in the dark valley
  I fear no evil; for you are at my side
  With your rod and your staff
  that give me courage.

SIDE 2: You spread the table before me
  in the sight of my foes;
  You anoint my head with oil;
  my cup overflows.
  Only goodness and kindness follow me
  all the days of my life;
  And I shall dwell in the house of the LORD
  for years to come.

Psalm 23

WE CARE *About Creation*

Caring for God's Creatures

Erv, an eighty-nine-year-old man whose wife of sixty years recently died, lives in an apartment in a retirement residence with Moe—his goldfish. From the small fishbowl that rests on the table next to Erv's favorite chair, Moe provides Erv with constant companionship. Though he's just a tiny goldfish, Moe has become quite important to Erv. Erv frequently finds himself talking to Moe, even though he knows Moe can't talk back. He carefully changes Moe's water every couple of days and feeds him regularly. The little goldfish, a gift from some friends in Erv's parish, helps Erv feel less lonely.

People who study ancient civilizations tell us that pets have been part of human life since the beginning of history. Pets can provide us with affection, companionship, protection, and hours of fun.

Many nursing homes now provide pets for their residents. The special friendship of pets seems to help the elderly physically as well as emotionally—cheering them up, lowering their blood pressure, and drawing them out of isolation and loneliness. Animal experts often speak about how to properly care for pets, and many parishes now encourage families to have their pets blessed at the parish on the feast of Saint Francis Assisi. All of this has helped raise awareness about the importance of pets and the treatment of animals in general. Caring for our pets is part of our responsibility to God's creation.

How do you accept your responsibility to care for animals?

Think About It

Saint Francis called animals our brothers and sisters and treated them with great respect. Although God did not create animals with souls or free will as he did human beings, animals are God's creatures, too, deserving of our love and care. The world of animals is varied, and animals can touch our lives in special ways.

Do you have, or have you ever had, a pet that you feel a special affection for? Design the pet's ID card at right. If you have never had a pet, write about a pet that you would like to have.

A Special Pet

Pet Name: _____

Type of Animal: _____

Special Characteristics: _____

Tricks or Uncanny Abilities: _____

_____

Ways to Care for My Pet: _____

_____

Learn About It

The Book of Genesis in the Bible tells the story of Creation. In this story, we read that God gave the first man, Adam, the task of naming all the animals and that God entrusted the care of the animals to human beings. In making us stewards, or caretakers, of creation God meant for us to protect animals and treat them as humanely as possible.

Do Something About It

You have probably heard about situations in which animals were not treated humanely.

Write something your religious education group might do to address such problems.

On your own, perhaps you might volunteer to help at a local animal shelter or see if a local nursing home has a program allowing pets to be brought in for the residents.

The Meaning of the Kingdom

Jesus taught us about our relationship with God and revealed the kingdom of God. We are called to spread the Gospel by living the values of God's kingdom.

Blessed are the poor in spirit,
*   for theirs is the kingdom of heaven.*

Matthew 5:3

Jesus compared the kingdom of God to a net cast into the sea and to a farmer who sows seed in his field. Both images illustrate how Jesus gathers his followers into the kingdom.

We Are the Hope

Paul A. Tate

Get Connected

with family and friends

The Kingdom of God

In the Lord's Prayer, we pray, "Thy kingdom come; thy will be done on earth as it is in heaven." God's kingdom is his reign of peace, justice, and love. As Catholics, we believe that Jesus began the kingdom here on earth by coming into the world. We do the work of God's kingdom when we treat others with love, compassion, and mercy.

Find Your Own Calcutta

An American woman once wrote to Mother Teresa to ask if she could come to Calcutta, India, to join the Missionaries of Charity and serve the poor and suffering. In response, Mother Teresa said that the woman should stay in the United States and serve the poor and suffering there.

By being kind and loving to those around us, we prepare for the coming of God's kingdom. Look around your home, school, or community, find your own Calcutta, and get to work.

Activity

Do one of the following:

(1) Have the members of your family decide on an activity to do together to serve the community in which you live.

(2) As a family, pray for the fulfillment of God's kingdom and for God to show each member of your family how he or she is being called to serve.

Check It Out

This cross is the emblem for the Catholic bishops of the United States. The bishops prepare documents and letters that help us understand the Church's social teaching. The bishops teach us about important issues such as the sanctity of human life, family life in the Church and society, the rights of workers, our responsibility to the poor and vulnerable, and the importance of caring for the earth. When we follow the Church's social teaching, we share the goodness of God's kingdom with others.

Did you know...?

Catholic social teaching reminds us that as Christians we are called to respond to the suffering of all our brothers and sisters, especially those with the greatest needs.

Holy Humor!

Signs of Wit

Seen on signs outside churches:

FREE TRIP TO HEAVEN. DETAILS INSIDE.

THIS IS A CH __ __ CH. WHAT IS MISSING? (U R)

FIGHT TRUTH DECAY - STUDY THE BIBLE DAILY.

SEVEN DAYS WITHOUT PRAYER MAKES ONE WEAK.

LIFE IS FRAGILE; HANDLE WITH PRAYER.

SIGN BROKEN. MESSAGE INSIDE THIS SUNDAY.

All-Star Profile

Name: Archbishop Oscar Romero
Born: 1917
Died: 1980
Occupation: archbishop of the diocese of San Salvador, courageous leader, peacemaker
Quote of a Lifetime: "The Church would betray its own love for God and its fidelity to the Gospel if it stopped being a defender of the rights of the poor, a humanizer of every legitimate struggle to achieve a more just society, one that prepares the way for the true reign of God in history."
Claims to Fame: Was the voice for the poor and suffering in El Salvador. Condemned military violence and abuses of political power that oppressed the poor. Died a martyr; assassinated while celebrating Mass.

Something To Do

On Sunday

During the Prayer of the Faithful, pray for people throughout the world who are victims of war, poverty, or famine.

Through the Week

Show the ways of God's kingdom by performing small acts of kindness for your family, friends, and neighbors.

Wired

Visit Our Web Site
www.blestarewe.com

Web Site Spotlight
www.usccb.org

Discover more about your faith and ways that Catholics are being called to action by reading the documents and teachings of our U.S. bishops.

✝ A Prayer for the Week

Lord, help us use our gifts and talents to serve others in a spirit of love and charity. Through our actions, may we show your love to others and do the work of your kingdom here on earth.
Amen.

5 The Kingdom of God

You shall love your neighbor as yourself.

Matthew 22:39

Share

Our world does not always reflect peace or happiness. People in many countries face poverty, sickness, and war. Yet there are people who are working to make a difference. In the news, we often hear about people who respond quickly to the needs of others and take a stand against injustice. We hear about organizations that send money, supplies, and volunteers to assist people who are suffering. Through such volunteer efforts, people are making a difference in creating a just and peaceful world.

Activity

In the box below, list of some of the injustices that exist in our society today. Then select one of the injustices you listed and write a change that could be made to help create a better society.

What does Jesus teach us about God's kingdom?

Hear & Believe

✝ Scripture Parables of the Kingdom

A *parable* is a story that teaches a moral or religious lesson. Jesus often spoke in parables to help people understand his teachings. In order to pass on Jesus' message, I have retold some of Jesus' greatest parables. Some of these parables describe God's wonderful kingdom. Through these stories, Jesus tells us of the value and greatness of the kingdom and helps us understand that God is a loving Father who desires that all his children live with him forever.

Throughout his ministry, Jesus told parables to illustrate how God calls us to share in his love. Parables often use everyday events and objects, especially from nature, to explain important truths. In the following parables, found in Matthew's Gospel, Jesus describes the **kingdom of God**.

The kingdom of heaven may be likened to a man who sowed good seed in his field. While everyone was asleep, his enemy came and sowed weeds all through the wheat, and then went off. When the crop grew and bore fruit, the weeds appeared as well.

The slaves asked, "Master, do you want us to go and pull up the weeds?"

He replied, "No, if you pull up the weeds you might uproot the wheat along with them. Let them grow together until harvest; then at harvest time I will say to the harvesters, 'First collect the weeds and tie them in bundles for burning; but gather the wheat into my barn.'"

He who sows good seed is the Son of Man, the field is the world, the good seed the children of the kingdom. The weeds are the children of the evil one, and the enemy who sows them is the devil. The harvest is the end of the age, and the harvesters are angels.

The kingdom of heaven is also like a net thrown into the sea, which collects fish of every kind. When it is full, fishermen haul it ashore and sit down to put what is good into buckets. What is bad they throw away.

The kingdom of heaven is like a tiny mustard seed that becomes a large bush, and the birds of the sky come and dwell in its branches.

The kingdom of heaven is like a treasure buried in a field, which a person finds and hides again and out of joy goes and sells all that he has and buys that field.

The kingdom of heaven is like a merchant searching for fine pearls. When he finds a pearl of great price, he goes and sells all that he has and buys it.

Based on Matthew 13:24–30, 36–39, 47–48, 31–32, 44–46

God's Plan for His Kingdom

The kingdom of God, or heaven, is God's reign of peace, justice, and love. Jesus began the kingdom of God on earth. The Church is the beginning of God's kingdom. We continue Jesus' work by following his example, and God's kingdom grows within us like a tiny mustard seed.

Only at the end of time will the kingdom of God be fully realized. Jesus Christ will judge how well we have served God and others. The angels, spiritual creatures who glorify and serve God, will separate the good from the bad. Those who follow Christ will enjoy everlasting happiness. The parable about the weeds among the wheat illustrates how Jesus will gather his followers into his kingdom.

The Church, a Sign of God's Kingdom

The Church is a sign of God's kingdom. Christ, the head of the Church, teaches us to reach out to all people, especially those who are poor or suffering.

He showed us how to treat others with love, compassion, and mercy. Jesus also encourages us to not allow the "anxieties and riches and pleasures of life" (Luke 8:14) to lead us away from God.

As members of the Church, the Body of Christ, we are united to each other. Each member of the Body has differences, yet we join together to work for the kingdom. We respond to our vocation by using our unique talents to bring God's justice and mercy to others. We believe that all salvation comes from Christ through the Church. We also believe that God both willed and destined all creatures for the good of humanity and God's glory.

A Closer Look

The Mustard Seed

The mustard seed is a very small seed. In Jesus' time it may have been the smallest seed known. In Palestine, a variety of mustard seed could grow into a tree whose size was comparable to that of a dogwood. The image  of the small, insignificant mustard seed growing into a large tree was a familiar image that Jesus could use to explain the growth of God's kingdom.

Faith Words

parable A parable is a story that teaches a moral or religious lesson. Parables often use everyday events and objects to explain important truths.

kingdom of God The kingdom of God is God's reign of peace, justice, and love, initiated on earth by Jesus and reaching perfect fulfillment at the end of time.

How can we bring God's truth to others?

Our Church Teaches

Out of love, God created the universe. He keeps it in existence through his Son, Jesus Christ, and the Holy Spirit. God created all creatures to share in his truth, goodness, and beauty. As a sign of his love, God made an everlasting covenant with Noah and all his descendants. Then he called Abraham and made a covenant with him and his descendants. As a sign of this covenant, God revealed his law to us through Moses. God fulfilled the promises of his covenant by sending Jesus Christ, who saved us from sin. Always faithful to his covenant, God continues to guide and protect us as we do the work of his kingdom.

We do the work of the kingdom through the Church, especially when we care for the poor and the suffering. By using our abilities to serve the needs of others, we grow in faith and live the joy of God's kingdom.

> **We Believe**
> United in Christ, the members of the Church use their varied talents to serve others, particularly the poor and the suffering.

Respond

The Turnaround Team

With only eight seconds to go, Troy Bell, point guard of the Boston College Eagles, found himself guarded by two University of Southern California Trojan defenders. He passed the ball to Kenny Harley, a senior, who drove to the basket but missed the layup. Then Bell missed an attempted dunk, ending the second-round game of the 2001 NCAA Basketball Tournament with a score of 74–71. The Eagles' hopes for a trip to the Final Four were cut short.

Of course, the Eagles were disappointed, but their coach, Al Skinner, reminded them that they had enjoyed a good season. In fact, it had been a "fairy tale" season. The Eagles had become the first team in their conference's history to go from last place to first place in one year and had ended up being the 2001 Big East Champions. In previous years, the team's win-loss records were 15–16, 6–21, and 11–19.

Everyone asked, "How did a team that was neither unusually quick nor strong end up winning twenty-six games and rank as the number-ten team in the country?" Some said the Eagles had a strength that could be felt but not seen. Some said

that what Al Skinner and his coaching staff had accomplished that year was "miraculous."

Coach Skinner said that what had made the difference was that during the losing years, his players had accepted the fact that it would take time to improve. He had challenged them to work hard and to add one new skill each year to improve as a team. Coach Skinner had also taught the players to be patient with themselves and with each other. He had inspired them to make sacrifices for the team.

Coach Skinner had done another important thing to turn the team around: After the team's third losing season, the coach had taken the Eagles to Europe to play against some European teams. There, he encouraged his players to spend their free time together in the hope that they might get to know one another better. His plan worked. The players grew closer. They learned to listen to one another and appreciate their differences. Above all, the players learned how to have compassion for one another. When the B.C. Eagles returned from Europe to Boston, they were ready to play as a team. The rest is NCAA history.

Activities

1. How did the Boston College team reflect the way people treat each other in the kingdom of God?

_____

_____

_____

2. Describe ways that people you know or have heard about have reflected God's kingdom.

_____

_____

_____

3. Explain how the kindom of God is like a treasure buried in a field.

_____

_____

_____

_____

How can we ask for God's help in doing the work of his kingdom?

 **Prayer Celebration**

Doing the Work of God's Kingdom

When we join together to promote justice, we become a powerful force in doing the work of God's kingdom.

Group 1:	Thank you, God, for sending your beloved Son to proclaim the good news of your kingdom. May we always receive Christ's message with loving hearts.
Groups 1 and 2:	May your seed of love and unity grow in our hearts and transform the lives of those around us. Help us make a difference so that through us others may know your love.
Groups 1, 2, and 3:	Guide us in doing the work of your kingdom here on earth. Help us be aware of the needs of the poor and the suffering, the young and the elderly. May we use the talents with which you have blessed us to bring your joy and love to others. We pray with joy and hope for the fulfillment of your kingdom. Amen.

Get CONNECTED

with family and friends

Servants of the Kingdom

Every baptized person has a special role, or vocation, in doing the work of God's kingdom. Our vocation is a way of using our gifts to love and serve others. The Church's sacramental life nourishes us so that we can find our vocation. Matrimony and Holy Orders are among the many ways to faithfully live out our vocation.

What's the Plan?

What are your hopes, dreams, and plans for your life? As you grow up, you begin to consider your future profession, such as chef, musician, or doctor. As you imagine your life ahead, it is important to ask God about his plan for you. You have particular gifts and talents that only you can contribute in doing the work of God's kingdom. God already knows the deepest desires of your heart, so ask him to reveal his plan to you and try to respond faithfully.

Activity

Do one of the following.

(1) Ask your parents or godparents about their work and vocation in life. Find out what role God played in their choices.

(2) Have a discussion with family members about one another's career goals and vocations. Share ways of supporting one another's dreams.

Brain Teaser

Circle seven things you could do to discover your vocation.

```
Z P  I N J K P G V
O T  R U S T N O H
B Z  D A G B L H A
S N O R Y U I F Y
E M C E N O S O D
R T Y T Y L T O U
V S E F X C E M T
E E L J B P N R S
R E S E A R C H Q
```

Did you know...?

Simeon of Syria (390–459) was the first stylite, an extremely religious person who lived on top of tall, narrow pillars. His preaching from pillars, as high as sixty-six feet, converted many to Christianity.

Spirit-Filled and Hopeful

Leon C. Roberts brought the energy and emotion of gospel music into the Church's tradition. His music ministry began in 1968 while he was a Baptist. Nine years later, Roberts became the conductor of a gospel choir at St. Augustine's Church in Washington, D.C. He became a Catholic, and he was hopeful that his music would help people of other faith traditions understand our Church's heritage. Roberts's work included being a composer and workshop presenter for Oregon Catholic Press. *The Coming* is a collection of new Mass music for Advent and Christmas. His final collection, *Come, Bless the Lord,* presents Scripture-based themes that give glory to God.

One of Roberts's workshops, titled *Save Our Youth, Enliven Our Liturgy,* explored ways of enabling young people to become full participants in the liturgy. Leon Roberts died of cancer at age forty-eight in 1999. His hope-filled spirit lives on in his music.

All-Star Profile

Name: Saint Katharine Drexel
Born: 1858
Died: 1955
Family Background: born into a wealthy family whose home was always open to people in need, with a prayerful father and a mother who died when Katharine was five weeks old
Occupation: foundress and superior of the Sisters of the Blessed Sacrament
Quote of a Lifetime: "The patient and humble endurance of the cross, whatever nature it may be, is the highest work we have to do."
Claims to Fame: Founded a religious order of women devoted to helping Native and African Americans. Used her inheritance to open convents, religious education centers, and more than sixty schools. Founded Xavier University of Louisiana, a predominantly African-American institution. Canonized in 2000.

Wired

Visit Our Web Site
www.blestarewe.com

Web Site Spotlight
www.christusrex.org

This site is a favorite for art lovers. See some of the world's most beautiful religious art.

Something To Do

On Sunday

While at Mass, notice the various ministries in which people in your parish are involved. Imagine yourself in such roles, and pray to the Holy Spirit for guidance in finding your own unique way to serve the Church.

Through the Week

Choose a person of faith whom you respect and admire. Spend a day with this person to observe how he or she lives by faith.

A Prayer for the Week

Lord, I want to love you and serve you, but I am not always sure how. There are so many choices that sometimes I feel confused. Teach me to listen to you in the many ways that you reveal yourself.
Amen.

Answer Key: ask, volunteer, observe, pray, listen, trust, research

6 Servants of the Kingdom

As the Father loves me, so I also love you. Remain in my love.

John 15:9

Share

Who are you? Most likely, when someone asks you this question, you respond with your name. You might also describe yourself by listing your physical characteristics, such as your facial features, hair color, and height.

But who are you really? You have a distinctive identity that includes your personality traits, likes and dislikes, values, and even your dreams for the future.

Activity

Imagine that you have been asked to complete a special ID card. List some of your strengths (inner and outer), goals for this year, and ambitions for the future. You may also wish to create a symbol that represents who you are.

God has a special place for each of us in his kingdom. We come to know our vocation in life through prayer and reflection. By exploring who we really are, we develop a sense of how we can best serve God and others.

My strengths:

courageous and brave

smart and strong

Goals: to get good grades

in school

Ambition: to help people

and become a firefighter

My strengths:

cheerful and creative

talented artist

Goals: to learn how to

develop my artistic ability

Ambition: to become an

artist or fashion designer

Why is choosing a vocation so important?

Hear & Believe

Worship   A Marriage Blessing

Marriage and the priesthood are among the ways to live out a vocation. Through the sacrament of Holy Orders, a man can serve the Church as a **disciple**, or follower of Christ. Men and women can also live out their vocation as Christ's disciples through the sacrament of Matrimony, as explained in the following marriage blessing.

"Father, by your plan man and woman are united, and married life has been established
as the one blessing that was not forfeited by
    original sin
or washed away in the flood.

"Look with love upon this woman, your daughter,
now joined to her husband in marriage.
She asks your blessing.
Give her the grace of love and peace.
May she always follow the example of the holy
    women
whose praises are sung in the scriptures.

"May her husband put his trust in her
and recognize that she is his equal
and the heir with him to the life of grace.
May he always honor her
and love her as Christ loves his bride, the Church.

"Father, keep them always true to your
    commandments.
Keep them faithful in marriage
and let them be living examples of Christian life.

"Give them the strength which comes from the
    gospel
so that they may be witnesses of Christ to others.
(Bless them with children
and help them to be good parents.
May they live to see their children's children.)
And, after a happy old age,
grant them fullness of life with the saints
in the kingdom of heaven.

"We ask this through Christ our Lord.

"Amen."

Rite of Marriage

A Loving Commitment

"If we love one another, God remains in us, and his love is brought to perfection in us" (1 John 4:12). In marriage, a man and a woman make a lifelong commitment to love and respect each other. This commitment is more than just a contract between two people; it is a holy covenant sealed by God. The couple's mutual love is a sign to others of God's love and forgiveness. For this reason, Jesus raised marriage to the dignity of a sacrament. Couples considering marriage should prepare for such a serious commitment. To be joined together in the presence of Christ, the man and woman must freely choose to marry, promise to be faithful to each other, and raise their children in a caring Christian environment.

Holy Orders

The Twelve Apostles were commissioned by Jesus to preach the Gospel and to bring God's healing touch to others. Today, God calls men to continue Jesus' mission by leading the Church as bishops, priests, and deacons. These are the three degrees of Holy Orders. They are essential to the very nature of the Church. Through this sacrament, the Holy Spirit enables chosen baptized men recognized by the Church and accepted to receive Holy Orders to serve as ordained ministers of the Church.

The Role of Priests

Through Baptism, all Christians share in Christ's priesthood and are called to spread the Gospel message and participate in the liturgy. However, a priest's role is different from that of the rest of the faith community. Priests undertake a sacred mission to serve the faithful. Priests are given the responsibility to oversee a parish community, instruct it in the faith, and lead it in prayer and worship. Furthermore, only an ordained priest can preside at the Eucharist and **consecrate** the bread and wine.

Through the sacrament of Reconciliation, or **Penance**, priests forgive sins in the name of the Father, Son, and Holy Spirit. Only priests and bishops can bring God's healing and forgiveness to people through the sacraments of Reconciliation and Anointing of the Sick. Priests and the sacraments are Christ's instruments for the forgiveness of sin, for helping us grow in holiness, and for giving us a share in everlasting life.

 GO TO *pages 239–240 to learn more about the sacraments at the service of communion.*

Faith Words

disciple A disciple is a follower of Christ who carries on Christ's mission by showing others the love of God.

consecrate To consecrate is to make sacred. The priest calls upon the Holy Spirit to consecrate the bread and wine, or change them into the Body and Blood of Christ.

Penance Penance is another name for the sacrament of Reconciliation. With a lowercase *p,* it refers to a prayer or kind act that we do as an expression of sorrow for our sins.

How do we serve God's kingdom through our vocations?

Our Church Teaches

There are many ways to serve the Lord in single, married, or religious life, all with the common mission of living and spreading the Gospel.

Marriage is a public celebration of the love that a man and a woman have for each other. Because they exchange wedding vows with each other, they are the ministers of the sacrament. On behalf of the Church, the priest and the assembly witness

We Believe

In the sacraments of Matrimony and Holy Orders, men and women make lifelong commitments to carry on Christ's mission.

the couple's union. In the presence of Christ, the man and woman promise to be faithful in their love and to share this love in service to others.

In the sacrament of Holy Orders, the bishop lays his hands on the head of the man being ordained and prays that God will help him in his ministry. The new priest promises to assist the bishop in carrying on Christ's mission.

Respond

Pope John Paul II

Pope John Paul II is known for having traveled to many countries, and millions of people have gathered to hear him speak. He has traveled more than any other pope in history, visiting the rich and the poor. When he visited a slum in Nairobi, Kenya, Mary Kamati, who was dying of AIDS, said, "This is the only pope who has come to this part of the world."

In addition to his travels, Pope John Paul II wrote several books. His book of meditations, *Crossing the Threshold of Hope*, quickly became a bestseller in twelve countries. The pope's Latin recitation of the Rosary on CD is very popular in Europe. The pope even used the Internet to spread the message of Christ. In a 1989 statement regarding World Communications Day, he challenged young people to use modern technology in "promoting greater universal justice . . . and the freedoms essential for a fully human life."

Pope John Paul II also called for the writing of a new catechism to summarize the Church's teachings, something that had not been done in more than 400 years. The *Catechism of the Catholic Church* was published in 1994 and is considered one of the outstanding accomplishments of his papacy.

Pope John Paul II is known for having spoken out and confronted the problems

of society. When Vatican delegates attended the United Nations population conference in Cairo, Egypt, in 1994, the pope guided the delegates from Rome. Pope John Paul II made it clear to the world that the Catholic Church strongly opposes abortion as a method of controlling population growth.

When he was recognized in 1994 as *TIME Magazine*'s man of the year, Pope John Paul II stated, "The pope must be a moral force." Indeed, Pope John Paul II is an example of a pope who spent his life defending human rights.

Activity

There is a story about a young boy who tries to improve the world by helping three people. He instructs them not to pay him back but to "pay it forward" by helping three other people. His idea spreads and soon many people are performing good deeds.

Share stories of people you know or have read about who spread goodwill. Then list different ways you can be of service to others this week for each category below.

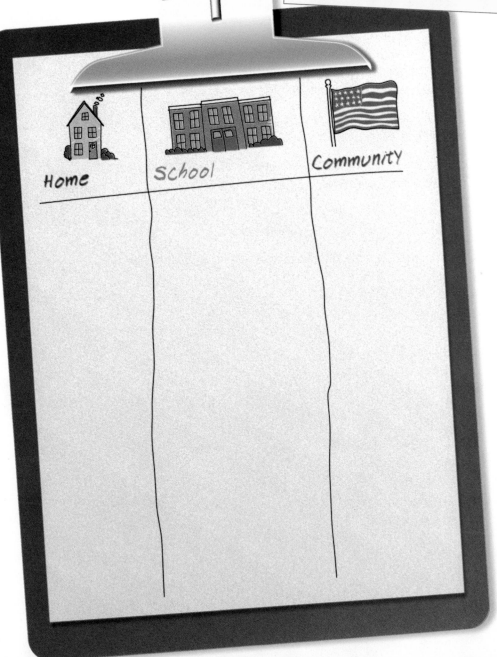

Home	School	Community

How can we answer God's call to serve?

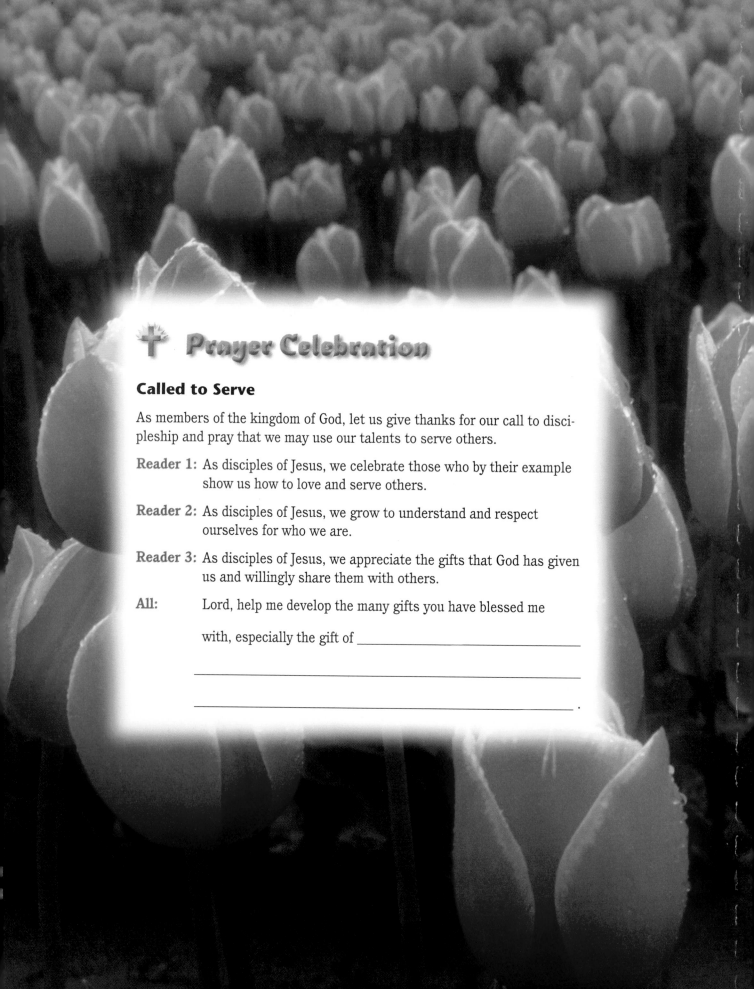

✝ Prayer Celebration

Called to Serve

As members of the kingdom of God, let us give thanks for our call to discipleship and pray that we may use our talents to serve others.

Reader 1: As disciples of Jesus, we celebrate those who by their example show us how to love and serve others.

Reader 2: As disciples of Jesus, we grow to understand and respect ourselves for who we are.

Reader 3: As disciples of Jesus, we appreciate the gifts that God has given us and willingly share them with others.

All: Lord, help me develop the many gifts you have blessed me

with, especially the gift of _____

_____

_____ .

Get Connected

with family and friends

Justice in the Kingdom on Earth

Who are our neighbors? Our Church teaches that all people are our neighbors. All people are made in God's image. Because of this, we must uphold the dignity of all people by working for justice, ensuring that people everywhere have what they need to live a life of dignity. Jesus' parable about the Good Samaritan, discussed in this chapter, inspires us to act.

Justice in Your Own Community

Have you ever ridiculed or excluded someone who seemed different? In your school and community, you may encounter people whose cultural or ethnic backgrounds, skills, ways of dressing or speaking, physical abilities, and choice of friends seem very different from yours. One of the wonderful realities of God's creation is that he did not make everyone the same. Treating someone poorly because he or she is different from you goes against the ways of Jesus, who sought justice for everyone, including those who were different. How can you do the same?

Activity

Do one of the following.

(1) Be friendly toward a person whom you consider different from you. Ask the person how he or she feels about a current event or something important to you. Listen closely, and try to understand and respect that person's point of view.

(2) Ask your family to help you research what life is like for people your age in a developing part of the world. What is unique about the young people's country and culture? What prejudices and conflicts do they experience? Finally, in what ways are these young people similar to you?

F.A.Q.

Dear Mr. F.A.Q.,
Some kids in my class are always picking on people. They picked on me for a while, but now they have targeted someone else. What should I do about this?

Signed,
Safe-at-the-Moment Steve

Dear Safe,
Always picking on others is called "bullying." Bullying may include verbal harassment, ridicule, or even physical violence. You should not stand by and let others suffer as you did. Talk to a trusted adult about the situation. Being a faithful Christian requires that you speak up truthfully when people are getting hurt. It is the right thing to do.

God bless,
Mr. F.A.Q.

Did you know...?

In Jesus' time, the Samaritans were a group of people who came from Samaria, an area between Judea and Galilee. The Jews and Samaritans did not get along, as the Samaritans worshiped God differently from the Jews.

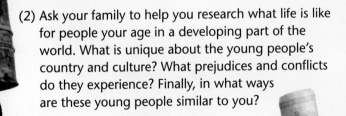

Holy Humor!

Bulletin Bloopers

Seen in actual announcements in church bulletins:

The cost for attending the Fasting and Prayer Conference includes meals.

Thursday Night: Potluck Supper. Prayer and medication to follow.

Sunday Gospel reading: Jesus walks on the water. Sermon tonight: "Searching for Jesus"

Next Thursday there will be tryouts for the choir. They need all the help they can get.

The seventh graders will present Shakespeare's *Hamlet* in the church basement on Friday at 7 p.m. All parishioners are invited to attend this tragedy.

All-Star Profile

Name: Dietrich Bonhoeffer
Born: 1906
Died: 1945
Family Background: sixth child in a family with strong moral beliefs, with a father who was a professor of psychiatry and a mother who held a university degree

Occupation: Protestant religious leader, teacher, writer, and peace activist

Quote of a Lifetime: "It is our duty to remind ourselves of the stand which we have taken as [a movement] against anti-Semitism in all its forms."

Claims to Fame: Spoke out against the Nazi regime during World War II. Worked with many people to end the evil and violence of Hitler. Was executed for his beliefs and for helping Jews escape to freedom.

Wired

Visit Our Web Site
www.blestarewe.com

Web Site Spotlight
www.youmagazine.com/peer_pressure_index.html

This site has a monthly advice column that often discusses how to deal with problems you might encounter from your peers when you try to be kind to people who seem different.

Something To Do

On Sunday

During the Gospel reading, reflect on how Jesus led a life of justice and peace. Think about the times that you brought justice and peace to your family and friends. Thank God for the gifts of courage and wisdom.

Through the Week

Remember that each person you meet is created in the image of God. Treat each person fairly and with respect.

A Prayer for the Week

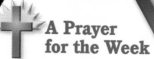

Lord, there is violence between people and nations simply because they are different from each other. Open my mind and heart and show me how to make this world a better place, a place where all people are respected.
Amen.

7 Justice in the Kingdom on Earth

 Whoever does the will of God is my brother and sister and mother.

Mark 3:35

Share

We all have the same basic needs. There are people in our own communities who suffer because such needs are not met. There are others who suffer because of people who disrespect life. We must reach out to all in need and promote justice.

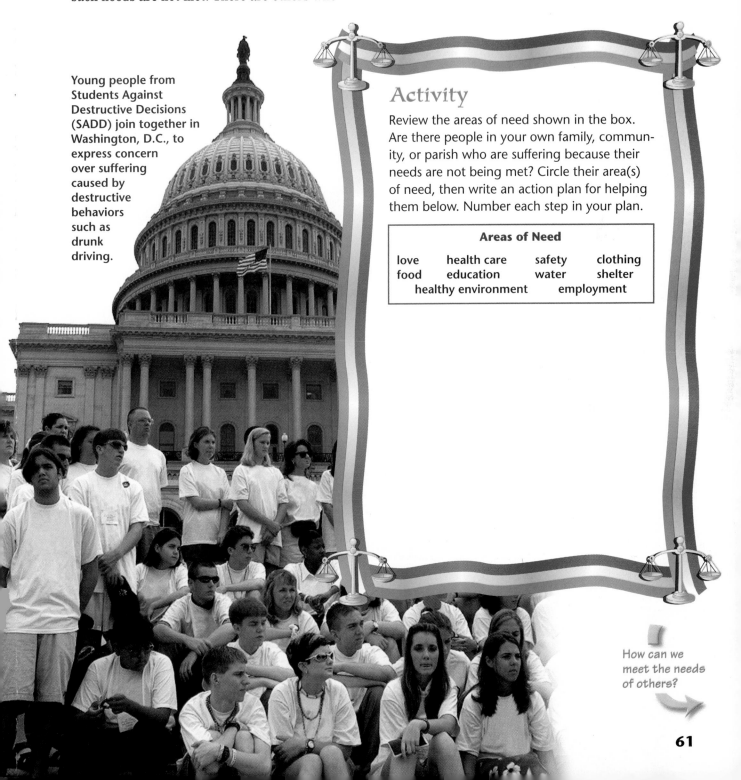

Young people from Students Against Destructive Decisions (SADD) join together in Washington, D.C., to express concern over suffering caused by destructive behaviors such as drunk driving.

Activity

Review the areas of need shown in the box. Are there people in your own family, community, or parish who are suffering because their needs are not being met? Circle their area(s) of need, then write an action plan for helping them below. Number each step in your plan.

Areas of Need			
love	health care	safety	clothing
food	education	water	shelter
healthy environment		employment	

How can we meet the needs of others?

Hear & Believe

✝ Scripture Loving Your Neighbor

The **Pharisees** often tried to test Jesus' knowledge of the law by asking him questions. They hoped that his answers would prove that he misinterpreted God's law.

The Pharisees gathered together and one of them, a scholar of the Law, tested Jesus by asking, "Teacher, which commandment in the law is the greatest?"

Jesus said to him, "You shall love the Lord, your God, with all your heart, with all your soul, and with all your mind. This is the greatest and the first commandment. The second is like it: You shall love your neighbor as yourself. The whole law and the prophets depend on these two commandments."

The scholar of the Law then asked, "And who is my neighbor?"

Jesus replied, "A man fell victim to robbers as he went down from Jerusalem to Jericho. They stripped and beat him and went off leaving him half-dead. A priest happened to be going down that road, but when he saw the man, he passed by on the opposite side. Likewise, a Levite came to the place, and when he saw the man, he passed by on the opposite side. But a Samaritan traveler who came upon the man was moved with compassion at the sight. He approached the victim and

poured oil and wine over his wounds and bandaged them. Then he took him to an inn and cared for him. The next day he took out two silver coins and gave them to the innkeeper with the instruction 'Take care of him. If you spend more than what I have given you, I shall repay you on my way back.' Which of these three, in your opinion, was neighbor to the robbers' victim?"

The scholar of the law answered, "The one who treated him with mercy."

Jesus said to him, "Go and do likewise."

Based on Matthew 22:34–40 and Luke 10:29–37

Respecting Human Dignity

When the Samaritan helped the beaten man, he was acting out of genuine concern for another human being. He did not expect recognition or reward. We are also called to act for the good of others without expecting personal gain.

"Who is my neighbor?" we might ask, just as the scholar of the Law in the Scripture story asked. For us, the wounded man in Jesus' parable, which is known as the Parable of the Good Samaritan, represents anyone who might be suffering and need our help. Samaritans, in Jesus' time, were people who were disliked. They did not share the accepted ways of worshiping God. For that reason, a Samaritan would have seemed an unlikely "neighbor" to a Jewish person listening to Jesus' parable. Jesus' parable teaches us that all people deserve our respect and love regardless of race, religion, and culture. Created by God and in God's image, all people have dignity. We have equal rights as members of God's family. Because of this, we must respect the dignity of all people.

When Jesus told his listeners which of God's laws was the greatest, he revealed that God's law, expressed in the Ten Commandments, is based on love for God, our neighbors, and ourselves. We show our love by respecting our own dignity and the dignity of each person created by God. We work to protect the rights of others and try to promote justice. We show compassion just as the Samaritan did.

Responding to God's Grace

Our conscience, which enables us to sense what is right and wrong, tells us which actions go against the natural sense of morality that God gave us in creating us. A morally good act is more than something that happens to turn out all right in the end. It is something that we start, continue, and finish with good intentions toward ourselves, others, and God. If we have properly formed our conscience through prayer and the guidance of the Holy Spirit, the Scriptures, the Church, and the adults in our lives, our conscience will lead us toward actions that are good.

God's **grace**, the power of his love within us, enables us to love ourselves and others fully. At Baptism, the Holy Spirit gives us the gift of grace. Through this sacrament, we are united to Christ, who frees us from sin, renews our hearts with his love, and gives us **sanctification**. Through the love of Christ that lives within us, we have the grace we need to bring justice to our neighbors.

Jesus Christ promised that those who follow him by loving God and their neighbors will enjoy everlasting happiness in heaven. It is important to understand, however, that we do not gain the joy of heaven purely through our efforts but through Jesus Christ. It is only by God's grace, gained for us through Christ's death and Resurrection, that we have merit in God's eyes. God's grace is his free gift to us, and through it, we can live a life of doing good works. As Catholics, we believe that by a life of grace we gain the true reward of everlasting life.

Faith Words

Pharisees Pharisees were Jewish people who accepted the written laws of the Old Testament and tradition (the spoken teachings of religious leaders).

grace Grace, a gift that God freely gives us, is God's life within us, which fills us with his love and enables us to live according to his will.

sanctification Sanctification is the act of making or of being made holy.

How do we show love for our neighbors?

Our Church Teaches

God's kingdom begins with the Church. The Church's unity reflects the unity of God the Father, Son, and Holy Spirit. As members of the Church, we work for justice, remembering that every person has dignity as a child of God. We recognize this dignity by sharing what we have with others. Aside from sharing material things, we must share our time and our faith. As citizens we must not obey leaders who promote moral disorder but rather obey God. We must work with public officials, entrusted with protecting human rights, to create a just society that protects our freedom. Society must be guided by the light of the Gospel or it risks losing its freedom. Our media must promote truth, freedom, and justice. Together, we must work for the good of all God's children and live the values of the kingdom.

We Believe

We are called to work for justice in God's kingdom on earth. With God's grace, we can build a society that honors and protects human dignity.

Respond

Anne Frank

When she was thirteen years old, Anne Frank kept a diary, as many young people do. Her writings, however, did not include accounts of normal, everyday activities in the life of a young teen. Hidden in an attic in the Netherlands, Anne wrote about the atrocities of the Holocaust. Many of her writings express a deep concern for humanity.

Anne and her family had gone into hiding after the German army occupied the Netherlands. The freedom they enjoyed had been taken away once the Nazis issued anti-Jewish decrees. Forced to wear a yellow star, Jewish people had to restrict their activities, and they were carefully monitored. They lived in constant fear of being arrested and sent to German labor or prison camps.

With the help of friends, Anne's family lived in their secret hideaway along with four other people. Although they lived apart from the rest of the world, they were not sheltered from the harsh reality of the war. They listened to radio broadcasts, which Anne later recorded in her diary. On November 19, 1942, she wrote, "In the evening

when it's dark, I often see long lines of good, innocent people accompanied by crying children, walking on and on, ordered about by a handful of men who bully and beat them until they nearly drop. No one is spared. The sick, the elderly, children, babies, and pregnant women—all are marched to their death."

On August 4, 1944, the Nazis raided the attic that was Anne's family home for two years. Anne and the others were arrested and sent to concentration camps. At the age of sixteen, Anne died at a concentration camp. Her father survived and published excerpts from the diary that meant so much to his daughter.

Anne Frank's diary is widely read and has been translated into many languages. Despite the prejudice and hatred that Anne experienced, her diary shows the hope she had in humanity. She wrote, "It's a wonder I haven't abandoned all my ideals, they seem so absurd and impractical. Yet I cling to them because I still believe, in spite of everything, that people are truly good at heart."

Activities

1. Anne Frank's diary is an example of the "power of the pen." She wrote about the injustices she saw, and her words have had a lasting impact. Do you know of any saints, people in your parish or community, leaders in the Church, or other Catholics whose writings have made an impact on humanity? Below, explain how their words have demonstrated the power of the pen and how they have inspired you.

_____

_____

2. In the Declaration of Independence, Thomas Jefferson wrote, "We hold these truths to be self-evident, that all men were created equal; that they are endowed by the Creator with certain inalienable rights; and that among these are life, liberty, and the pursuit of happiness. That to secure these rights, governments are instituted" (based on the Declaration of Independence). By writing to government officials, we can help create and uphold laws that protect our rights. Below, write a sample letter to a government representative about a public issue that needs attention. Later, send a real letter on your own. Don't underestimate the power of the pen!

Date: _____

Official (senator, governor, president, or other): _____

Address: _____

City, State, and ZIP Code: _____

Dear _____:

I am writing to you regarding _____,

an issue that is very important because _____

_____.

I urge you to support laws that will help address this issue by _____

_____.

Sincerely,

Name: _____

Address: _____

City, State, and ZIP Code: _____

How can we show mercy to others?

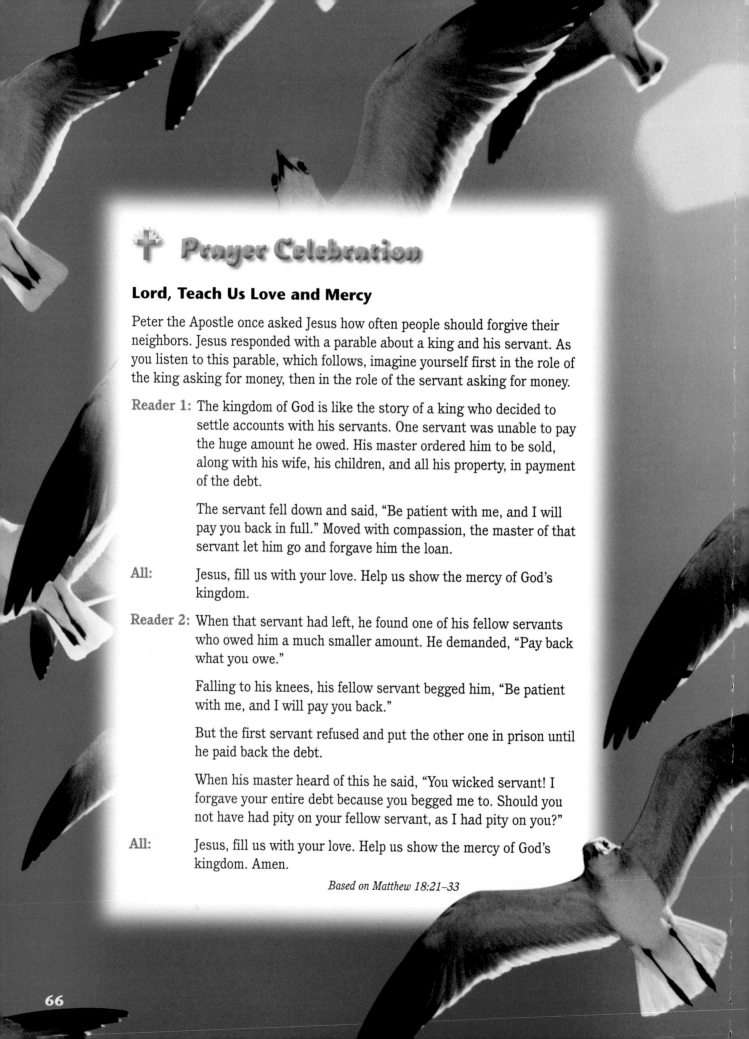

✝ Prayer Celebration

Lord, Teach Us Love and Mercy

Peter the Apostle once asked Jesus how often people should forgive their neighbors. Jesus responded with a parable about a king and his servant. As you listen to this parable, which follows, imagine yourself first in the role of the king asking for money, then in the role of the servant asking for money.

Reader 1: The kingdom of God is like the story of a king who decided to settle accounts with his servants. One servant was unable to pay the huge amount he owed. His master ordered him to be sold, along with his wife, his children, and all his property, in payment of the debt.

The servant fell down and said, "Be patient with me, and I will pay you back in full." Moved with compassion, the master of that servant let him go and forgave him the loan.

All: Jesus, fill us with your love. Help us show the mercy of God's kingdom.

Reader 2: When that servant had left, he found one of his fellow servants who owed him a much smaller amount. He demanded, "Pay back what you owe."

Falling to his knees, his fellow servant begged him, "Be patient with me, and I will pay you back."

But the first servant refused and put the other one in prison until he paid back the debt.

When his master heard of this he said, "You wicked servant! I forgave your entire debt because you begged me to. Should you not have had pity on your fellow servant, as I had pity on you?"

All: Jesus, fill us with your love. Help us show the mercy of God's kingdom. Amen.

Based on Matthew 18:21–33

Get Connected

with family and friends

A Prayer for the Kingdom

The Lord's Prayer is a prayer that is shared by all Christians. It is the prayer Jesus himself taught us. The Lord's Prayer is a summary of the Gospel. It states the truths of our faith and includes petitions that ask God to give us what we need to make his kingdom come on earth. Take some time to reflect on and pray this prayer.

Peace Amidst the Pieces

Nancy felt as if her world was crashing around her. Her friends were always fighting and trying to get her to take sides. Her parents often argued, and she was worried that her dad might leave again. Writing in a journal at night brought Nancy peace. It seemed like she was writing to God, a friend who always loved and listened without judging. God is always ready and waiting to hear from us through prayer.

Activity

Do one of the following.

(1) Draw a square, and write your name in the middle. On each of the four sides, write one thing that is bothering you. Ask God how to handle these pressures. Try to listen and respond faithfully.

(2) Ask your family and friends if there is anything that you can pray about for them. Pray in your own words, then say the Lord's Prayer.

The Password Is

petition

A petition is a solemn prayer of request. The word *petition* comes from the Latin *petere*, meaning "to seek or rush at." Petitions are prayers in which we ask for what we need. An old Hebrew custom is to always pray a prayer of thanksgiving before making a petition.

Did you know...?

A pretzel is shaped like a pair of arms folded in prayer. Some say the pretzel was once a Lenten snack. The word *pretzel* supposedly came from a Latin word meaning "with little arms."

Finding Your Place in This World

Singer/songwriter **Michael W. Smith** has been writing songs, performing at concerts, and playing music for years. His songs speak to the heart about the hopes, fears, and yearnings that we share. He works in several ministries, not the least of which is assisting with the Rocketown Club, a youth haven that offers help and hope to searching teenagers. In the song "Place in This World," Smith sings about his own life as much as the lives of teenagers in search of meaning. Through his music ministry, Smith tried to help people who suffered the tragedy at Columbine High School in Colorado in 1999 to heal. Inspired by the faith of the young victims, Smith produced the CD *This Is Your Time*. Smith has recorded several CDs. He has won two Grammies and several Dove awards. He says, "I'm an entertainer, but I try to use the platform to say something that could be lifesaving to somebody."

All-Star Profile

Name: César E. Chávez
Born: 1927
Died: 1993
Family Background: from a family of migrant farmers in the Southwest, worked the fields at ten years old and left school after eighth grade to help support his family
Occupation: migrant worker, community and labor organizer, farm workers' advocate
Quote of a Lifetime: "If you are outraged at conditions, then you can't possibly be free or happy until you devote all your time to changing them."
Claims to Fame: Served as National Director of the Community Service Organization. Founded the National (now "United") Farm Workers of America. Received the Aguila Azteca award, Mexico's highest honor, and the Presidential Medal of Freedom, the highest honor awarded in the United States.

Wired

Visit Our Web Site
www.blestarewe.com

Web Site Spotlight
www.usccb.org/cchd
This is the site for the Catholic Campaign for Human Development. Find out what the organization is doing to help others and learn how you can get involved.

Something To Do

On Sunday
Read the front page of the Sunday paper before Mass, and pray for anyone you read about who seems to be in need of help.

Through the Week
Choose a time during your daily routine to quietly pray the Lord's Prayer several times. This will help you stay close to God and find strength in him.

✝ A Prayer for the Week

Thank you, God, for giving us a love that is as gentle and strong as that of a loving parent. Thank you for allowing us to call you our Father and for teaching us how to be your children. Help us to live in your love.
Amen.

8   A Prayer for the Kingdom

Your heavenly Father knows all of your needs. Seek first the kingdom of God, and these things and more will be given to you.

Based on Matthew 6:32–33

Share

Babies are not able to satisfy their basic needs on their own. Babies and small children are very dependent on others for care. As children grow, however, they become more independent and take on more responsibilities. As you get older, you probably notice that your needs begin to change and to include needs other than physical ones. You also become more aware of the needs of people around you.

Activity

Jesus told his followers, "What father among you would hand his son a snake when he asks for a fish? If you know how to give good gifts, how much more will the Father in heaven give the Holy Spirit to those who ask him?" (based on Luke 11:11–13). Imagine that you had to send an e-mail to the Father about your needs and the needs of people you love. What would you ask of God?

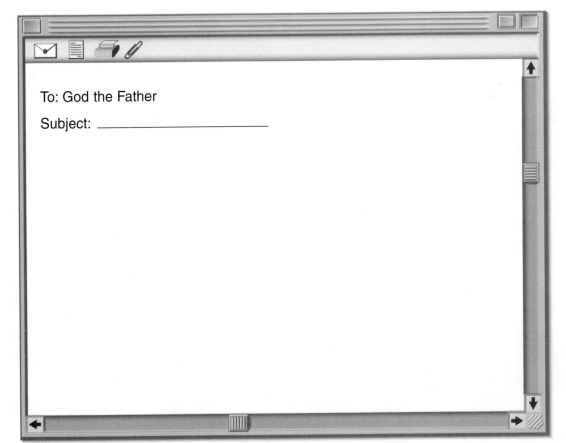

To: God the Father

Subject: _____

What prayer did Jesus give us for asking God to meet our needs?

Hear & Believe

Scripture The Sermon on the Mount

Great crowds gathered from Galilee, north of Jerusalem, and from surrounding areas to hear Jesus teach about God's kingdom. He taught his followers the **Beatitudes**, a guide to bringing God's peace, justice, and forgiveness to others and to finding true happiness. Jesus also taught his followers how to pray for God's help in practicing the Beatitudes.

The Beatitudes

Blessed are the poor in spirit,
   for theirs is the kingdom of heaven.
Blessed are they who mourn,
   for they will be comforted.
Blessed are the meek,
   for they will inherit the land.
Blessed are they who hunger and thirst for
      righteousness,
   for they will be satisfied.
Blessed are the merciful,
   for they will be shown mercy.
Blessed are the clean of heart,
   for they will see God.
Blessed are the peacemakers,
   for they will be called children of God.
Blessed are they who are persecuted for
      the sake of righteousness,
   for theirs is the kingdom of heaven.

Matthew 5:3–10

The Lord's Prayer

Our Father in heaven,
   hallowed be your name,
   your kingdom come,
your will be done,
   on earth as in heaven.
Give us today our daily bread;
and forgive us our debts,
   as we forgive our debtors;
and do not subject us to the final test,
   but deliver us from the evil one.

Matthew 6:9–13

A Prayer for the Kingdom

The Sermon on the Mount consists of teachings that Jesus gave his followers, including the Beatitudes and the Lord's Prayer. Just as Moses ascended a mountain in Sinai to receive the commandments of God, Jesus went up a mountain in Galilee to teach his followers how to keep the commandments in a spirit of love. The Beatitudes tell us that we will find true happiness in the kingdom of God by loving God, loving each other, seeking justice, and spreading peace. The Beatitudes are a guide to the way we should live. By living them, we reveal to others the glory and love that will be found in God's kingdom, as well as experience some of the glory and love of God's kingdom in our own lives.

"Your kingdom come," Jesus said when teaching the Lord's Prayer. In this prayer, we ask God to make his kingdom a reality. We pray with trust, addressing God as our Father. When praying, Jesus actually used the name **Abba** for God, which meant "Daddy" to the Jewish people. When we pray as Jesus did, we show that we understand that we are God's children and trust in his ability to meet our needs.

The Lord's Prayer (see page 264) summarizes the teachings of Jesus in the four Gospels. If we look closely at the prayer, we see seven petitions, or requests. In the first three petitions, we praise God and ask that God always be praised and glorified. In the final four petitions, we express our needs and our desire to be close to God.

The Glory of God (Petitions 1–3)

When we pray "hallowed be thy name" in the first petition of the Lord's Prayer, we offer praise to God, who is all-holy. God revealed his holiness first to Moses, then in and through Jesus, his Son. Baptism calls us to live a life of holiness in imitation of Christ, who is God. Every day, we strive to give glory to God in prayer and holy works.

In the second petition of the Lord's Prayer, when we pray, "Thy kingdom come," we are asking that the love and justice of God already present in the lives and actions of God's people continue to grow each day. When we try to imitate God's goodness toward people, we are working for the coming of the kingdom. Also in this petition, we pray for Christ's coming, when we will be with God for all eternity.

The third petition, just as the first two, expresses our love for God. It also expresses our complete faith in his will for us. "Thy will be done on earth as it is in heaven" is a petition that we will obey God in all things, as Jesus did. It is a prayer, as well, that we will help fulfill God's plan through our vocation.

Our Needs (Petitions 4–7)

When we ask God to "give us this day our daily bread," we are praying that God will nourish us in the Eucharist and that all his people's needs will be met. By sharing our goods with those in need, we help fulfill this request.

In the fifth petition, which asks God to "forgive us our trespasses as we forgive those who **trespass** against us," we pray that we might show the same mercy toward others that God does toward us.

In the sixth petition, in which we pray that we will not be led into temptation, we ask God to help us avoid sin.

Finally, in the seventh petition, we ask God to "deliver us from evil," a request that God will lead us to his everlasting kingdom of heaven and protect us from harm.

Faith Words

Beatitudes The Beatitudes are Jesus' teachings about how to live and find real happiness in God's kingdom. They teach us to love God, love each other, seek justice, and spread peace.

Abba *Abba* is the word that Jesus used to teach people to call God "Father" in prayer. The word meant "Daddy" to the Jewish people.

trespass *Trespass* means "to commit a sin."

How can we place our faith in God?

Our Church Teaches

Jesus had a loving and trusting relationship with his Father, and he prayed often for the fulfillment of God's kingdom. We show our faith in God's plan for us when we pray the Lord's Prayer in imitation of Jesus Christ. This is a prayer of confidence in God's goodness and mercy. It expresses our desire to live holy lives.

The Lord's Prayer contains seven petitions that summarize the whole Gospel. When we pray the first three petitions we focus on God, whom we love above all things. We glorify God as we pray that his name be honored and blessed by all people, that his kingdom come, and that his will be carried out. The other four petitions relate to our needs. We ask God to nourish our lives both physically and spiritually and to forgive our sins. We pray that our Father will guide and strengthen us in our struggle against evil.

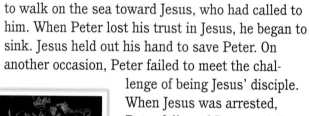

We Believe
We pray the Lord's Prayer to give glory to God and express our needs. The Lord's Prayer is a prayer for the kingdom of God.

Respond

Peter, the Rock

Jesus gave Peter a tremendous responsibility. Jesus entrusted Peter with the "keys of the kingdom": the reponsibility to lead Christ's Church. How could this simple fisherman become the leader of the Church? Was Peter a natural leader or did he have to work at it?

Peter did possess leadership qualities. Often, he was the first to ask Jesus questions about his ministry. Sometimes Jesus even spoke directly to Peter when all the apostles were present.

Jesus chose Peter to play a crucial role in the Church's mission. At their very first meeting Jesus changed Peter's name from Simon to Peter, which means "rock." Jesus also made sure that Peter was present at significant events. For example, Peter, along with James and John, saw the glory of Jesus at the Transfiguration.

But Peter did not always live up to his role as leader. There were times when he disappointed Jesus. For example, one stormy night, Peter tried to walk on the sea toward Jesus, who had called to him. When Peter lost his trust in Jesus, he began to sink. Jesus held out his hand to save Peter. On another occasion, Peter failed to meet the challenge of being Jesus' disciple. When Jesus was arrested, Peter followed Jesus and the soldiers from a distance. When Peter was questioned about his friendship with Jesus, Peter did what he told Jesus he would never do. Three times he denied even knowing Jesus!

Tears of St. Peter by El Greco

Despite many moments of weakness, Peter became a model leader. Instead of feeling sorry for himself because of his mistakes, he grew stronger and knew that in Jesus Christ he could find forgiveness. Peter became the rock upon which Jesus built his Church. We honor Saint Peter when we celebrate the Feast of Saints Peter and Paul on June 29.

Do you seek God's forgiveness when you make mistakes? Do you reach out to God when you feel you are sinking?

Activities

1. Create symbols for the first three petitions from the Lord's Prayer to illustrate their meaning.

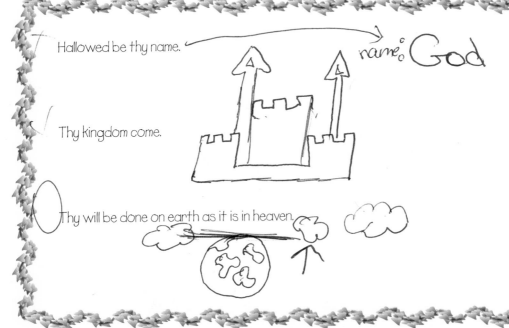

Hallowed be thy name.

Thy kingdom come.

Thy will be done on earth as it is in heaven.

2. Create symbols for the final four petitions from the Lord's Prayer to illustrate their meaning.

Give us this day our daily bread.

Forgive us our trespasses as we forgive those who trespass against us.

Lead us not into temptation.

Deliver us from evil.

How can we celebrate our trusting relationship with God?

✝ Prayer Celebration

In the Words That Jesus Taught Us

The Lord's Prayer has been a liturgical prayer in the Christian community since the first century. We pray it during every Mass. It is a prayer that unites us with God—the Father, the Son, and the Holy Spirit. It is a prayer that expresses our love for God and our hope for eternal happiness with him.

Look at the symbols that you designed on page 73. You might share the meaning of one of your symbols with your religious education group.

Leader: Let us now pray the Lord's Prayer, the prayer given to us by Jesus, God's Son.

GO TO *page 264 for the Lord's Prayer.*

Words from the Heart

Ana was eating dinner with her family when the phone rang. Her mother answered the phone, then began to talk in hushed tones. She brought the phone into the next room. Ana looked at her father, puzzled. After a few minutes, Ana's mother returned, hung up the phone, and sat down, looking serious.

"Ana," she said, "that was Mrs. Joseph. She was calling to say that she just learned that the mother of your classmate Denise died in that building fire we heard about in the news today."

There was silence at the dinner table. Ana did not know Denise very well, but she felt incredibly sad for her. Ana thought about her aunt's sudden death in a car accident two years ago. She remembered how shocked and upset she and everyone else had been.

Before they continued eating, Ana's father led the family in a short prayer for peace for Denise's mother and comfort for the family. When dinner was over, Ana asked her mother, "Do you think there is something I could do to make Denise feel better? Should I send her a card? She'll probably be out of school for a while."

"Why don't you just approach her when she comes back? You could tell her about Aunt Margaret and how you felt."

"But what should I say? I don't want to make her feel worse," Ana said. "What if she thinks I can't really understand how she feels? What if she thinks I'm being phony?"

Ana's mother smiled. "Don't worry, Ana. Just try to remember the kind words that comforted you when your aunt died. What did you need to hear in order to feel at peace?"

"Yeah, but . . . what if I say something really stupid because I can't think of anything?"

"You won't say anything stupid," Ana's mother replied gently, "if your words come from your heart."

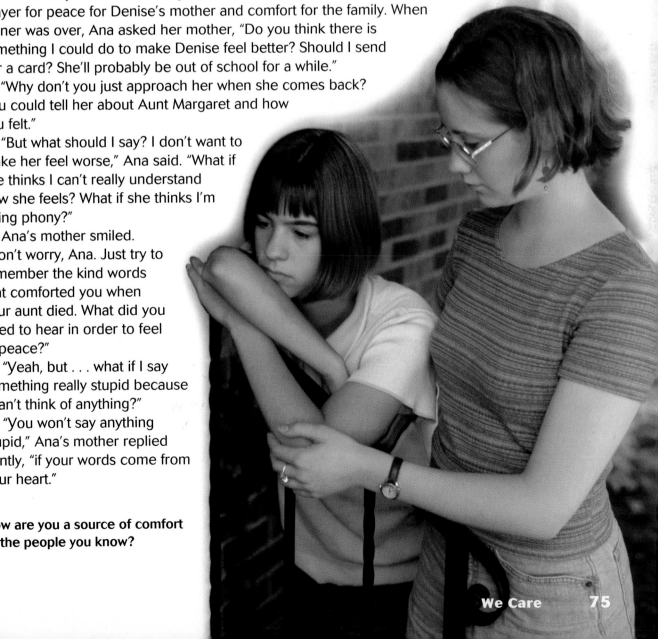

How are you a source of comfort to the people you know?

Think About It

Sometimes we prevent ourselves from reaching out to people who need us because we are afraid of how they or others will react.

Recall a time you had the courage to reach out to someone you know who needed help. List the good things that happened as a result.

Learn About It

You have learned about the Beatitudes, the ways to true happiness that Jesus taught in his Sermon on the Mount. The Beatitudes describe true Christian behavior, behavior that belongs to the kingdom of heaven. Jesus said, "Blessed are they who mourn, /for they will be comforted" (Matthew 5:4). In the kingdom of heaven, there is abundant comfort for the sorrowful. Jesus himself reached out to people who were sorrowful or facing the death of a loved one, such as his friends Mary and Martha (see the Scripture story in Chapter 12). God calls all of us who seek his kingdom to be sources of comfort for others, just as Jesus is.

Do Something About It

As followers of Jesus we need to challenge ourselves to reach out to others who are suffering. Many parishes offer support groups for people who are coping with death. Some parishioners make special visits to people who are grieving.

In the greeting card at right, write something you can do with the members of your religious education group or parish to comfort others.

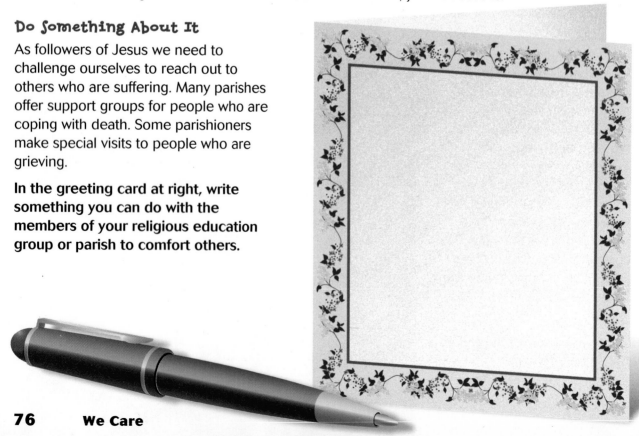

The Christian Life

Jesus made it clear to his followers that they were to model their lives after his. Our own call to discipleship involves putting the Gospel first in our relationships with God and our neighbor.

Father, I thank you for hearing me. I know that you always hear me.

Based on John 11:41–42

The center of worship and moral teaching for Jews in Jesus' time was the Temple in Jerusalem. Today, one of the most revered places of worship for Jews is the Western Wall—the only part of Herod's Temple that remains.

In Remembrance of You

Paul A. Tate

VERSE 1
Jesus, hope for all
  teach us to believe.
Reach us, hope for all,
  in water, wine, and wheat.

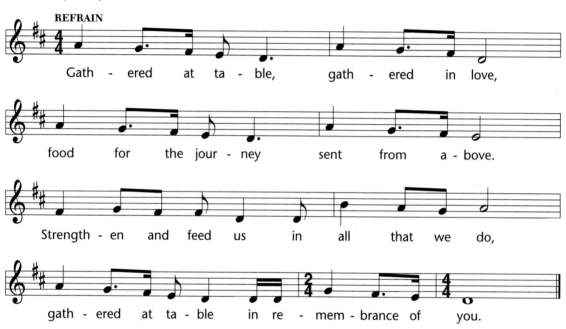

REFRAIN

Gath - ered at ta - ble, gath - ered in love,

food for the jour - ney sent from a - bove.

Strength - en and feed us in all that we do,

gath - ered at ta - ble in re - mem - brance of you.

VERSE 2
Jesus, Son of God,
  you are living Word.
Teach us, Son of God,
  to share what we have heard. *(Refrain)*

VERSE 3
Jesus, Lamb of God,
  bearer of our sin,
Free us, Lamb of God,
  come heal us from within. *(Refrain)*

Get Connected

with family and friends

Living in Christ's Service

In this chapter about almsgiving, we learn about a poor widow whose small Temple offering Jesus contrasted to the showy contributions of wealthier people. When we think about almsgiving, we might recall Mother Teresa's suggestion that we give from the heart when we "give until it hurts." Jesus taught that loving others means serving them and placing their needs above our own.

The Time Is Now!

Jim and Mark had been best friends since kindergarten. Then Anthony moved to town. He quickly became their friend. The three boys spent much of their free time together. After a while, Mark noticed that Anthony rarely had spending money. Anthony's family lived in what others called the "dangerous" part of town. It began to bother Mark that he and Jim could buy new CDs and computer games while Anthony sometimes didn't have enough money for lunch. But Anthony never asked for help. Mark and Jim decided that they wanted to do something. As Christians, what could they do?

Activity

Do one of the following.

(1) Meet with a parent, godparent, or family member to discuss what you would do for Anthony. Plan how to get involved in a real-life situation and make things better.

(2) Whenever you receive a gift of new clothing, donate an article of clothing to someone who needs it more than you. You can give it to a relative or to a charitable organization, such as the St. Vincent de Paul Society.

Check It Out

Sharing Catholic Social Teaching: Challenges and Directions by the U.S. Catholic Bishops identifies the main themes of Catholic social teaching—ways to follow Jesus' teachings about loving and serving. Catholic social teaching themes include: the life and dignity of the human person; involvement in family and community life; people's rights and responsibilities; the poor and vulnerable; the rights of workers; solidarity; and care for God's creation.

As Catholics, we are challenged to learn and follow Catholic social teaching principles.

Did you know...?

Living in Christ's service can simply mean being welcoming to people you meet. Venerable Solanus Casey was noted for simple acts of kindness, such as offering sandwiches to visitors at the parish where he worked.

Holy Humor!

Prayers Overheard

"Dear God, so far today, I've done all right. I haven't gossiped, and I haven't lost my temper. I haven't been grumpy, nasty, or selfish, and I'm really glad about that!

Gee, I've been such a GOOD Person today!

"But in a few minutes, God, I'm going to get out of bed, and from then on, I'm going to need a lot of help. Amen."

"God, please pray for our Little League team. We need God's help, or a new pitcher. Amen."

All-Star Profile

Name: Father James Healy
Born: 1830
Died: 1900
Family Background: born into slavery as one of eight children of an Irish immigrant and a black slave, but taken North with his brothers by his father, and baptized and educated in a free society
Occupation: priest, pastor, teacher, bishop-elect
Quote of a Lifetime: "The almost inevitable result of denunciation is to extinguish whatever little faith is in the heart of the denounced person and to wound the feelings of friends and relatives."
Claim to Fame: as the child of an interracial marriage, faced racism and rejection all his life but always exercised forgiveness
Hobbies: teaching, being an example of tolerance, serving the poor in his community

Something To Do

On Sunday

The second collection at Mass is often for the needs of people outside your parish who are poor or need assistance. Offer your prayers, and donate whatever you can.

Through the Week

To care for God's creation, set up a recycling project at home. Arrange containers for newspapers, plastics, and glass. Help take the items collected to a recycling center.

Wired

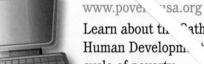

Visit Our Web Site
www.biblestarewe.com

Web Site Spotlight
www.povertyusa.org

Learn about the Catholic Campaign for Human Development. Help break the cycle of poverty.

✝ A Prayer for the Week

Lord, let us serve you as you deserve, give and not count the cost, toil and not seek for rest, labor and not seek reward, except knowing that we do your will. Amen.

Based on a prayer by Saint Ignatius of Loyola

9 Living in Christ's Service

If you wish to be perfect, go, sell what you have and give to [the] poor, and you will have treasure in heaven. Then come, follow me.

Matthew 19:21

Share

When Makenzie Snyder was in the second grade, she attended the Children's World Summit in France and met two boys who had been in the foster care system. They told her that brothers and sisters were often separated from each other when placed in foster homes. In addition to losing their families, such children had to leave behind most of their toys and clothes. Social workers would give each child only a single trash bag in which to place a few belongings. With this trash bag, the child would travel from home to home.

Moved by this story, Makenzie went to local garage sales and collected suitcases and duffel bags for foster children. She also collected stuffed animals to place in each bag. Gradually, her efforts expanded. During a local "Make a Difference Day," Makenzie held a luggage drive. People heard about her efforts and sent her donations. She received positive responses from individuals as well as organizations. With the support of many,

Makenzie was able to send thousands of stuffed-animal–filled luggage bags to children in the foster care system.

Based on a story from Chicken Soup for the Preteen Soul

Activity

Read and reflect on the words of Jesus from Matthew 19:21 at the top of the page. In the left column below, list three ways that Makenzie Snyder responded to Jesus' message. In the right column, list ways you might respond.

_____   _____

_____   _____

_____   _____

How can we serve people in need?

Hear & Believe

✝ Scripture Giving Alms

In my writings, I tried to encourage Christians to stand faithful in the face of persecution. I also told stories about Jewish customs and their connection to Christian traditions. I wanted all people to know that Christ has called them to journey through life in imitation of him. I invited people to discover how to imitate Jesus by learning the stories about Jesus' care and concern for the poor, the sick, the sinners, and all those seeking the kingdom.

In the Scriptures, Jesus explained that we must not be attached to our material possessions. Jesus used the following story, which appears in Mark's Gospel, to teach us about **almsgiving**, or giving money or goods to people who are in need. Men and women practiced almsgiving in the Temple. They placed their offerings in one of the thirteen chests commonly known as the treasury.

The Poor Widow's Contribution

Jesus was teaching in the Temple area. In the course of his teaching, he said, "Beware of the scribes, who like to go around in long robes and accept greetings in the marketplaces, seats of honor in synagogues, and places of honor in banquets."

Jesus sat down opposite the treasury and observed how the crowd put money into the treasury. Many rich people put in large sums. Then a poor widow came by and put in two small coins worth a few cents.

Calling his disciples to himself, Jesus said to them, "Amen, I say to you, this poor widow put in more than all the other contributors to the treasury. For they all contributed from their excess wealth, but she, from her poverty, contributed all she had—her whole livelihood."

Based on Mark 12:35, 38–39, 41–44

Teaching About Almsgiving

Jesus also said, "Take care not to perform righteous deeds in order that people may see them; otherwise, you will have no recompense from your heavenly Father. When you give alms, do not blow a trumpet before you, as the hypocrites do in the synagogues and in the streets to win the praise of others. Amen, I say to you, they have received their reward. But when you give alms, do not let your left hand know what your right is doing, so that your almsgiving may be secret. And your Father who sees in secret will repay you."

Based on Matthew 6:1–4

Giving of Ourselves

Jesus called people who did good works for selfish reasons "hypocrites" because they did not act out of a sincere love for others. Jesus was pleased with the widow's offering, even though it was worth only a few cents, because she gave all she had. Each of us is called to serve others by using all of the special gifts God has given us. Our gifts include not only our talents, unique abilities, and personality traits but our time, possessions, and other privileges with which God has blessed us, perhaps enabling us to live a more comfortable life than others can. We should offer these gifts for the service of others.

Practicing Virtues

God invites us to respond to Christ's call to love and serve by using our gifts in the work we do. Whatever work we do that has Christian love as its goal brings us more fully into Christ's saving grace. Through our work, we participate in and benefit from creation. As we strive to imitate Christ, with God's grace, we grow in the ability to make morally good decisions that lead to the habit of doing good. We call this type of ability a **virtue**. The more we practice virtues, the more they become part of our everyday lives.

Faith, hope, and charity are known as the **theological virtues**. These virtues connect us with the Trinity because they come from God, are signs of Christ's example, and show that the Holy Spirit lives within us. Through the virtue of faith, we believe in God, in everything God has revealed, and in all that the Church teaches us to believe. We accept God as the source of all truth and goodness. The virtue of hope is the trust that we place in God's promise of everlasting life. We also trust in God to remain with us in this life. The virtue of charity is the love we show for others and for God. Through it, we love God with all our hearts and we reach out to people who are suffering. We are even able to love people whom we find difficult to love, just as Jesus taught us.

Because God is at the center of all the theological virtues, practicing them will enable us to grow in the **moral virtues**, spiritual qualities that help us avoid sin, which separates us from God's grace. The moral virtues are **temperance**, **prudence**, **justice**, and **fortitude**. Through understanding, constant practice, and God's grace, these virtues can increase.

 page 242 to learn more about the moral virtues.

Faith Words

almsgiving Almsgiving is the act of giving time, money, or goods to people who are poor or in need.

virtue A virtue is an ability to make morally good decisions that lead to the habit of doing good. Christian virtues are considered gifts from God that we can develop into habits of Christian living.

theological virtues The theological virtues are three spiritual qualities—faith, hope, and charity—that come from God and help us become more holy.

moral virtues The moral virtues are four spiritual qualities—temperance, prudence, justice, and fortitude—that we receive through the Holy Spirit. They help us avoid sin.

How can we practice charity and serve others?

Our Church Teaches

We are all part of God's family. God loves us all. God did not create human beings to live alone, without the love of one another. He created us male and female, and he meant for man and woman to share God's love with each other and with all living beings. This represents the first form of fellowship among human beings. God created man and woman in his image and calls each person to accept his or her identity.

We Believe

As disciples of Christ, we are called to a life of service. With charity, we work for the needs of others.

Charity, or love, is considered the greatest virtue. We can practice the virtue of charity by giving alms.

We shape our economic and social conditions in a positive way through almsgiving and sharing what we have with others. Works of charity help ensure that everyone receives his or her fair share of the world's resources and goods, which God created for everyone. Practicing almsgiving is a work of justice that pleases God.

Respond

Saint Francis of Assisi

More than 800 years have passed since Saint Francis was born in Assisi, Italy, yet his life still interests us. Born into a wealthy family, Francis enjoyed spending money on himself. His teenage years were filled with fun and adventure. By the time he was about twenty-five, however, Francis had decided to give it all up.

The change within Francis began after he participated in a battle between the cities of Perugia and Assisi. He was a prisoner of battle for

a year and became seriously ill. During this time, Francis heard a voice directing him to go home and "serve the master rather than man."

Francis did return to Assisi, but he wasn't quite sure what he was supposed to do. Then one day he met a leper on the road. The leper's body was covered with sores. Francis, although horrified at the sight, was filled with compassion. From that point on, Francis understood that he could serve God by helping others.

Francis began to visit sick patients in the hospital and donate money and clothes to the poor. He also worked to restore churches that needed repair. Francis' father was so outraged by his actions that he beat Francis and brought him before the bishop. But instead of returning to his old way of life, Francis gave up his inheritance and the very clothes he was wearing.

Those who knew Francis as a carefree young man had trouble accepting his change of lifestyle. However, they soon came to admire his dedication to the poor. When others joined Francis in his life of simplicity and poverty, Francis wrote a short rule book to guide them. Today, the members of the Franciscan Order continue to turn away from worldly goods so that they can better follow Christ. We celebrate the feast day of Saint Francis of Assisi on October 4.

Activities

1. Again reflect on the quote at the top of page 85. In what ways did Saint Francis respond to Jesus' message in the quote?

_____

_____

_____

_____

2. Did you ever think about how many people you may have helped in your own life? In the inner circle, write something you have done to help others. In the outer circle, list people who directly benefited from your actions.

How can we express charity through our prayers?

✝ Prayer Celebration

In Giving We Receive

In the Concluding Rite of the Mass, we bow our heads as the priest blesses us in God's name. Bowing our heads is a posture that shows our reverence for God. Bow your head as you pray the Prayer of Saint Francis of Assisi.

Lord, make me an instrument of
your peace; where there is hatred,
let me sow love;
where there is injury, pardon;
where there is doubt, faith;
where there is despair, hope;
where there is darkness, light;
where there is sadness, joy.

Grant that I may not so much seek
to be consoled as to console;
to be understood as to understand;
to be loved as to love.

For it is in giving that we receive, it is
in pardoning that we are pardoned,
it is in dying that we are born to
eternal life.

Prayer of Saint Francis of Assisi

Get Connected

with family and friends

Jesus, Our Eucharist

How amazing it is that 2,000 years after Jesus shared the Last Supper with the Twelve Apostles in a simple room in Jerusalem we—his disciples today—share his sacrifice in our own languages and cultures in churches around the world. When we celebrate the Eucharist, we express our unity with Christ and one another and go forth as living signs of God's love in the world.

Not Just Any Old Day

Imagine the following. It's Sunday. All the stores are closed. There are no soccer games or little league practices. Your parents don't have to work. All your cousins, aunts, and uncles get together with your family for a big gathering that lasts for hours. You all tell stories and play games, and there seems to be more food than anybody can eat. This describes what a typical Sunday was like for most American Catholics a few decades ago. While we can't go back in time and experience this again, we can look at our own Sunday schedules and traditions and consider how our families celebrate the Sabbath.

Activity

Do one of the following.

(1) Help plan a family meal for Sunday. Check with your family members to see what they would like, and add your own ideas. The meal can be fancy or simple, served in either the kitchen or the dining room. Enjoy your meal together and, above all, enjoy the gift of your family.

(2) Play a game with your family. It can be a simple card game or a favorite board game. Form teams if that will help younger siblings. Have fun playing together.

Brain Teaser

Number the following items according to their order in the Mass.

___ homily

___ second reading

___ Lord's Prayer

___ Profession of Faith

___ greeting

___ communion

Did you know...?

Adoration of the Eucharist is a devotion with a long history. As early as A.D. 325, convents and monasteries set aside the Eucharist for the sick and dying. Displaying the Eucharist specifically for adoration probably began in medieval times.

Rock Star to Troubadour

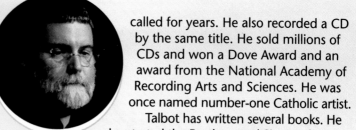

John Michael Talbot once played guitar in a successful band called Mason Proffit. One night after a concert, the sight of leftover liquor bottles, beer cans, and drug paraphernalia caught his attention and made him feel sad. The fast-track rock-star lifestyle suddenly seemed empty. It was time for a change.

After some soul-searching, Talbot became a Christian recording artist. In 1992, Talbot founded his own record label, Troubadour for the Lord, a name he had been called for years. He also recorded a CD by the same title. He sold millions of CDs and won a Dove Award and an award from the National Academy of Recording Arts and Sciences. He was once named number-one Catholic artist.

Talbot has written several books. He also started the Brothers and Sisters of Charity at Little Portion Hermitage at Arkansas. This is a Franciscan community of lay people and religious brothers and sisters, committed to living a simple life and serving the poor.

All-Star Profile

Name: Doctors Without Borders
Begun: 1971
Purpose: delivering emergency aid to victims of armed conflict or disasters
Quote of a Lifetime:
"We are by nature an organization that is unable to tolerate indifference. We hope that by arousing awareness and a desire to understand, we will also stir up indignation and stimulate action" (Rony Brauman, MD, former president).
Claims to Fame: Serves people in more than eighty countries total and more than twenty countries in which war is taking place. Demands access to victims of war during armed conflict. Has more than 15,000 staff workers and 2,000 volunteers who provide medical care for the poor. Gains public support for its work. Won the Nobel Peace Prize in October 1999.

Wired

Visit Our Web Site
www.blestarewe.com

Web Site Spotlight
www.youthapostles.org

Find out how young people can carry out their mission as members of the Body of Christ, focusing especially on prayer and the sacraments.

Something To Do

On Sunday

Prepare for the transformation of the bread and wine into the Body and Blood of Christ by praying that God will show you how you can be more like Jesus.

Through the Week

Spend five minutes each day praying in front of a cross in your home. Pray that you will be as willing to accept your struggles as Jesus was.

✝ A Prayer for the Week

Lord, at the end of every Mass we say, "Thanks be to God," in response to the words "Go in peace to love and serve the Lord." May our actions truly illustrate the faith that we proclaim.
Amen.

Answer Key: 3, 2, 5, 4, 1, 6

10 Jesus, Our Eucharist

I am the bread of life; whoever comes to me will never hunger, and whoever believes in me will never thirst.

John 6:35

Share

The United States is often referred to as a "melting pot" because of the diversity of its people. While immigrants adapt to the culture of our nation, they also preserve many customs and traditions from their past. Their distinct cultural practices enrich our country.

Your own family reflects such wonderful differences. Your family has special ways of celebrating birthdays and holidays. Some of the foods you eat may be from recipes that have been handed down from generation to generation. Even the way your family spends time together expresses something unique about your family's identity and values.

Activity

Think about the customs that seem unique to your family. Which ones do you wish would remain part of your family's heritage for generations to come?

_____

_____

What special traditions do your friends follow that you might like to try in your family?

_____

_____

How do people from diverse backgrounds join together to praise God?

Hear & Believe
Worship Eucharistic Prayer

The Church is made up of people from various cultures and traditions. Despite our differences, we are united in the Eucharist, the center of all Christian life. Each Sunday, we join together in faith to celebrate the Eucharist. As you read the Eucharistic Prayer below, think about how the words honor God and express our shared joy in Christ.

Father, it is our duty and our salvation,
always and everywhere
to give you thanks
through your beloved Son, Jesus Christ...

For our sake he opened his arms on the cross;
he put an end to death
and revealed the resurrection.
In this he fulfilled your will
and won for you a holy people...

Holy, holy, holy Lord, God of power and might,
heaven and earth are full of your glory.
  Hosanna in the highest.
Blessed is he who comes in the name of the Lord.
  Hosanna in the highest.

Lord, you are holy indeed,
the fountain of all holiness.

Let your Spirit come upon these gifts to make them holy,
so that they may become for us
the body and blood of our Lord, Jesus Christ.

Before he was given up to death,
a death he freely accepted,
he took bread and gave you thanks.
He broke the bread,
gave it to his disciples, and said:
Take this, all of you, and eat it:
this is my body which will be given up for you.

When supper was ended, he took the cup.
Again he gave you thanks and praise,
gave the cup to his disciples, and said:
Take this, all of you, and drink from it:
this is the cup of my blood,
the blood of the new and everlasting covenant.
It will be shed for you and for all
so that sins may be forgiven.
Do this in memory of me.

Eucharistic Prayer II

A Eucharistic Community

As you can see, the Eucharistic Prayer recalls Christ's sacrifice and tells the story of the Last Supper. More than 2,000 years ago, Jesus Christ instituted the Eucharist at the Last Supper while celebrating a traditional Jewish meal with his apostles. He "took the bread, said the blessing, broke it, and gave it to them saying, 'This is my body, which will be given for you; do this in memory of me. And likewise the cup after they had eaten, saying, 'This cup is the new covenant in my blood, which will be shed for you'" (Luke 22:19–20). Catholics worldwide gather to celebrate this sacrificial meal in the Mass. Reflecting the universal nature of the Church, Catholic liturgies worldwide may include various cultural traditions and languages. But these liturgies all express the same mystery of Christ, and the Church recognizes them as faithful to apostolic tradition.

The Eucharistic Prayer is preceded by a short dialogue between the priest and the congregation. In this dialogue, the priest begins by blessing us, saying, "The Lord be with you," and we respond with a blessing ourselves, saying, "And also with you." Blessings are important in the worship and prayers of the Church. Blessings include prayers for the good of others, such as the blessings between the priest and the people before the Eucharistic Prayer. Blessings also include praising God for his works and his gifts. At the end of the dialogue, the priest prays, "Let us give thanks to the Lord our God," to which we respond, "It is right to give him thanks and praise."

Celebrating the Eucharist is a sign of our unity with Christ, with each other, and with Christians who have gone before us. We unite our voices with those of the saints in praising God.

Christ's Presence in the Eucharist

Jesus Christ, the eternal priest of the covenant that God made with all humanity through the death and Resurrection of his Son, is present in the ministry of the priest who presides over the liturgy. Jesus Christ acts through the priest, offering the eucharistic sacrifice, the sacrifice of his Body and Blood, in every Mass. Jesus Christ is also present in the people gathered at the Mass. Receiving the Body and Blood of Christ strengthens our bond with the Lord. When we share in the eucharistic meal, God forgives our venial sins and draws us closer to him. The Lord's presence within us helps protect us from mortal sins. In closer union with Christ, we are better able to love and serve others. When we experience this closeness and love between ourselves and Christ, our unity as the Body of Christ becomes even stronger.

Christ is present in both the consecrated bread and wine. When we receive Holy Communion in either form, we are receiving Christ whole and entire. Receiving in both forms, however, is a more complete sign of communion.

After the celebration of the Mass, the consecrated hosts—in which Christ is present—are kept in the tabernacle. We can spend time before the tabernacle in **adoration** of the Blessed Sacrament, allowing Jesus' love to penetrate our hearts. We can also show our devotion during the **exposition** of the Blessed Sacrament. This is when the eucharistic host is prominently displayed in a container called a **monstrance**. We can reflect on Jesus' presence in the eucharistic host and pray to him.

Faith Words

adoration Adoration is the act of worshiping or honoring God as divine.

exposition Exposition is a manner of honoring the Blessed Sacrament by placing it in view of worshipers for adoration.

monstrance A monstrance is a special container in which the Eucharist is placed for adoration.

How does the Eucharist transform our lives?

Our Church Teaches

As people who have received Christ in the Eucharist, we must be signs to all people, Christian and non-Christian, of the love of Christ that is within us. We must keep in mind the teachings of the Scriptures that we have heard at Mass, remember the instructions that the priest has given in the homily, and listen to the prompting of the Holy Spirit in our hearts and minds. We encounter the Lord in a special way when we receive the Eucharist. We are healed of our venial sins and strengthened to avoid sin in the future.

Jesus Christ, in instituting the Eucharist and dying on the cross, offered himself for the forgiveness of our sins. When we respond, "Thanks be to God," at the end of Mass, we reaffirm our gratitude for this wondrous gift from God. Then we go forth to serve God and others.

We Believe

As members of the Body of Christ, we join together to praise and thank God. The Eucharist unites us to Christ and to one another.

Respond

Saint Paul

Those who write about Saint Paul often describe him as "zealous." That's because nothing seemed to keep Paul from traveling and spreading the message of Christ. Despite being beaten, stoned, and shipwrecked, he was determined to

speak boldly about the risen Lord. Even after being arrested, Paul continued his mission by writing about Christ from prison.

What got Paul so fired up? It certainly wasn't hearing Jesus preach. Paul was born in the city of Tarsus, which is part of present-day Turkey. Trained as a strict Pharisee, he thought of Christians as heretics. In fact, after Jesus' crucifixion, Paul beat and arrested those who believed in Christ. He stood by as Stephen, the first Christian martyr, was killed.

How did someone who persecuted the Christians come to speak so forcefully about Jesus Christ as the Savior? One day, on his way to arrest more Christians, Paul encountered the risen Lord in a vision. This encounter transformed his life, and for many years he traveled extensively, establishing many Christian communities along the way. He invited various groups to unite themselves to Christ. He stressed that Jesus came to save all people.

In the Second Letter of Paul to Timothy we read: "I have competed well; I have finished the race; I have kept the faith."

Saint Paul's feast day is June 29.

Activities

1. Think about the story of Saint Paul, then complete the sentences.

Jesus Christ appeared to Saint Paul in a _____. This experience of Christ's

presence _____ Paul's life. Paul was able to keep the _____ because

Christ was with him, just as Christ is with _____ when we receive the Eucharist.

2. Think about Jesus' presence in your life. When you think about Jesus, do you imagine him to look a certain way? The way that we picture Jesus often reveals certain aspects of our relationship with him. For example, we might picture Jesus as the Good Shepherd, revealing that it is important for us to see Jesus as our caretaker.

Many artists have tried to capture certain qualities of Jesus in order to reach people with different points of view. Examine the images of Jesus on this page. On the lines, write about the picture you identify with the most, and explain why.

Salvator Mundi by Vivarini

Black Jesus Blesses the Children by unknown artist

Christ the Healer by G.E. Mullan

_____

_____

_____

_____

_____

How can we celebrate the presence of Jesus in the Eucharist?

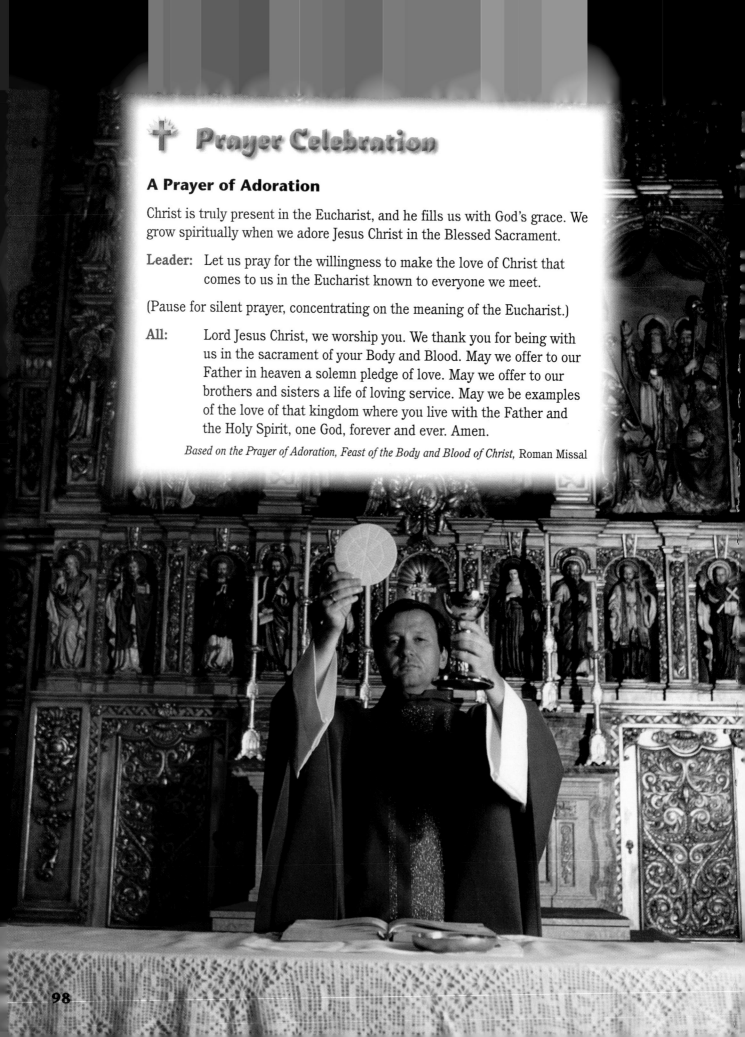

✞ Prayer Celebration

A Prayer of Adoration

Christ is truly present in the Eucharist, and he fills us with God's grace. We grow spiritually when we adore Jesus Christ in the Blessed Sacrament.

Leader: Let us pray for the willingness to make the love of Christ that comes to us in the Eucharist known to everyone we meet.

(Pause for silent prayer, concentrating on the meaning of the Eucharist.)

All: Lord Jesus Christ, we worship you. We thank you for being with us in the sacrament of your Body and Blood. May we offer to our Father in heaven a solemn pledge of love. May we offer to our brothers and sisters a life of loving service. May we be examples of the love of that kingdom where you live with the Father and the Holy Spirit, one God, forever and ever. Amen.

Based on the Prayer of Adoration, Feast of the Body and Blood of Christ, Roman Missal

Get Connected

with family and friends

Living in Christ's Love

Jesus made it clear that loving one another as he loves us is not easy. He said, "Whoever wishes to come after me must deny himself, take up his cross, and follow me" (Matthew 16:24). We must take up our "crosses" to live a Christian life. The Ten Commandments are a moral guide to Christian life.

Daring to Live the Truth

A group of friends was outside playing "Truth or Dare." Each person had to reveal the worst thing he or she ever did or complete a dare. Five minutes into the game, Lily started to feel uncomfortable. People were daring each other to do things Lily knew were wrong, and the "truth" questions were about topics she didn't want to waste time talking about. She wanted to walk away, but she knew people would talk about her. Finally, her turn came. "Truth or dare?" she was asked.

"Truth," she replied.

"Did you ever steal?" someone asked.

The answer was no. But Lily was silent. She was going to "dare" to say something witty that would teach them what the "truth" really was.

Activity

Do one of the following.

(1) Cut out slips of paper for each person in your family. Have each person write an ending for the story above. Take turns reading each other's replies.

(2) Work with your friends and family members to create a new game for young people that would focus on positive activities instead of the kinds of activities in the game Lily played.

F.A.Q.

Dear Mr. F.A.Q.,

I live in a small town. Lately, a homeless man has been hanging around the bus shelter. Everyone's afraid to go near him. But yesterday, my mom picked up the homeless guy, drove us to a diner, and bought the man a meal. He was so thankful. I'd like to start a group to raise money to help the man. But I'm afraid that everyone will make fun of me.

Signed,
Feeling Cowardly

Dear Feeling Cowardly,

Your mother gave you a wonderful example of following Christ. Jesus helped people whom others avoided or ignored, such as lepers or beggars. Sometimes we worry about what others might say, but can you live with yourself knowing that the man is still suffering? Would Jesus want that?

God bless,
Mr. F.A.Q.

Did you know...?

People often misunderstand the Golden Rule, which is based on Matthew 7:12. The Golden Rule means "Treat others *the way you would like to be treated*," not "Treat others the way they treat you."

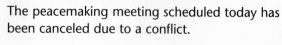

Holy Humor!

Bulletin Bloopers

Seen in actual announcements in church bulletins:

The pastor would appreciate it if the ladies of the congregation would lend him their electric girdles for the pancake breakfast next Sunday morning.

The peacemaking meeting scheduled today has been canceled due to a conflict.

This being Easter Sunday, we will ask Mrs. Lewis to come forward and lay an egg on the altar.

The concert held in the parish hall was a great success. Special thanks to Sister Geraldine, who labored the whole evening at the piano, which, as usual, fell upon her.

All-Star Profile

Name: Father Mychal Judge
Born: 1933
Died: 2001, during the collapse of the World Trade Center, while assisting with emergency efforts
Occupation: Franciscan priest, chaplain for the New York City fire department, head of New York City Bread Line, organized by friars to feed the homeless
Quote of a Lifetime: "He was a priest in love with Jesus. Where there was Father Mike, there was Jesus. He brought Christ's message of love and forgiveness" (Steven McDonald, New York City police detective).
Claims to Fame: Consoled firefighters in the midst of tragedy. Helped grieving families of the TWA flight 800 disaster in 1996. Stood beside officer Steven McDonald as he forgave a youth who had shot and nearly killed him.

Something To Do

On Sunday

Consider how water, bread, wine, fire, darkness, and light are used during Mass to say something wonderful about the world God has created.

Through the Week

Blessed John XXIII said, "Even if Jesus lays on us some part of the Cross, he is there to help us bear it." List the ways you feel Jesus' support when you do something good or take a stand for what you believe.

Wired

Visit Our Web Site
www.blestarewe.com

Web Site Spotlight
www.lifeway.com/tlw

This is the site for True Love Waits, an abstinence program. Thousands of teens have taken a stand on respecting their bodies and made a pledge online to live their Christian values.

✝ A Prayer for the Week

Lord, help us be true to you, the commandments, and our faith. Show us good ways to spend our time as Christians. Guide us in making good choices. May we inspire others to make good choices. Amen.

11 Living in Christ's Love

If you keep my commandments, you will remain in my love, just as I have kept my Father's commandments and remain in his love.

John 15:10

Share

God created the earth with abundant natural resources to be used for the good of all people. However, human beings have wasted, polluted, or destroyed many of the earth's natural resources. Water is a prime example.

Human survival depends on the availability of clean water. Without consuming water, we become dehydrated and unable to survive. We also need water for cleaning and for cooking. It is also necessary for the irrigation of the crops from which we get our basic foods. As world populations increase, water is in more demand than ever. Unfortunately, water is being used faster than it can be replenished by rain. In addition, bodies of water continue to be polluted with chemicals or contaminated with diseases because of the improper disposal of hazardous wastes.

As Christians, we are responsible for the care of the earth. We must protect its resources for our generation and future generations. We live in Christ's love when we are aware of environmental problems and work to solve them.

According to a 1999 report from the United Nations, about 2.7 billion people will experience severe water shortages within the next twenty-five years.

Activity

We have a moral obligation to protect the earth's resources for our use today and the use of future generations. Below, suggest ways you can stop the abuse of water, one of our most valuable resources.

_____

_____

_____

_____

Reflect on other environmental issues in which your actions can make a difference.

In what other ways can we show that we live in Christ's love?

Hear & Believe

 Scripture The Conditions of Discipleship

Choosing to use our resources responsibly is just one way we carry out our mission as Catholics. We make many choices in our day-to-day living that affect those around us. With Jesus' help, we can make good decisions.

Jesus said to his disciples, "Whoever wishes to come after me must deny himself, take up his cross, and follow me. For whoever wishes to save his life will lose it, but whoever loses his life for my sake will find it. What profit would there be for one to gain the whole world and forfeit his life? Or what can one give in exchange for his life? For the Son of Man will come with his angels in his Father's glory, and then he will repay everyone according to his conduct. Amen, I say to you, there are some standing here who will not taste death until they see the Son of Man coming in his kingdom."

Matthew 16:24–28

Leading a Moral Life

To live as disciples of Jesus, we must be willing to make sacrifices and overcome temptations.

Since we are baptized in Christ, we are called to live a chaste, or morally pure, life. Jesus is our model of **chastity** because he was pure in his thoughts and conduct. Chastity requires working to control our desires and being careful not to give into the temptation to use God's gift of sexuality to satisfy our own selfish wants. For people who are unmarried, chastity includes respecting and following the teaching that sexual love is meant for the lifelong commitment of marriage. For married people, being chaste includes remaining faithful to one's spouse. Chastity also involves understanding that sexuality is part of our identity. The way we express our sexuality cannot be separated from our lives as faithful Christians. The ninth commandment, "You shall not commit adultery," obliges us to live a life of chastity.

We live moral lives by basing our actions and words on those of Jesus, who always followed God's law. Christian **morality** includes keeping the Ten Commandments, God's laws that guide us in our relationship with God and other people. Jesus said, "If you wish to enter into life, keep the commandments" (Matthew 19:17). The commandments are a gift from God in which he has revealed his will. God gave the commandments as signs of his covenant with people. They are signs of God's love, because keeping them draws us closer to him. They express the natural law, the understanding of right and wrong that God gave to humanity. The natural law, an understanding of how to do good and avoid evil, is the basis of all morality.

 page 249 to learn more about chastity and pages 247–250 to learn about the Ten Commandments.

The Natural Law and the Church

The Catholic Church teaches on questions of natural law, guiding us in living a moral life. Jesus Christ established the Church and gave the apostles and their successors the authority to preach the faith. Jesus said to the apostles, "Whoever listens to you listens to me. Whoever rejects you rejects me. And whoever rejects me rejects the one who sent me" (Luke 10:16). Because of this, the pope and the bishops, as the apostles' successors, continue to teach us about the faith and guide us in making moral decisions. The pope, in communion with the bishops, is the teaching authority, or **Magisterium**, of the Church. Guided by the Holy Spirit, the pope and the bishops preserve and preach Jesus' message. The teachings of the Magisterium on questions of morality come from the Holy Spirit and thus are without error. These teachings help keep us faithful to the saving truths of our Catholic faith.

Moral Growth Through Worship

We grow in morality by participating in the sacraments and the Mass because they fill us with Jesus Christ's presence. Faithfully celebrating the Sunday liturgy is essential to our moral life, and it fulfills the third commandment: to keep holy the **Lord's Day**. The Sunday liturgy is our celebration of Christ's Resurrection. For Christians, Sunday is the Lord's Day, a time to rest and to enrich our family relationships, our spirituality, our cultural experiences, and our social lives.

Faith Words

chastity Chastity is a virtue that helps us express our sexuality in a mature and unselfish manner. The word *chastity* describes a state of being morally pure in thought and conduct.

morality Morality is a system of rules for good conduct based on our beliefs. Christian morality includes keeping the commandments in response to God's love.

Magisterium The pope, in communion with the bishops, is the teaching authority, or Magisterium, of the Church.

How does God help us with our moral growth?

Our Church Teaches

God created us to be good. Our human reason enables us to know and follow the natural law. In his goodness, God continues to guide us in developing our moral life.

God revealed the Ten Commandments to us, giving further expression to the natural law. The Church, established by Christ, guides us in applying the commandments in our everyday living. For example, the seventh commandment teaches us not to take another person's property. The Church not only helps us understand that such an action is morally wrong but requires us to make amends. It is our moral duty to return stolen goods or to compensate the owner for them. The Church also teaches that the seventh commandment's meaning for us goes beyond the command not to steal. It also means protecting and preserving the world's goods for everyone.

> **We Believe**
> The Church guides us in our faith and moral issues. The pope and the bishops help us apply Jesus' teachings to our moral life.

Respond

Following in Jesus' Footsteps

We can accomplish a great deal when we join together as Jesus' disciples. Many Catholics organize themselves into groups that work to make positive changes in society. One such group is the Catholic Worker Movement, which began with the printing of a newspaper in New York City in 1933. Journalist Dorothy Day and her friend Peter Maurin began publishing *The Catholic Worker* to make people aware of the social teachings of the Catholic Church. They charged only one cent per copy. Dorothy Day saw the Catholic Church as "the church of the immigrants, the church of the poor." She said *The Catholic Worker* was a "little paper" written for those who were unable to find a sense of hope in the future.

One time, a homeless woman who read the first issue appeared at Dorothy's door asking for help. Dorothy welcomed her into her apartment, thus beginning the first Catholic Worker house of hospitality. Today, there are about 130 Catholic Worker communities in the United States. There are also Catholic Worker houses of hospitality in Canada, Europe, and Australia. Each one operates independently and ministers to homeless individuals and families. The houses of hospitality also help refugees, disabled adults, and those suffering from alcoholism. They welcome anyone who has lost his or her way in society.

All of the houses are founded on the belief that it is our moral duty to help our neighbors. Catholic Workers recognize the dignity of each person, and they leave behind the material things of this world to live and work with the poor. They provide food, shelter, and clothing to people in need.

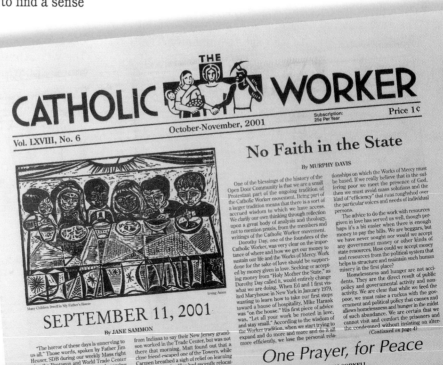

Activity

Jesus taught us to observe God's commandments and live according to the Gospel. Read the following moral dilemmas, then write what you think Jesus would do in each situation.

Tom really wasn't friends with Jack. In fact, no one in the class talked to Jack—except to tease him about his clothes or his unusual mannerisms. But Tom got to know Jack when they were assigned to work on a class project together. To his surprise, Tom discovered that he and Jack shared some of the same interests.

The day after their project was completed, Jack walked over to Tom and his friends. Tom's friends started to tease Jack. Tom usually joined in, but now he felt uncomfortable. Then, in front of all Tom's friends, Jack invited Tom to his house to shoot some baskets. Tom didn't know what to say.

What would Jesus do?

_____

_____

_____

Erin just couldn't seem to do anything right lately. Her parents were upset with her for coming home late one night after a movie. They also didn't like the fact that she had tried to complete in one night a science project that she had known about for three weeks. Her parents called her behavior "irresponsible."

One day, Erin's mother asked her to find a videotape she had rented from the video store so that they could return it together. Erin suddenly became uneasy. She had accidentally stepped on the tape, and it was cracked. Her parents would be annoyed that she had been so careless. Considering all her recent troubles, she wasn't sure what to do.

What would Jesus do?

_____

_____

_____

How can we celebrate Jesus' love as his disciples?

✝ Prayer Celebration

Becoming True Disciples of Jesus

Using the words of a song, let us now pray that we can be true disciples of Jesus by sharing his love with others. As you say the words, use the sign language shown for words that are in bold.

Refrain: We have been told, we've seen his face
and heard his voice alive in our hearts;
"Live in my love with all your heart,
as the Father has loved me; so **I have loved you**."

Reader 1: I am the **vine**; you are the **branches**
and all who live in me will bear great fruit. (Refrain)

Reader 2: You are my friends, if you keep my commands,
no longer slaves, I call you friends. (Refrain)

Reader 3: No greater love is there than this:
to lay down one's life for a friend. (Refrain)

"We Have Been Told" by David Haas © 1983 GIA Publications, Inc., 7404 South Mason Avenue, Chicago, IL 60638-9927. All rights reserved. Used with permission.

vine   branches   I love you

Get Connected

with family and friends

A Prayer for Christ's Healing

The Gospels describe ways that Jesus healed people and gave them a fresh start in life. Jesus' healings included freeing people from fear and sin as well as curing their physical ailments. In this chapter, we learn about John's account of an important fresh start: Jesus' raising of Lazarus from the dead. Jesus' healings involved praying to God the Father. Prayer and healing are central to our faith.

A New Beginning

Gianna and Graciella were crushed when their grandmother had a stroke. For weeks, their grandmother was in the hospital recovering. She couldn't even walk and she had trouble speaking. When the doctor transferred her to an acute care center, the sisters thought they would never have the same relationship with their grandma again.

Graciella and Gianna asked God to heal their grandmother. They prayed often and asked others to join them in prayer. They also said prayers with their grandmother. Nurses and physical therapists starting having some success. Grandma started smiling more, and she was speaking more clearly. One day, Gianna and Graciella heard some good news: Grandma was ready to go home.

Activity

Do one of the following.

(1) Place pictures of family members, friends, and others for whom you wish to pray in a prominent place and invite your family to remember these people in prayer.

(2) Attend a healing Mass or prayer service in your parish. Invite your family and friends to join you. Pray for God's healing in your lives and in the world.

The Password Is

Gospel

The word *Gospel* came from the Old English *god*, meaning "good," and *spel*, meaning "news." These words were translations of the Latin *bona adnuntiatio*, meaning "reward for bringing good news." The word came to refer to the "good news" of the writings of Matthew, Mark, Luke, and John.

Did you know...?

Many doctors and researchers have studied the effects of prayer on healing. The results of their studies often show that sick people who pray, or for whom others pray, experience greater healing than other sick people.

Lyric Soul Food

Amy Grant is not only one of the most influential singers in contemporary Christian music but one of the reasons that Christian music has reached a global audience. She grew up in Nashville, Tennessee, in 1960—the youngest of four children—and released her first album at age fifteen. Throughout the 1980s, Grant's success continued, as her albums went gold and platinum and won awards, including five Grammy Awards.

"The attraction of Christian music is in its Gospel message," says Grant.

"Everybody wants to be re-inspired about life, hope, and faith, whether it's contemporary Christian music, whether it's Southern Gospel, or just hearing robust singing in a church setting," she says. "That is soul food. That is the real deal. The great thing about contemporary Christian music is that you can get that kind of lyric soul food in just about any kind of genre you like."

All-Star Profile

Name: Nkosi Johnson
Born: 1989
Died: 2001
Family Background: Born infected with AIDS because his mother was infected. Given up for adoption by his mother, who feared rejection by her community.
Occupation: young South African activist and speaker on the AIDS crisis
Quote of a Lifetime: "You can't get AIDS if you touch, hug, kiss, hold hands with someone who is infected. Care for us and accept us. We are all human beings."
Claims to Fame: Spoke internationally about the need for governments to give medicine to pregnant women infected with AIDS so babies do not become infected. Lived nine years longer than doctors had predicted. Used this time to campaign for the rights of people infected with AIDS and to break stereotypes about people with the disease. Helped shelter and care for babies infected with AIDS.

Wired

Visit Our Web Site
www.blestarewe.com

Web Site Spotlight
www.beliefnet.com

Visit this site and check out the sections on inspiration and health and healing. There are many interesting articles and prayers.

Something To Do

On Sunday

Check your church bulletin for the names of people who are sick or have died. Pray for God's blessings and healing for them and their families.

Through the Week

Use gentle and healing words with others this week. Try to let go of anger toward family or friends. Make forgiving others a priority.

✝ A Prayer for the Week

May we always have faith in your healing power, Lord, and may we be the bearers of healing to others, just as Nkosi Johnson was. Thank you for your compassion. Amen.

12 A Prayer for Christ's Healing

Your faith has saved you. Go in peace!

Based on Luke 8:48

Share

There are times in our lives when we need to put our trust in other people. When we are physically hurt or ill, we put our trust in doctors to help us get better. When we experience emotional hurt or distress, we go to our friends or parents for comfort and advice. Trust means believing in and having faith in another person's ability to care for us. To fully trust a person, our fears and doubts cannot get in the way. Rather, we need to be completely willing to allow other people's care and concern to make a difference in our lives.

Activity

Describe occasions in which you needed to trust in...

a) your parents.

_____

_____

_____

b) your friends.

_____

_____

_____

c) God.

_____

_____

_____

Why is it important to place our trust in Jesus?

Scripture The Raising of Lazarus

Mary and Martha and their brother Lazarus were friends of Jesus, and they trusted him completely. When Lazarus became very ill, the sisters sent a message to their friend Jesus.

When Jesus heard about Lazarus, he said, "This illness is not to end in death but is for the glory of God, that the Son of God may be glorified through it."

Jesus waited two days and then told his disciples, "Our friend Lazarus is asleep, but I am going to wake him." When Jesus saw that his disciples did not understand, he said clearly, "Lazarus has died. And I am glad for you that I was not there, so that you may believe. Let us go to him."

When Martha heard that Jesus was coming, she went out to meet him, but Mary sat at home.

Martha said to Jesus, "Lord, if you had been here, my brother would not have died. But even now I know that whatever you ask of God, God will give you."

Jesus said to her, "Your brother will rise."

"I know he will rise," Martha replied, "in the resurrection on the last day."

Jesus told her, "I am the resurrection and the life; whoever believes in me, even if he dies, will live, and everyone who lives and believes in me will never die. Do you believe this?"

"Yes, Lord," said Martha. "I have come to believe that you are the Messiah, the Son of God, the one who is coming into the world."

Then Mary came to Jesus and fell at his feet and said to him, "Lord, if you had been here, my brother would not have died."

"Where have you lain him?" Jesus asked when he saw Mary and the Jews who had come with Mary weeping. He was deeply moved.

"Sir, come and see," they replied.

Jesus wept, and the Jews said, "See how he loved him." But some of them said, "Could not the one who opened the eyes of the blind man have done something so that this man would not have died?"

So Jesus came to the cave that was Lazarus' tomb. A stone lay across it.

"Take away the stone," Jesus said.

Martha said to him, "Lord, by now there will be a stench; he has been dead for four days."

"Did I not tell you that if you believe you will see the glory of God?" Jesus said to her.

So they took away the stone. And Jesus raised his eyes and said, "Father, I thank you for hearing me. I know that you always hear me; but because of the crowd here I have said this, that they may believe that you sent me." And when he had said this, he cried out in a loud voice, "Lazarus, come out!"

The dead man, tied hand and foot with burial bands, came out, his face wrapped in a cloth.

Jesus said to the people gathered, "Untie him and let him go."

Based on John 11:1–44

The Miracles of Jesus

Mary and Martha sent for Jesus because they had a strong faith in his power to heal. Even though she was filled with grief over Lazarus' death, Martha expressed her faith in Jesus. Jesus performed the **miracle** of raising Lazarus from the dead as a sign that he was sent by God to save the world. In the Gospel of John, such happenings are actually called "signs" instead of "miracles" because each sign helps us better understand who Jesus is. God wanted people to recognize Jesus as Christ, the Anointed One and Messiah who had come to bring new life.

Before this, Jesus had also performed numerous miracles that people witnessed. They came to trust in Jesus, not only for his wondrous works, but also for the compassion and mercy he showed to those who were suffering. Here is a summary of some of Jesus' healing miracles:

Healing of the Paralytic (Luke 5:17–26)
Some men lowered their paralyzed friend through a roof so that he would be closer to Jesus. Because of the man's faith, Jesus forgave the man's sins and healed him, saying, "Rise, pick up your stretcher, and go home."

The Man Born Blind (John 9:1–17)
Jesus gave sight to a blind beggar on the streets by first smearing clay on his eyes. Then Jesus said to him, "Go wash in the Pool of Siloam."

The Man with a Withered Hand (Matthew 12:9–14)
Jesus said to a man in the synagogue, "Stretch out your hand." The man followed Jesus' command and his hand was healed.

The Cure of a Demoniac (Luke 4:31–37)
Jesus cured a man possessed by evil spirits when he said, "Be quiet! Come out of him!"

By his command or by his touch, Jesus cured illnesses. His healing and miracles were visible signs of God's love. More important, Jesus brought peace to those he healed, the peace that comes from being embraced by Jesus' love. Restored to wholeness, those who were healed followed Jesus faithfully.

Healing is still an important part of our Christian life. We all need Christ's healing, both physically and spiritually. If we pray with complete trust in Jesus Christ, we can experience God's healing in our lives. The Church also offers the sick and the elderly the sacrament of the Anointing of the Sick, in which Christ's healing can be experienced in a special way. The priest, acting in Christ's name and in the name of the Church, anoints those who are sick or near death with **holy oil**.

A Closer Look

Holy Oil
Disciples of Jesus Christ anointed the sick with oil as they traveled to preach the Gospel message.  Oil was used in the ancient world as a remedy. Today, priests anoint the sick with holy oil that has been blessed by the bishop on Holy Thursday.

The Expression of Faith

Jesus' healing miracles are signs that faith can heal. We express our faith by praying to the Father. We pray not only for ourselves, but on behalf of others as well. In a prayer of **intercession**, we ask God to help our families, friends, and other people who need Christ's peace and healing.

Faith Words

miracle A miracle is a wondrous sign or event that can only have happened through the power of God.

holy oil Holy oil is oil blessed by the bishop and used in the Anointing of the Sick and other sacraments.

intercession An intercession is a prayer that we say on behalf of others in need of God's help.

How can we satisfy our spiritual needs?

Our Church Teaches

Prayer is an important part of our journey of faith. The Holy Spirit helps us understand what Jesus taught us about prayer and guides us in our prayer life. There are five basic forms of prayer: blessing or adoration, petition, intercession, thanksgiving, and praise.

Because God has blessed the human heart, we offer prayers of blessing to God as a way to acknowledge him for blessing us. We address all our prayers primarily to God, our Father, who is the source of all our blessings. Through our prayers of petition, we ask God to help us with our own needs. In our prayers of intercession, we remember the needs of others.

Christians express themselves in prayer by using vocal prayer, meditation, or contemplation. We are in God's presence regardless of which method we choose to use.

We Believe
Guided by the Holy Spirit, we express the power of our faith in Christ's peace and ability to heal through our prayers.

Respond

Saint Pio of Pietrelcina

In the mountains of southern Italy in 1956, Saint Pio saw his vision of a special hospital become a reality. This Capuchin Francisan priest established a facility where patients were considered part of a family. He stressed the importance of building trust with the patients and attending to both their physical and spiritual needs. To reflect his philosophy of care, Saint Pio named the hospital the House for the Relief of Suffering.

Saint Pio was born in a town called Pietrelcina in Italy and he died more than thirty years ago, but patients continue to receive loving and compassionate care at the hospital complex he created. Saint Pio is known throughout the world for living a life of faith and prayer. He constantly prayed for others, whom he called his "spiritual children." He also formed prayer groups because he strongly believed in the power of prayer. He once said, "Prayer is the oxygen of the soul!"

When Saint Pio was a young priest, something quite miraculous happened to him. While he was praying in front of a crucifix, the wounds of Christ appeared on his hands, feet, and side. People turned to Saint Pio to receive healing miracles.

When Saint Pio died at the age of eighty-one, more than 100,000 people attended his funeral. After his death, Pope Paul VI said that people admired Saint Pio because "he said the Mass

Saint Pio and His Stigmata by Professor Angelo Marelli

humbly. He heard confessions from morning to night…. He was a man of prayer and suffering."

In 1999 the *Daily Catholic* ranked Saint Pio number three in a list of the top 100 Catholics of the twentieth century. Pope John Paul II canonized Pio on June 16, 2002.

Activities

1. Saint Pio said, "Prayer is the oxygen of the soul!" Are there people you know who need prayers for Christ's healing? Write a prayer of intercession asking God to help them.

_____

_____

_____

_____

2. Jesus showed compassion not only for people who were suffering physically but for those who were experiencing the pain of sin, loneliness, or uncertainty. Matthew's Gospel says that, as Jesus preached the good news of the kingdom to crowds in towns and villages, "his heart was moved with pity for them because they were troubled and abandoned, like sheep without a shepherd" (Matthew 9:36).

Read the following story about Jesus from the Scriptures. At the end of the passage, write how you think Jesus responded, based on what you know about Jesus' compassion.

Mary Magdalene Washing Christ's Feet by Giovanni da Milano

A Pharisee invited Jesus to dine with him, and Jesus entered the Pharisee's house and reclined at a table. There was a sinful woman in the city who learned that Jesus was at the house of the Pharisee. Bringing ointment with her, the woman stood behind Jesus at the table and wept. She bathed Jesus' feet with her tears, wiped them with her hair, kissed them, and anointed them with the ointment.

When the Pharisee who had invited Jesus saw this, he said, "If this man were a prophet, he would know who and what sort of woman this is who is touching him. He would know that she is a sinner!"

Jesus said to him in reply,   *Based on Luke 7:36–40*

"_____

_____

_____

_____."

How can we experience Jesus' mercy and love?

113

✝ Prayer Celebration

Touched by Jesus' Mercy and Love

Reflect on your own hurts and the things that keep you from living your faith. Write a prayer for healing below, then pray it silently.

_____

_____

Leader: May the Lord in his love and mercy help you with the grace of the Holy Spirit. May the Lord who frees you from sin save you and raise you up.

Rite of Anointing of the Sick

All: Lord Jesus Christ, Son of God, have mercy on me, a sinner. Amen.

The Jesus Prayer

WE CARE *About Ourselves*

A Temple of the Holy Spirit

Charlie was trying to make the middle-school wrestling team. All the boys had to weigh in before each tryout match. Charlie had been jogging to the point of collapse every morning, but he just couldn't reach the weight that the coaches were demanding.

Monique was feeling pretty self-conscious. When did all the other girls in her gymnastics class start looking so thin and perfect? As she stepped onto the exercise mat, she glanced at her reflection with disgust.

Both Monique and Charlie heard about people who starve themselves, or force themselves to throw up after they eat, to stay thin. Fortunately, however, Monique and Charlie refused to take such extreme measures to get thin. Something didn't seem right about putting their bodies through so much torture.

They were correct, because God made us beautiful just as we are. Each of us is sacred—a temple of the Holy Spirit. When we think of ourselves in this way, we can avoid doing things that harm our bodies. Unfortunately, many young people give in to temptation and risk serious harm to their bodies in an attempt to be someone they were not meant to be.

One seventh grade girl—when she heard about an older girl who ended up in the hospital because of anorexia nervosa— always tries to reassure friends who express dislike for their own appearance. She collects articles about people who have suffered or even died because of eating disorders, and she tries to spread the word about the dangers of eating disorders around her school.

How can you remember that you are a temple of the Holy Spirit?

Think About It

Name five ways that young people sometimes try to change who they are or how they appear.

1.

2.

3.

4.

5.

Name reasons why young people might want to change themselves.

_____

_____

Learn About It

Have you heard the expression "God doesn't make junk"? Each of us is precious in God's eyes. Of course, there is nothing wrong with experimenting with new hairstyles, clothing, and so on. But there is a difference between trying out new looks and physically harming ourselves. Jesus taught us that we are to love our neighbor just as we love ourselves. Yes, God is commanding us to love ourselves. People who obey this command recognize that they are made in God's image and feel good about themselves just as God made them.

Do Something About It

List five reasons for feeling good about yourself just as you are.

1. _____

2. _____

3. _____

4. _____

5. _____

UNIT 3 Organizer

The topics of the Unit 3 chapters are listed in the center below. In the boxes on the left, write examples of what Jesus said about each topic in the Scriptures. In the boxes on the right, write about an action that is an example of the topic for today.

What Jesus Taught

Examples for Today

Topic

Living in Christ's Service

Jesus, Our Eucharist

Living in Christ's Love

A Prayer for Christ's Healing

A Complete the puzzle using the clues.

Across

2. the place in the Temple where Jews placed their offerings

6. people who are not sincere in performing good acts

7. the theological virtue that enables us to believe in God

Down

1. the saint who dedicated himself to the poor

3. the theological virtue of love

4. the poor woman who contributed all she had

5. the Son of God

8. the theological virtue of trust in God's promise of everlasting life

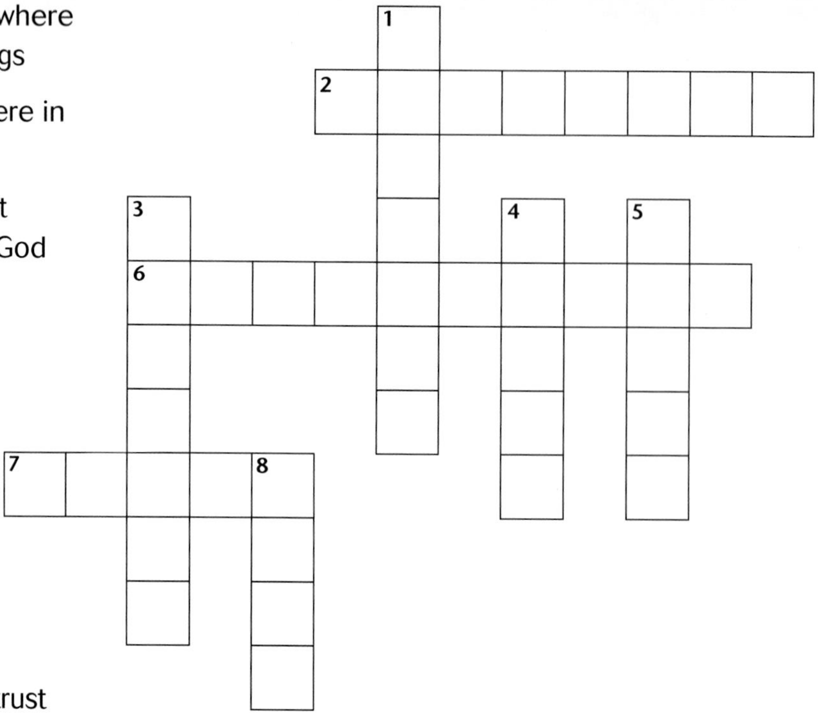

B Complete the sentences by selecting the correct words from the box below.

Body	language	Pharisee	Christ's	Tarsus	Blood

1. The _____ and rituals of the Mass may differ from

   culture to culture, but they always express the same mystery of

   _____ sacrifice.

2. Receiving the _____ and _____ of Christ
   strengthens our bond with the Lord.

3. Saint Paul was born in _____ and trained as a strict

   _____.

C Circle the letter of the correct answer.

1. God created the earth with abundant natural resources

   a. to be used any way people desire.

   b. to be used for the good of all people.

   c. to be used by the rich who know how to invest them wisely.

2. The natural law is a human understanding that tells us how

   a. to do good and avoid evil.

   b. to treat animals in the jungle.

   c. to celebrate the Eucharist.

3. Dorothy Day is known for

   a. being a movie star.

   b. writing children's stories about the poor.

   c. making people aware of the social teachings of the Church.

D Identify the person to whom Jesus spoke each message by writing the correct name of the person or phrase describing the person on the line next to the message. Select names and phrases from the box.

Martha	the paralytic
the disciples	the man possessed by evil spirits
the man born blind	Mary

1. _____ "Go wash in the Pool of Siloam."

2. _____ "Be quiet! Come out of him!"

3. _____ "Where have you lain him?"

4. _____ "Our friend Lazarus is asleep, but I am going to awaken him."

5. _____ "Rise, pick up your stretcher, and go home."

6. _____ "Your brother will rise."

E Match the Faith Words in Column 1 with the definitions in Column 2.

Column 1

a. monstrance

b. virtue

c. chastity

d. intercession

e. morality

f. theological virtues

g. Magisterium

h. adoration

i. almsgiving

j. exposition

k. miracle

l. holy oil

m. moral virtues

Column 2

1. ____ oil blessed by the bishop and used in the Anointing of the Sick and other sacraments

2. ____ a system of rules for good conduct based on our beliefs

3. ____ an ability to make morally good decisions that lead to the habit of doing good

4. ____ a virtue that helps us express our sexuality in a mature and unselfish manner

5. ____ the four spiritual qualities of temperance, prudence, justice, and fortitude

6. ____ a wondrous sign or event that can only have happened through the power of God

7. ____ the act of worshiping or honoring God as divine

8. ____ the teaching authority of the Church, which consists of the pope in communion with the bishops

9. ____ a prayer that we say on behalf of others in need of God's help

10. ____ the three spiritual qualities of faith, hope, and charity

11. ____ the act of giving time, money, or goods to people who are poor or in need

12. ____ a manner of honoring the Blessed Sacrament by placing it in view of worshipers for adoration

13. ____ a special container in which the Eucharist is placed for adoration

F What is the Jesus Prayer, and on what occasion might you pray this prayer?

_____

_____

_____

UNIT 4

The Paschal Mystery

Begun with the events celebrated in the Easter Triduum, our salvation in Christ was made complete by the coming of the Holy Spirit, which we commemorate with the feast of Pentecost.

On that day you will realize that I am in my Father and you are in me and I in you.

John 14:20

This Palm Sunday procession down the Mount of Olives recalls the first steps of Jesus' Easter journey. The sixth-century icon shows Mary and the disciples receiving the Holy Spirit at Pentecost.

Hold Us in Your Mercy

Words by Rory Cooney

Music by Gary Daigle

Cantor: Hold us in your mer - cy. **All:** Hold us in your mer - cy.

Cantor: Hold us in your mer - cy. **All:** Hold us in your mer - cy.

Cantor:
1. Mak - er's love poured out from heav - en. **All:** Hold us in your mer - cy.
2. Born as one of home - less pil - grims.
3. You who shared the sin - ner's ta - ble.
4. You who shared our life and la - bor.
5. You who si - lence rag - ing de - mons.
6. You whose cross has gone be - fore us.
7. In - no - cent, you faced the guilt - y.
8. Come and break the chains that bind us.
9. Break the pow - er of the dark - ness.
10. Ky - ri - e e - le - i - son!
11. Ky - ri - e e - le - i - son!

Cantor:
1. Mer - cy's word - made-flesh a - mong us. **All:** Hold us in your mer - cy.
2. Sent to bring the poor good news.
3. You who cleansed the lep - er's flesh.
4. You who chose to walk our roads.
5. You who bid the storm be si - lent.
6. You who bear our cross with us.
7. One in death with us for - ev - er.
8. Free us from ad - dic - tion's pris - on.
9. Let us rise to life with you.
10. Chri - ste e - le - i - son!
11. Ky - ri - e e - le - i - son!

Get Connected

with family and friends

Jesus' Persecution

After Jesus raised Lazarus from the dead, he had even more followers. But some people, including some of the chief priests of the Temple and the Pharisees, could not accept Jesus. Those who could not accept Jesus' teachings, healings, and miracles began to plot his death. When Jesus arrived in Jerusalem, people welcomed him as their king. Soon after, however, Jesus sacrificed his life.

Standing Up for What Is Right

Angela was up all night studying for the history test. There was so much information to remember. Suddenly she got a call from Caren, someone she knew from school—not one of her closest friends. Caren knew Angela got good grades, so she asked Angela to make a cheat sheet for her for the test. Angela didn't want to refuse and become unpopular, so she asked for time to think it over. The next day, word got out, and several people approached Angela to help them get through the test. It took all of her courage, but Angela refused to make cheat sheets for anyone, even though she knew that this might make her unpopular. How would you have handled this pressure?

Activity

Do one of the following.

(1) Ask your friends and members of your family to talk about a time they had to stand up for something they believed in. Was it difficult for them? How did they feel afterward?

(2) You and your family can take up the cause of someone undergoing persecution who needs your help. For information on how to help, visit the Web site for Amnesty International (see the next page).

Check It Out

The cross is one of the most familiar signs of Christianity. Crucifixion—execution by being nailed or bound to a cross and left to die—was a method for punishing slaves and criminals in the Roman Empire. Because of the crucifixion of Jesus, the cross is a sign of victory for Christians. By the fourth century, the Roman Empire was Christian, and the cross became a recognizable sign of Christianity. The crucifix, a cross showing the crucified Christ, became an important symbol in the fifth century.

Did you know...?

The inscription *I.N.R.I.* on Jesus' cross means *Iesus Nazarenus Rex Iudaeorum,* or "Jesus of Nazareth, King of the Jews."

Holy Humor!

A Joke to Share

A four-year-old boy is in church one Sunday. He holds his mother's hand as she goes up to receive communion. He watches with interest as she eats the bread and drinks the wine.

As the boy and his mother are walking back to their pew, the boy tries to break free and get back on line. His mother leans down and tells him, "You're not old enough to receive communion yet."

Later, during the second collection, his mother gives him a nickel. But when the basket passes by, he steadfastly refuses to put his coin in.

"If I can't eat," he says, "I'm not paying."

All-Star Profile

Name: Sister Barbara "Bobbie" Ford
Born: 1939
Died: 2001
Occupation: nurse, missioner, member of the Sisters of Charity of St. Vincent de Paul
Quote of a Lifetime: "Sister Barbara Ford laid down her life for her friends—and there is no greater love than this. Another grain of wheat has fallen into the ground, source of new life for the people of Guatemala, and for the community of faith in the United States" (Father Flynn at Sister Barbara's funeral Mass).
Claims to Fame: Worked as a missioner for the poor in Guatemala and other locations worldwide. Organized mental health services for people who lost loved ones to violence from military groups. Learned the language of the Mayan people in the diocese where she served the poor. Operated literacy programs and helped with projects promoting safe drinking water. Recruited doctors and engineers to help people in poor areas.

Wired

Visit Our Web Site
www.blestarewe.com
Web Site Spotlight
www.amnesty.org
Visit this Web site to learn about Amnesty International, an organization that protects those who are persecuted.

Something To Do

On Sunday

To be persecuted is to be oppressed, harassed, injured, or distressed because of the actions of other people. Pray for people you know who are being persecuted, and ask God to help you comfort them.

Through the Week

Be attentive to those who have not been welcomed or accepted into your group of friends. Make an effort to extend your friendship.

A Prayer for the Week

Lord, we pray for the victims of persecution all over the world. Make us aware of people who are suffering, and help us make a difference in their lives. Grant that we may bring dignity, hope, and the love of Jesus to everyone we meet. Amen.

13 Jesus' Persecution

 Christ became obedient to the point of death. Because of this, God greatly exalted him and bestowed on him the name above every name.

Based on Philippians 2:8–9

Share

When you make a sacrifice, you put someone else's needs above your own. Even a child who shares a favorite toy is making a sacrifice. A teenager who mows an elderly neighbor's lawn for free is also making a sacrifice. A man or woman who decides to serve in the military makes a great sacrifice.

Being generous with what you have, including your time and talents, is part of making sacrifices. Every sacrifice is significant because it shows your love and concern for others.

Activity

Write *A* next to the statements with which you agree and *D* next to the statements with which you disagree.

_____ I have nothing to sacrifice.

_____ Making sacrifices is a sign of love.

_____ People never appreciate sacrifices.

_____ A person should make a sacrifice for another person only if the other person returns the favor.

_____ Sacrificing something for someone can make you feel good.

_____ Sacrificing things is difficult.

Imagine how difficult it would be to sacrifice your own life. Yet Jesus accepted the sacrifice of his life for us. Write about a time you had to make a difficult sacrifice to help someone. Write about the good things that resulted.

_____

_____

_____

_____

What events led to Jesus' sacrifice?

Hear & Believe

 Scripture   Jesus Prepares for His Sacrifice in Jerusalem

I have written about Jesus' signs and deeds so that you may know that Jesus is the Messiah, the Son of God (based on John 20:30–31). He has led us to a new Exodus. God's great acts to save his people—the parting of the Red Sea, the manna in the desert— have found their fulfillment in Christ (based on John 6:31). When we saw signs of Jesus' coming trials, Jesus told us, "Do not let your hearts be troubled. You have faith in God; have faith also in me. In my Father's house there are many dwelling places" (John 14:1–2).

You have read John's account of Jesus' raising of Lazarus, a sign of the new life that Jesus would give to all who believe. John also wrote about opposition that grew after Jesus performed that sign:

When Jesus raised Lazarus from the dead, many of the Jews who had seen what he did began to believe in him. But some of them went to the Pharisees and told them what Jesus had done.

The chief priests and the Pharisees met and said, "What are we going to do? This man is performing many signs. If we leave him alone, all will believe in him, and the Romans will come and take away both our land and our nation." From then on, they planned to kill Jesus.

Jesus no longer walked in public among the Jews. He went to a town called Ephraim, near the desert, and remained there with his disciples.

The chief priests and the Pharisees ordered that anyone who knew where Jesus was should inform them so that they could arrest him. Passover was approaching. People went to Jerusalem to purify themselves. They looked for Jesus in the Temple area and said to one another, "Do you think he will come to the Passover feast?"

Meanwhile, Jesus visited Lazarus and his sisters Martha and Mary. A large crowd of Jews followed Jesus there not only because of Jesus but to see Lazarus. The chief priests then plotted to kill Lazarus, too, because many Jews were believing in Jesus because of him.

The next day, the great crowd heard that Jesus was coming to Jerusalem. They took palm branches and went out to meet him, crying, "Hosanna! Blessed is he who comes in the name of the Lord, the king of Israel!"

Meanwhile, Judas Iscariot was plotting to hand Jesus over to those who wanted to arrest him. Jesus knew that his hour had come. Dining with his disciples at the Last Supper, Jesus prepared them for his death and strengthened them in faith.

Jesus raised his eyes to heaven and prayed, "Father, the hour has come. Give glory to your Son so that your Son may glorify you and give eternal life to all you gave him."

After the meal, Jesus and the disciples went across the Kidron and entered a garden there.

Based on John 11:1–45—12:13, 13:1–2, 17:1–2, 18:1

Jesus' Suffering and Glory

Jesus prepared his disciples for his coming suffering, crucifixion, and death. As Christians, we know that Jesus' suffering on the cross marked his victory over sin and evil. The story from John's Gospel reveals signs of this triumph of Jesus. For example, in John's account of Jesus' meal with Lazarus and his sisters, John writes that Lazarus' sister Mary anointed Jesus' feet with expensive oils and wiped his feet with her hair—actions that represented the anointing of a king and messiah. Palm branches, which the people in Jerusalem used to greet Jesus as he entered their city, were used in Jesus' time to welcome great conquerors. As the people welcomed Jesus, they called him the "king of Israel" and cried, "Hosannah!" *Hosannah* means "O Lord, grant salvation" in Hebrew. When the time of Jesus' suffering came, the chief priests would condemn Jesus for being known as "the King of the Jews."

The joy that marked Jesus' welcome into Jerusalem soon turned to sorrow, but with the sacrifice of his life, Jesus Christ conquered sin and death. Despite his pain and humiliation, Jesus freely offered his life for our salvation. We refer to Jesus' suffering and death as his **Passion**.

Life Without End

Jesus Christ, who was the Son of God, experienced humanity in all ways but sin. He truly died and was buried. In the Apostles' Creed, we profess that Jesus "descended into hell," which means that Jesus truly experienced death and suffering for sin. Through his death and **Resurrection**, Jesus freed us from the power of sin and everlasting death.

Jesus' sacrifice on the cross made it possible for us to have **life everlasting**. Jesus Christ rose from the dead and lives forever. Because of Christ's Resurrection, we wait in hope for our own resurrection. Our bodies decay at our deaths, but our souls live forever. At the end of time, we must appear in our own bodies before Christ, our judge, and give an account of how well we have followed him. If we chose to love God and others, we will have new life. God will transform and glorify our bodies, and we will live in God's everlasting kingdom of happiness. This new life given to us when our bodies reunite with our souls at the end of time is called "the resurrection of the body." This is a doctrine we profess each time we pray the Nicene Creed at Mass.

All followers of Christ—living and dead—are part of the Church. This is what we mean when we say that the Church is the **Communion of Saints**. The Eucharist joins us together so that we form one Body of Christ. United in Christ, we pray together for the salvation of all people.

Faith Words

Passion Jesus' Passion is the suffering, crucifixion, and death he endured for our sins.

Resurrection The Resurrection is Jesus' victory over death as he rose to new life. On the last day there will be a resurrection of our bodies as we rise to new life with Christ.

life everlasting Life everlasting is the life that Jesus' faithful followers will share for all eternity.

Communion of Saints The Communion of Saints is the union of all those, both living and dead, who believe in Christ.

How can we respond to Jesus' sacrifice of love?

127

Our Church Teaches

Because God loves us, he desires that we live forever with him in perfect happiness. Jesus Christ, in his death, opened the gates of heaven for the just souls who went before him and offered himself for the salvation of all who would come after. Jesus Christ offers us salvation, but it is up to us how we respond. We can respond by imitating Christ. We can have compassion and mercy just as Jesus did.

We Believe
Out of love for us, God sent his only Son to suffer and die for our sins. Through his death and Resurrection, Jesus won salvation for us.

We must use our free will wisely. If we choose to reject Christ's call to imitate him in this life, we choose separation from God in eternal life. If we die in a state of mortal sin, we will be removed from God's love forever. Rather than rise to the glory of Christ, we will experience everlasting death. Being eternally separated from God, whose life and happiness we long for and were created for, is known as hell.

Respond

Saint Joan of Arc

Jeanne d'Arc (Joan of Arc) was born in a small village in France in the fifteenth century. Neighbors and friends described her as a generous girl who would offer her own bed to a homeless stranger. Although she could not read or write, Joan learned about God and the lives of the saints from her mother. Joan lived simply, helping her mother with sewing and housekeeping.

Quite unexpectedly, Joan felt a calling from God. When she was about fourteen, she became convinced that the voices of Saints Michael, Catherine, and Margaret were instructing her to do something important. In time, she came to believe that she was being asked to save France from invading English troops and to help Charles VII regain control of France and become king.

Joan of Arc by Hillingford

Naturally, Joan was confused by this calling. But being devoted to God, she disguised herself as a man for protection and traveled to where Charles lived. Using a secret sign revealed by the saints, Joan convinced Charles to let her lead his soldiers into battle.

Dressed in armor, she carried a banner that read *Jesus, Mary.* Joan reclaimed French territory, including Orléans in 1492, and later stood by Charles's side as he was crowned king of France. She continued fighting for her country until she was captured and sold to the English. Sadly, King Charles deserted her, and she was put on trial by people who accused her of witchcraft and heresy.

Alone to defend herself, Joan was eventually sentenced to death by burning at the stake. At her request, a Dominican friar held a cross in front of her. As the flames surrounded her, Joan cried out to Jesus, her Savior. She was only nineteen years old.

More than twenty-five years after her death, Joan's name was cleared. Pope Benedict XV canonized Joan of Arc in 1920. On May 30, we honor Joan for her devotion to God and the sacrifice she made in his name.

Activities

1. In the puzzle below, find and circle six words that describe why the cross is an important symbol for Christians. The words may appear across, down, and backwards.

```
T H V I C T O R Y
E W Y A Y T H E T
R U R T E V O L H
A N O I S S A P N
S A L V A T I O N
D T G H E E F I L
```

Now write the uncircled letters in order on the lines below to reveal a message about Jesus.

Jesus says, "I am __ __ __ __ __ __ , __ __ __ __ __ __ __ __ ,

__ __ __   __ __ __ **life"** (based on John 14:6).

2. Write a letter thanking Jesus for dying for our sins and giving us new life.

How can we honor Jesus for sacrificing his life for us?

✝ Prayer Celebration

The Way of the Cross

To help us live as Jesus taught us, we can reflect on his great sacrifice for us. One way to do this is by meditating on the Passion. The Stations of the Cross, or Way of the Cross, is an important prayer in which we meditate on fourteen events of the Passion, beginning with the moment Jesus was condemned to death and ending with the moment he was laid in the tomb. You have probably noticed images of the fourteen events, or stations, lining the walls of your church. In the Stations of the Cross, we walk with Jesus as we look at images that help us follow the story of his Passion. Walk with Jesus now by reading each station below and praying the response each time.

Response: We adore you, O Christ, and we bless you, because by your holy cross you have redeemed the world.

Way of the Cross prayer, attributed to Saint Francis of Assisi

1. Jesus is condemned to death.
2. Jesus accepts the cross.
3. Jesus falls the first time.
4. Jesus meets his mother.
5. Simon helps Jesus carry the cross.
6. Veronica wipes the face of Jesus.
7. Jesus falls the second time.
8. Jesus meets the women of Jerusalem.
9. Jesus falls the third time.
10. Jesus is stripped of his garments.
11. Jesus is nailed to the cross.
12. Jesus dies on the cross.
13. Jesus is taken down from the cross.
14. Jesus is buried in the tomb.

Which of the stations has the most meaning for you? Draw that station here.

Getting ready for Chapter 14

Get Connected

with family and friends

Jesus' Passion

In this chapter, you will learn how the Church remembers and celebrates the events of Jesus' Passion. You will focus on Jesus' suffering and the great sacrifice he made for us by giving up his life. Christ is alive in the Church today. He reaches out to us with love and forgiveness. Holy Week and the season of Lent are the perfect times for us to respond to Christ's call to repentance.

Feeling Hopeless

Mary couldn't believe what she was hearing. She felt terrible. She knew things with her parents weren't so good, but did they have to get a divorce? Being in junior high had enough challenges without *this*. Mary wondered if she could do anything to change her parents' minds. Both parents told her that it wasn't her fault and they still loved her. They also said their decision was final. When Mary prayed, she wondered if Jesus understood what she was feeling. Did Jesus know what it was like to feel that a situation was hopeless?

What hope could you offer Mary?

Activity

Do one of the following.

(1) Think of someone you know who suffers from loneliness, rejection, or illness. With your family, plan to do something specific to alleviate the person's suffering.

(2) Gather with your family or friends. Light a candle and pray for people who are going through difficult times.

Brain Teaser

Write four other names for the sacrament of Reconciliation by filling in the missing consonants. **Hint:** Each word has at least one *N*.

PENANCE
CONFESSION
CONVERSION
_O_ _I_E_E_ _

Did you know...?

The Stations of the Cross, representing the events of Jesus' Passion and death, ranged in number from five to thirty-seven until the eighteenth century. Then Pope Clement XII set the number at fourteen.

131

Hart to Heart

Sarah Hart's musical experience began when she started studying the piano, organ, flute, and guitar at the age of six. Her love of music grew, and she went on to receive a degree in music composition and theory.

"Music is one medium that consistently draws people together," says Hart. "In light of that, my vision is to sing wherever I am given an opportunity to share." Hart has toured with well-known Christian artists, such as Kathy Troccoli.

Hart has also performed at several Catholic youth conferences, including a national one held in Indiana in 2001. Hart's CD *Obvious* contains twelve original songs that invite listeners to discover God's presence in their everyday lives. Among the songs are "I Will Have Faith in You", "Faces of Our Friends", "Make Me a Channel", and "You Alone".

Hart is also an accomplished folk musician, and she has been a finalist at various folk music competitions.

All-Star Profile

Name: Sister Mary Frances Seeley, O.S.F.
Born: 1931
Occupation: suicidologist, comforter of people who are suffering and suicidal, director of international hot-line consulting agency

Quote of a Lifetime: "Helping others is the most rewarding work you will ever do—besides fulfilling the most important commandment."

Claims to Fame: Started Crisis Line, a suicide helpline in Illinois, in 1976, which, as of this writing, has not knowingly lost a caller in an active suicidal state. Acquired funding that enabled the helpline to become a twenty-four hour service, assisting more than 90,000 people a year. Provides extensive training for volunteers. Holds a master's degree in education and a doctorate in law and public policy. Has given speeches in several countries. Was chief certification examiner for the American Association of Suicidology for three years.

Wired

Visit Our Web Site
www.blestarewe.com

Web Site Spotlight
www.frpat.com/stations/statsopen.htm

Visit this site to pray the Stations of the Cross in either English or Spanish. Seventh graders in Wisconsin illustrated each station.

Something To Do

On Sunday

Listen for words about Jesus' suffering, death, or Resurrection during the Eucharistic Prayer. Believe that Jesus understands our suffering and is there to help us.

Through the Week

Make an effort to be there for others when they are dealing with difficult or challenging issues in their lives.

✝ A Prayer for the Week

Lord, your Passion and Resurrection remind us of the unimaginable depths of your love for us. Teach us to love and serve others in ways that please you. May your dying and rising set us free. Amen.

Answer Key: penance, confession, conversion, forgiveness

132

14 Jesus' Passion

No one has greater love than this, to lay down one's life for one's friends.

John 15:13

Share

If a friend is really important to you, you make an effort to include that person in your activities, and your friend does the same for you. Good friends usually exchange acts of kindness, remember important events in each other's lives, leave time for each other, and try to spend equal time listening and helping each other.

Activity

Using the letters in the word *friend*, write words or phrases that describe ways you remember your friends and leave time for them. You may wish to add a design around these words to illustrate the meaning of true friendship.

F un

R ~~friend~~ relationship/respect

I nteresting

E nergetic

N ice

D ependible

How do Christians remember their relationship with Jesus Christ?

Hear & Believe

Worship Remembering the Passion of Our Lord

Holy Week is the holiest week of the liturgical year. We celebrate God's great love for us as demonstrated in the sacrifice of his Son, Jesus Christ. Holy Week begins with Palm Sunday of the Lord's Passion and includes Holy Thursday, Good Friday, and Holy Saturday.

On Palm Sunday, we remember Jesus' entry into Jerusalem to begin the events we know as the **Paschal mystery**. With palm branches in hand, we celebrate Mass and hear the story of Jesus' Passion. Here is an example of this reading.

The Passion of our Lord according to Mark.

Narrator: Jesus and his apostles came to a place named Gethsemane. Jesus took with him Peter, James, and John. He began to be troubled and distressed.

Christ: "Abba, Father, all things are possible to you. Take this cup away from me, but not what I will but what you will."

Narrator: Then, while Jesus was still speaking, Judas, one of the Twelve, arrived with a crowd of the chief priests, scribes, and elders, carrying swords and clubs. Judas, Jesus' betrayer, had arranged a signal with them, saying,

Judas: "The man I shall kiss is the one; arrest him and lead him away securely."

Narrator: Judas went to Jesus and said,

Judas: "Rabbi."

Narrator: and kissed Jesus. At this they laid hands on Jesus and arrested him. As soon as morning came, the chief priests, with the elders and scribes, held a council. They bound Jesus, led him away, and handed him over to Pilate, who questioned him,

Pilate: "Are you the king of the Jews?"

Narrator: Jesus said to him in reply,

Christ: "You say so."

Narrator: The chief priests accused him of many things. Again, Pilate questioned him,

Pilate: "Have you no answer? See how many things they accuse you of."

Narrator: Jesus did not answer. On Passover, Pilate used to release one prisoner. A man called Barabbas was then in prison along with rebels who had committed murder. The crowd began to ask Pilate to release one prisoner. Pilate answered,

Pilate: "Do you want me to release to you the king of the Jews?"

Narrator: But the chief priests stirred up the crowd to have Pilate release Barabbas for them instead. Pilate said,

Pilate: "Then what do you want me to do with the man you call the king of the Jews?"

Narrator: They shouted,

Crowd: "Crucify him."

Narrator: Pilate said to them,

Pilate: "Why? What evil has he done?"

Narrator: They only shouted the louder,

Crowd: "Crucify him."

Narrator: So Pilate, wishing to satisfy the crowd, released Barabbas. After he had Jesus scourged, he handed Jesus over to be crucified. The soldiers led Jesus away inside the palace. They clothed him in purple and placed a crown woven out of thorns on his head. They began to salute him, saying,

Crowd: "Hail, king of the Jews!"

Narrator: and kept striking his head with a reed and spitting upon him. They knelt before him in homage. When they had mocked him, they stripped him of the purple cloak, dressed him in his own clothes, and led him out to the place of Golgotha, translated "Place of the Skull," to crucify him. They nailed him to a cross and divided up his garments by casting lots. On the cross, they inscribed the charge against him: *The King of the Jews.* Those passing by said,

Crowd: "Save yourself by coming down from the cross."

Narrator: The chief priests, with the scribes, mocked him among themselves, saying,

Crowd: "He saved others; he cannot save himself. Let the Christ, the King of Israel, come down now from the cross that we may see and believe."

Narrator: At noon, darkness came over the land and lasted until three in the afternoon. At three o'clock, Jesus cried out in a loud voice,

Christ: "My God, my God, why have you abandoned me?"

Narrator: Some of the bystanders said,

Crowd: "Look, he is calling Elijah."

Narrator: One of them soaked a sponge with wine, and put it on a reed for Jesus to drink, saying,

Bystander: "Wait, let us see if Elijah comes to take him down."

Narrator: Jesus cried out and breathed his last. *Here all kneel and pause for a short time.*

Narrator: The veil of the sanctuary was torn in two from top to bottom. When the centurion who stood facing Jesus saw how he breathed his last he said,

Centurion: "Truly this man was the Son of God!"

Based on Mark 14:32—15:39

The Gospel of the Lord.
Praise to you, Lord Jesus Christ.

The Call to Repent

By his suffering and death, Jesus destroyed the power of sin and death, and restored our friendship with God. By his Resurrection, Jesus brought us the promise of life everlasting. When we reflect on this Paschal mystery throughout Lent, and especially during Holy Week, we experience a call to repent. The Church carries on Jesus' work of forgiveness and salvation, particularly in the sacraments of Reconciliation and the Anointing of the Sick.

Before receiving the sacrament of Reconciliation, we examine our conscience and express sorrow for our sins. Feeling sorrow because of our love for God, rather than because of fear of punishment, is called "perfect contrition." The next step is conversion; we make a firm promise to avoid sin in the future. In this state of mind, we are ready to confess our sins to a priest in the sacrament of

Reconciliation. Only a priest has the power to forgive our sins in the name of Christ. If we commit a mortal sin, receiving this sacrament is ordinarily the only way we can be reconciled to God and the Church. Although it is not necessary to confess venial sins, the Church encourages us to do so.

After we receive absolution from the priest, he describes an act of penance that we must do for the sins we have committed. This penance may be a prayer or an act of charity that helps us to follow Jesus more closely.

In the sacrament of the Anointing of the Sick, people suffering from illness or old age receive special grace. In this sacrament, which can be received more than once, the priest anoints the people's forehead and hands and prays for their healing, comfort, strength, and forgiveness.

The Easter Triduum

Holy Week concludes with the **Easter Triduum**. The Triduum includes the Mass of the Lord's Supper on Holy Thursday, the remembrance of Jesus' crucifixion on Good Friday, and the celebration of Jesus' Resurrection at the Easter Vigil. Holy Week ends with the holiest celebration in the Church's litugical year—Easter—rejoicing in the mystery of Christ's passover from death to life.

Faith Words

Holy Week Holy Week is the week that begins on Palm Sunday of the Lord's Passion.

Paschal mystery The Paschal mystery is God's plan for our salvation through the Passion, death, Resurrection, and Ascension of Jesus.

Easter Triduum The Easter Triduum is the holiest celebration of the liturgical year. It begins on Holy Thursday evening and concludes with the evening prayer on Easter Sunday.

Why is it so important to receive Jesus' forgiveness?

Our Church Teaches

Lent is a time of penance. In repenting of sin, we grow closer to God. If we commit mortal sin, the sacrament of Reconciliation reconciles us with God and the Church. It brings us into God's grace and excuses us from punishment for mortal sin. It brings us peace of mind, comfort, and the strength to avoid temptation and to continue our Christian journey through life. Reconciliation also excuses us from some of the punishments we might suffer in purgatory, a purification process we undergo after death for the effects of our sins. Although we receive complete forgiveness in Reconciliation, if we die without having fully atoned for all sin, we may be purified in purgatory. But through prayers and good works in this life, we can lessen this suffering both for ourselves and for the souls already in purgatory and find spiritual strength.

We Believe

We rejoice in the risen Christ who brings us his love and forgiveness. Through Reconciliation and the Anointing of the Sick, Jesus heals us.

Respond

Saint John the Apostle

It's not very easy to stick by a person who is mocked for his beliefs or who is not very popular. According to tradition, John, the youngest of Jesus' disciples, did just that. In the Gospel of John we learn that when others ran away from Jesus in his time of need, John stuck around. He was the only disciple who stood at the foot of the cross as Jesus was being crucified. Do you stand by Jesus even when it's not the popular thing to do?

John was with Jesus almost from the very beginning of his ministry and is often referred to in John's Gospel as the "beloved disciple." Along with Peter and his brother James, John was part of Jesus' inner circle of friends. In the Gospel of John we read that the three of them were with Jesus during the important moments of his life. Now, as Jesus was dying, only John remained a faithful friend. Before Jesus died, he even asked John to take care of his mother, Mary.

According to tradition, John lived for about seventy years after Christ's Resurrection. It is believed that during that time, he traveled with Peter, preaching the good news of salvation and healing the sick. The Gospel of John is believed to have been based on the memories of John, the beloved disciple. The symbol for the Gospel writer John shows an eagle in the background, representing the majesty of his Gospel.

According to legend, John the Apostle died when he was very old. He is honored as the patron saint of friendships, and we celebrate his feast day December 27.

Do you try to remain a friend to Jesus by living a good and holy life?

Activities

1. List some reasons why John would be known as the beloved disciple.

_____

_____

_____

_____

_____

_____

_____

2. Choose one day of the Easter Triduum and design a symbol that shows its significance in our lives.

GO TO *page 210 to read more about the Easter Triduum for help with this activity.*

How can we celebrate the presence of the risen Lord in our lives today?

Jesus: A Brother, a Friend

Leader: Being born, he gave himself to all.
He lived a human life as a brother, a friend.
He died on Calvary's hill because he loved, loved without end.

Based on a passage from Verbum Supernum Prodiens

Reader 1: Throughout his life, Jesus was a friend and a brother to others. One time, the apostle Peter asked Jesus, "Lord, if my brother sins against me, how often must I forgive him? As many as seven times?" Jesus answered, "I say to you, not seven times, but seventy-seven times."

Based on Matthew 18:21–22

Reader 2: Jesus Christ showed this great mercy by giving up his life for us. On Good Friday, a day in the Triduum (which means *three*, signifying the three holy days of the Easter Triduum), we meditate on Jesus' suffering and sacrifice. We spend time with Jesus as he walks to Golgotha with his cross, scorned and mocked, suffering for the sins of humanity.

Leader: This is something we can do all year round. In thinking about Jesus' suffering, we can consider the weight of our sins and feel in our hearts the desire to do better. Reflect on your actions today. How well have you responded to Christ's great mercy and love?

All: Grant me, O Lord my God, a mind to know you,

a heart to seek you,
wisdom to find you,

conduct pleasing to you,
faithful perseverance
in waiting for you,

and a hope of finally
embracing you. Amen.

From A Prayer Before a Picture of Christ

Get CONNECTED

with family and friends

The Resurrection and the Call to Discipleship

Like the first disciples of Christ, we are called to spread the good news of Christ's Resurrection. God calls us to holiness and to live as virtuous people at the service of others. Living as faithful disciples of Jesus Christ presents us with many responsibilities and challenges. Through the Holy Spirit, God gives us the grace and the gifts we need to be true disciples.

A Call to Action

José was making the most of his summer. But one day he witnessed a terrible thing. A cognitively impaired young man who walked to the bus stop every day was being ridiculed. Neighborhood bullies were throwing stones at him. The young man looked down and kept walking. José was upset and told his parents. He decided that he would walk with the young man to the bus stop from that day forward. Although the ridicule continued, the stone-throwing stopped. How was José a faithful disciple of Jesus? Would you have done the same thing José did?

Activity

Do one of the following.

(1) Volunteer for an organization that actively serves others. Invite your family and friends to join you in helping others.

(2) Help people in your family. Do some chores without being asked. Make yourself available to spend time with people in your family. Visit an elderly relative who needs company.

F.A.Q.

Dear Mr. F.A.Q.,

Everyone in my class makes fun of a new student named Rebecca. They don't like her clothes, her hair, or her accent. But Rebecca keeps trying to be my friend. I want to help, but I don't want people to think I'm friends with her.

Signed,
Hesitating in Houston

Dear Hesitating,

It is good that you want to help Rebecca. Opportunities to follow Jesus come to us in the ordinary situations of our lives, such as in school. What kinds of things are wonderful about Rebecca? Ask the Holy Spirit for the courage and strength to "spread the word" about Rebecca's wonderful abilities and traits to your classmates. Challenge yourself to be an example of Christ to others.

God bless,
Mr. F.A.Q.

Did you know...?

A sand dollar is a symbol of the good news of Christ. It has five holes, symbolic of the five wounds of Christ. It has the markings of an Easter lily on one side. Inside are five dove-shaped shells, symbolizing peace.

Holy Humor!

Children's Letters to God

Dear God,
Thank you for the baby brother, but what I prayed for was a puppy.
Joyce

Dear God,
Who does your job when you are on vacation?

Neil

ON VACATION-
ANY QUESTIONS,
CALL SAINT PETER

Dear God,
Please send me a pony. I've never asked for anything before. You can look it up.
Josh

Dear God,
We read in school that Thomas Edison made light. But the Bible said you did it. I bet he stole your idea.
Amy

All-Star Profile

Name: Olympic Aid
Begun: 1994, after Olympic speed skater Johann Olav Koss of Norway challenged Norwegians to donate a small amount of money every time a Norwegian won a gold medal
Purpose: helping children using sports and play, raising money to help those afflicted by war and poverty
Quote of a Lifetime: "Every child has the right to play" (Olympic Aid motto).
Claims to Fame: Raised more than 13 million dollars in Atlanta in 1996 for children afflicted by war. Builds hospitals for people living in poverty. Builds schools to serve the poorest children in Eritrea. Enabled women and children in Iraq and Afghanistan, and more than 12 million children around the world, to receive vaccinations against diseases. Supports the United Nations Rights of the Child and promotes values in sports.

Wired

Visit Our Web Site
www.blestarewe.com

Web Site Spotlight
www.disciplesnow.com/celebrate

Visit this site to view the Scripture readings for this Sunday's Mass, and learn how to apply their message to your life as a young disciple of Christ.

Something To Do

On Sunday

Before Mass consider what you have done during the past week that either helped or hurt others. Did you spread God's word? Do you need God's forgiveness? Pray for forgiveness and grace.

Through the Week

Each night when you go to bed, think about your day, and thank God for what went well. Ask God to help guide you the next day in being a better disciple.

A Prayer for the Week

Lord, help our family live as faithful disciples. May the gift of your grace through the Holy Spirit be our strength and guide. We will try to use our time and talents to serve you and love others.
Amen.

15 The Resurrection and the Call to Discipleship

Let us persevere in running the race that lies before us while keeping our eyes fixed on Jesus, the leader and perfecter of faith.

Based on Hebrews 12:1–2

Share

Do you sometimes think, *I would help people like Jesus did, if I only had the opportunity*? Well, the opportunity might be right under your nose. Often, we are not aware of the many opportunities to help others that are surrounding us. Our daily activities and concerns can keep us from thinking beyond ourselves and our lives. Sometimes we need to "open our eyes"—to make a conscious effort to be on the lookout for opportunities to help others. People in need are everywhere. We just need to keep our eyes open.

Use the following three steps to get on the way to helping people, in the spirit of Christ.

Step One: Make a mental list of the various groups or communities to which you belong: your family, your class, your school, your team, your neighborhood, and so on.

Step Two: Think about the people who are part of those groups.

Step Three: Ask yourself, "Do any of these people need my help? Is any one of them in trouble or in need?"

Activity

On the poster, describe the type of helper that might be needed by the person(s) who came to mind in Step Three. For example, if the person who needs your help is an elderly, housebound neighbor, you could write: *someone dependable and gentle, who can run errands to the grocery store and pick up prescriptions.*

NEEDED

What did Jesus require of his disciples?

The Resurrection of Christ was very much an "eye-opening experience." In the Gospel of Luke, the account of the Resurrection of Christ first focuses on what Jesus' disciples Mary Magdalene, Joanna, and Mary, the mother of James, saw when they came to the tomb in which Jesus' body had been lain. They were completely amazed. When the women returned to tell Jesus' apostles about what they had seen, the apostles responded with disbelief. Peter even returned to the scene to see for himself…

Now there was a virtuous and righteous man named Joseph who, though he was a member of the council, had not consented to their plan of action. He came from the Jewish town of Arimathea and was awaiting the kingdom of God. He went to Pilate and asked for the body of Jesus. After he had taken the body down, he wrapped it in a linen cloth and laid him in a rock-hewn tomb in which no one had yet been buried. It was the day of preparation, and the sabbath was about to begin. The women who had come from Galilee with him followed behind, and when they had seen the tomb and the way in which his body was laid in it, they returned and prepared spices and perfumed oils. Then they rested on the sabbath according to the commandment.

But at daybreak on the first day of the week they took the spices they had prepared and went to the tomb. They found the stone rolled away from the tomb; but when they entered, they did not find the body of the Lord Jesus. While they were puzzling over this, behold, two men in dazzling garments appeared to them. They were terrified and bowed their faces to the ground. They said to them, "Why do you seek the living one among the dead? He is not here, but he has been raised. Remember what he said to you while he was still in

Galilee, that the Son of Man must be handed over to sinners and be crucified, and rise on the third day." And they remembered his words. Then they returned from the tomb and announced all these things to the eleven and to all the others. The women were Mary Magdalene, Joanna, and Mary the mother of James; the others who accompanied them also told this to the apostles, but their story seemed like nonsense and they did not believe them. But Peter got up and ran to the tomb, bent down, and saw the burial cloths alone; then he went home amazed at what had happened.

Luke 23:50—24:12

He Has Been Raised

Just as with the stories of Jesus' birth, the Gospel writers wrote their stories about the first signs of the Resurrection of Christ with different audiences in mind. For example, Luke's Gospel tells a story about an appearance of the risen Christ to two disciples on the way to Emmaus, a place just outside of Jerusalem. The disciples walk with Jesus and talk with him about Scripture but do not recognize him until they share the eucharistic meal with him. Luke emphasized Jesus' appearances in and around Jerusalem, the Jewish holy city, because one theme of Luke's Gospel is the way in which Jesus fulfilled the Old Testament promises and the hopes of the Jewish people.

After his Resurrection, Jesus instructed his disciples about their future ministry. While they were gathered in Jerusalem, he suddenly appeared to them in his resurrected body, saying, "Peace be with you." They were terrified and thought they were seeing a ghost. But Jesus said, "Why are you troubled? And why do questions arise in your hearts? Look at my hands and my feet. It is I myself" (based on Luke 24:36–39). Jesus also said, "Behold, I am sending the promise of my Father upon you. Stay in Jerusalem until you receive power from on high" (based on Luke 24:49).

Although his time on earth would soon end, Jesus promised his disciples that he would be with them. After his **Ascension**, Jesus sent the Holy Spirit, or **Advocate**, to help them carry on his work.

"I Will Come Back to You"

Jesus had a special mission for his group of followers. He wanted them to spread his message of salvation. Before his death and again after his Resurrection, Jesus prepared his disciples for the time when he would no longer be on earth with them. Jesus said to them, "The Advocate, the holy Spirit that the Father will send in my name—he will teach you everything and remind you of all that [I] told you" (John 14:26). He added, "Do not let

your hearts be troubled or afraid. You have heard me tell you, 'I am going away and I will come back to you'" (John 14:27–28).

Empowered by his Spirit, Jesus' disciples would be able to spread his peace, love, and forgiveness throughout the world.

Called to Serve

Just as the first disciples, we receive the grace of the Holy Spirit. God freely offers his grace as a gift to help us cooperate in his plan for salvation. By the power of the Holy Spirit, we can merit for ourselves and others the graces needed to have life everlasting. Our ability to have such merit before God is a result of grace that only God can give. His loving presence guides us as we try to meet the challenges of being his disciples.

In the Church today, all people, through Baptism, are disciples of Jesus—called to serve and bring the Gospel message to other people in words and actions. We must model ourselves after Jesus and work as a community to spread his good news. As we grow, some of us may decide to proclaim Jesus Christ's message by serving in Holy Orders or in the religious life, while others may serve as lay people. Guided by the Holy Spirit, lay people bring God's love to their families, communities, and people throughout the world. Lay people may serve as eucharistic ministers, lectors, music ministers, catechists, and so on.

Faith Words

Ascension The Ascension was the moment when Jesus, in his resurrected body, returned to his Father in heaven. He will come again at the end of time.

Advocate The Advocate is another name for the Holy Spirit, the Third Person of the Trinity, who helps and guides us in following Jesus.

What are true disciples of Jesus willing to do?

Our Church Teaches

We are called to worship God through prayer and liturgy. It is against the first commandment to tempt God or show disrespect for the sacraments or other liturgical celebrations. It is also important for us to respect the truth. If we lie, we are responsible for correcting the damage we cause. We must also respect the reputation of others by not sharing false or private information about them. It is wrong for professionals, such as doctors, to share personal confidential information. A priest also must keep the sins we confess secret, under all circumstances.

In the Scriptures, we read that the first humans, Adam and Eve, lost their original holiness, justice, and friendship with God, not only for themselves but for all humanity. Even sins that are not serious create a habit of sin that weakens our friendship with God, who is love.

We Believe

The Holy Spirit gives us grace and strength to overcome temptations and accept our responsibilities as disciples of Christ.

Respond

Saint Paul Miki

Paul Miki was born in Japan in 1562, the son of a Japanese military leader. At the age of eighteen, he answered a call to religious life by joining the Society of Jesus. He became very well known for his preaching style and continued even when Japanese leaders began to strongly oppose Christianity.

Eventually, Paul was arrested for spreading Christ's message. With twenty-five other Christian men, Paul marched 600 miles to Nagasaki to be martyred. On February 5, 1597, the Japanese leaders had Paul, along with two other Jesuits, six Franciscans, and seventeen lay people, crucified and stabbed with a lance. In 1862, Pope Pius IX canonized Paul Miki and the faith-filled men who died with him.

As he was dying, Paul remained committed to his faith. He gave this final speech from the cross: "The only reason for my being killed is that I have taught the doctrine of Christ. I thank God it is for this reason that I die. I believe that I am telling the truth before I die. I know you believe me and I want to say to you all once again: Ask Christ to help you become happy. I obey Christ. After Christ's example, I forgive my persecutors. I do not hate them. I ask God to have pity on all, and I hope my blood will fall on my fellow men as a fruitful rain." Saint Paul Miki's feast day is February 6.

Activities

1. What part of the story of Saint Paul Miki has the most meaning for you? Why?

_____

_____

2. On the lines below, make a list of what is expected of you as a disciple of Jesus. Then, review the list and put a check mark by the requirement that is the most challenging but also the most rewarding.

_____

_____

_____

_____

_____

Resolve to work hard at the most challenging aspects of being a disciple.

3. Write about a group in your community whose members spread the Spirit of Jesus to others. How do they do this?

_____

_____

_____

_____

_____

How can we celebrate the action of the Holy Spirit in our lives today?

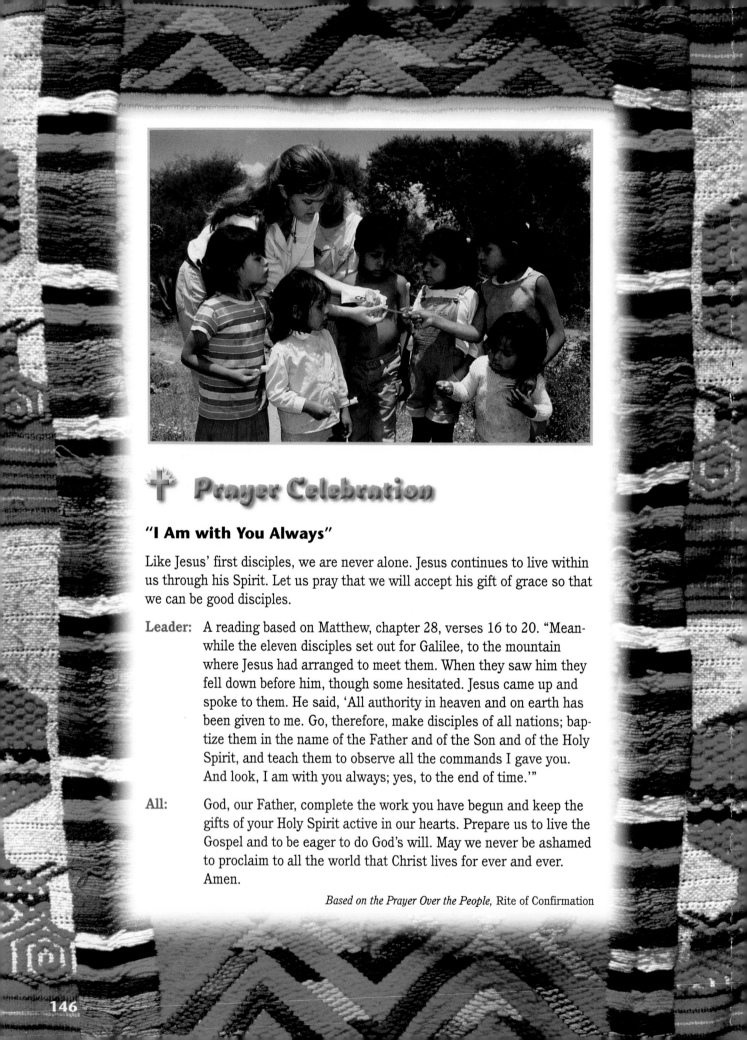

✝ Prayer Celebration

"I Am with You Always"

Like Jesus' first disciples, we are never alone. Jesus continues to live within us through his Spirit. Let us pray that we will accept his gift of grace so that we can be good disciples.

Leader: A reading based on Matthew, chapter 28, verses 16 to 20. "Meanwhile the eleven disciples set out for Galilee, to the mountain where Jesus had arranged to meet them. When they saw him they fell down before him, though some hesitated. Jesus came up and spoke to them. He said, 'All authority in heaven and on earth has been given to me. Go, therefore, make disciples of all nations; baptize them in the name of the Father and of the Son and of the Holy Spirit, and teach them to observe all the commands I gave you. And look, I am with you always; yes, to the end of time.'"

All: God, our Father, complete the work you have begun and keep the gifts of your Holy Spirit active in our hearts. Prepare us to live the Gospel and to be eager to do God's will. May we never be ashamed to proclaim to all the world that Christ lives for ever and ever. Amen.

Based on the Prayer Over the People, Rite of Confirmation

Get Connected

with family and friends

Pentecost

In this chapter, we learn about the beginning of the Church at Pentecost, when Jesus sent his Holy Spirit to his disciples as he promised. Filled with the Holy Spirit, they began to speak in many languages, yet all shared the same message. They went forth to spread this message of salvation to the world. Through the Holy Spirit, members of the Church today bring God's love and forgiveness to the world.

What Could I Do?

Father Bill called to say our help was needed. Mom called other parishioners right away to tell them that there was a fire and people needed our help. They made plans to handle the crisis. I wished that I could help, too.

As we left the house I brought along some of my stuffed animals. When I walked into the parish center I did not know what to do. Then I saw a young girl who was upset. I talked with her and shared my stuffed animals. Later, Father Bill thanked me for having made a difference in her life.

Activity

Do one of the following.

(1) Brainstorm ways in which you and your family can spread God's word in school, the workplace, or a social setting.

(2) As a family, meet with your pastor and ask him what your family can do for someone in your community who needs help.

The Password Is

Christian

The name *Christian* comes from the Greek word *christos*, meaning "anointed," and refers to those who have been baptized in Christ. Christian life is "life in the Spirit." Christians share in Christ's priestly, prophetic, and kingly roles, and are called by God to carry out his mission in the world.

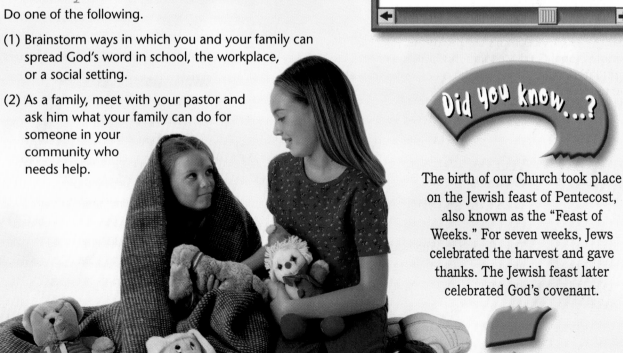

Did you know...?

The birth of our Church took place on the Jewish feast of Pentecost, also known as the "Feast of Weeks." For seven weeks, Jews celebrated the harvest and gave thanks. The Jewish feast later celebrated God's covenant.

Angelina, the "Singing Angel"

Have you ever heard of a twelve-year-old "singing angel"? That is how **Angelina** of Gulfport, Mississippi, was known to her fans. Angelina has been developing her talents for more than four years and is recognized as a leading contemporary Christian singer in the Southern United States. She is the youngest member of the Catholic Association of Musicians. Angelina's professional career began at age nine. After a year of vocal lessons, she released her first CD, *Angelina Prays the Rosary*. Some of the profits from this CD are donated to Catholic causes and charities of her choice, including the pro-life movement. Angelina's CD *Wake Up Call* is based on Matthew 14:27–33, in which Peter and the apostles are invited to courageously embrace their faith. Angelina's songs encourage people of all faiths to awaken their sense of spirituality. When Angelina is not singing God's praises, she listens to music, talks with her friends, practices guitar, and enjoys making pottery.

All-Star Profile

Name: Harry Chapin
Born: 1942
Died: 1981
Occupation: folk singer, writer, political activist, filmmaker
Quote of a Lifetime: "America stands for two things: aiding and abetting the quest of every human being for human rights, human dignity and human needs, and providing that individuals can make a difference."
Claims to Fame: Used his music and concerts to raise awareness about world hunger and asked others to join him in this cause. Raised more than 5 million dollars to end hunger. Co-founded "World Hunger Year" in 1975. Accomplished performer. Received the Congressional Gold Medal for his humane efforts. Foundation in his name, begun by his wife, addresses the problems of the disadvantaged and promotes educational programs and the arts.

Something To Do

On Sunday

At Mass, recall how God sent the Holy Spirit to be with the disciples and guide them. Pray that the Holy Spirit will help you know and do God's will.

Through the Week

When you say your prayers, always begin with the Sign of the Cross. Think about how you and your family are loved and blessed by God the Father, the Son, and the Holy Spirit.

Wired

Visit Our Web Site
www.blestarewe.com

Web Site Spotlight
www.christiananswers.net/spotlight

This Christian Web site has games, music, movie reviews, news, and lots more for you and your family to enjoy!

A Prayer for the Week

Lord, fill us with your Holy Spirit and help us know your love and see your presence in those around us. Teach us to use the gifts you have given us so that we may lead others to you.
Amen.

16 Pentecost

On that day you will realize that I am in my Father and you are in me and I in you.

John 14:20

Share

It was the first day of practice for the newly formed middle school band. Sonja had a new flute. She had been practicing for a few days to prepare for the band's first afterschool meeting. But she was a little nervous because she didn't know who the other kids in the band were. When she entered the room, she saw that she didn't know anybody. Sonja's school had students from many different ethnic neighborhoods around the city. A lot of the kids in the room were huddled in groups speaking to one another in their native languages. Sonja found a spot near the window and sat by herself.

For weeks, Sonja dreaded band practice. She didn't really have anyone to talk to before or after-practice. As time went on, however, the band improved and became more in tune. The students began to compliment one another's playing. Sonja befriended the drum major, who had moved all the way from Estonia when she was eight years old. It was fun learning about her new friend's culture.

The day of the band's first big event came. As the band leader stepped in front of them, Sonja remembered that first frightful day. And as all the different sounds of the band's many instruments came together and burst into a wonderful melody, she smiled to herself.

Activity

Think about a time when you had to do something that seemed overwhelming or frightening. What gifts do you have that helped you work through the difficult situation? Did another person or group of people help you overcome the problem? If so, how?

_____

_____

_____

_____

_____

_____

How did the Holy Spirit unite the first communities of believers?

Hear & Believe

✝ Scripture The Coming of the Spirit

After Jesus' Ascension, the disciples were confused and frightened because Jesus, their friend and Savior, was no longer with them. Although they feared for their lives, they remained in Jerusalem according to Jesus' instructions so that they could receive the Holy Spirit. Fifty days after his Resurrection, Jesus fulfilled his promise of sending his Spirit to his disciples.

When the time for **Pentecost** was fulfilled, they were all in one place together. And suddenly there came from the sky a noise like a strong driving wind, and it filled the entire house in which they were. Then there appeared to them tongues as of fire, which parted and came to rest on each one of them. And they were all filled with the Holy Spirit and began to speak in different tongues.

Now there were devout Jews from every nation under heaven staying in Jerusalem. When they heard the loud noise from the sky, they gathered in a large crowd, but they were confused because each one heard the disciples speaking in his own language. They were astounded, and in amazement they asked, "Are not all these people who are speaking Galileans? Then how does each of us hear them in his own native language? We come from many places throughout the Roman Empire, including Mesopotamia, Judea, Pontus, Asia, and Egypt. Among us are Jews and converts to Judaism, Cretans, and Arabs, yet we hear them speaking of the mighty acts of God in our own tongues." They were all astounded and bewildered, and said to one another, "What does this mean?" But others said, scoffing, "They have had too much new wine."

Based on Acts 2:1–13

Filled with the Holy Spirit

The Holy Spirit was not visible to the disciples in the same way that Jesus had been, but the disciples knew that something special was happening when they heard the powerful wind and saw the tongues of fire appear over each of their heads. The Holy Spirit empowered the disciples to speak in tongues, or different languages, which was a special gift of the Holy Spirit. Through this gift, the disciples were able to unite people from diverse cultural backgrounds, enabling the people to hear God's message. Those who gathered around the disciples spoke many languages, but all heard the very same message.

The message they heard was how Jesus suffered, died, and rose from the dead in fulfillment of the Scriptures. Jesus had done this willingly for the salvation of the whole world. With the power of the Holy Spirit, the disciples were now able to give witness to everything Jesus had done and said. His words and actions, as well as the silent moments and prayers they shared with him, had a great meaning they needed to share.

Jesus had taught the disciples the power and love of God through his miracles. By his prayerful life, he showed them how to have a personal relationship with God. He also showed them how to love and care for all people, especially the poor. His sacrifice on the cross to redeem the world and his Resurrection fulfilled everything God had revealed through the prophets. The disciples expressed all of this so that others could come to know Christ and know that Jesus had fulfilled God's convenant with his people. As disciples of Jesus, we also want to proclaim Jesus' message. The Holy Spirit gives us the power to do that.

The Holy Spirit is the Third Person of the **Trinity**. The mystery of the Trinity is that there is only one God, who is revealed to us as three divine Persons. The Holy Spirit is God, one and equal with the Father and the Son and of the same substance and the same nature as them, but is also the Spirit of both the Father and the Son.

The Birth of the Church

The Holy Spirit united the disciples and those who heard their message into a community of faith, hope, and love. Although they had cultural differences, they were united in their belief in the risen Lord. They received the love of God through the Holy Spirit. With God's grace, they could "boast in hope of the glory of God" (Romans 5:2). Pentecost was the day the Church was born!

The Holy Spirit gives the Church its life and unity. The Holy Spirit pours out many gifts upon the members of the Church. Within the Church, there are a variety of gifts that come from the Spirit. Through the power of the Holy Spirit, the many members of the Church are united to Christ and to each other.

The Church is the Body of Christ. Christ loves the Church with tremendous love, as a bridegroom loves a bride. This is why the Church is also called the Bride of Christ. Christ instituted the Church and gives it life through the Holy Spirit. Different traditions of Catholic spirituality and prayer that come from the Holy Spirit guide the spiritual life of the Church. The Church brings God's love and forgiveness to everyone. At the end of time, the Church will reach its final glory.

 page 225 to read more about the Trinity.

Faith Words

Pentecost Pentecost is the day on which Jesus Christ's disciples received the gift of the Holy Spirit, which empowered them to proclaim the good news. Pentecost is often referred to as "the day the Church was born."

Trinity The Trinity is the three Persons of God: the Father, the Son, and the Holy Spirit. We believe that there is only one God, who is revealed to us in these three divine Persons.

How does the Church fulfill Jesus' mission?

Our Church Teaches

During Jesus' time, many Jews thought that Jesus was trying to abolish the **Mosaic Law**. This was not Jesus' purpose. Jesus said, "Do not think that I have come to abolish the law or the prophets. I have come not to abolish but to fulfill" (Matthew 5:17). Jesus also said, "Keep the commandments" (Matthew 19:17).

Jesus lived the commandments, showing others how to love God and neighbor. By his words and actions,

Jesus fulfilled the Law of God to perfection. As members of the Church, we are called to imitate Jesus' loving ways. The Holy Spirit guides us in showing others the love of God.

Our Church has its origins in the Jewish faith. It is important to note that we do not blame the Jewish people today for Jesus' Passion and death. We remember that Jesus died for the sins of all. We pray that the Holy Spirit will unite all in Christ.

Respond

Reflecting on the Holy Spirit

The Holy Spirit is mentioned throughout the Scriptures. In the New Testament, Jesus tells his disciples about the Holy Spirit many times. Below are some of the things that Jesus said about the Holy Spirit. Read Jesus' words, and write what you think Jesus is teaching about the Holy Spirit.

"For the holy Spirit will teach you at that moment what you should say" (Luke 12:12).

_____

"Amen, amen, I say to you, no one can enter the kingdom of God without being born of water and Spirit" (John 3:5).

_____

"And I will ask the Father, and he will give you another Advocate to be with you always, the Spirit of truth, which the world cannot accept, because it neither sees nor knows it. But you know it, because it remains with you, and will be in you" (John 14:16–17).

_____

"The Advocate, the holy Spirit that the Father will send in my name—he will teach you everything and remind you of all that [I] told you" (John 14:26).

_____

"[Jesus] said to them again, 'Peace be with you. As the Father has sent me, so I send you.' And when he had said this, he breathed on them and said to them, 'Receive the holy Spirit'" (John 20:21–22).

_____

Activities

1. There are seven traditional qualities, or gifts, that come from the Holy Spirit, as discussed on page 175. Read the text about the qualities on that page, then choose one of the qualities and create a collage, drawing, or cartoon showing how we use this quality in our lives today.

2. Look at your responses to the Share activity on page 149. Write one gift that you listed for which you can thank God in the prayer celebration. If you wish, you may write one of the seven gifts instead.

_____

How can we celebrate the Holy Spirit's presence in our lives?

✝ Prayer Celebration

Come, Holy Spirit!

At the Mass of Pentecost, an ancient poetic prayer, "Veni Sancte Spiritus" ("Come, Holy Spirit"), is prayed or sung. Its author is believed to be Stephen Cardinal Langton, archbishop of Canterbury in the twelfth century. The poem has been called the "Golden Sequence" because of its beauty.

Veni Sancte Spiritus ("Come, Holy Spirit")

Come, Holy Spirit, come!
    And from Your clear celestial home,
    Shed a ray of light divine!
Come, Father of the poor!
Come, source of all our store!
    Come, within our being shine!
You, of comforters the best;
You, the soul's most welcome guest;
    Sweet refreshment here below;
In our labor, rest most sweet;
Grateful coolness in the heat;
    Solace in the midst of woe.
O most blessed Light divine,
Shine within these hearts of yours,
    And our inmost being fill!
Where you are not, we have naught,
Nothing good in deed or thought,
    Nothing free from taint of ill.
Heal our wounds, our strength renew;
On our dryness pour your dew;
    Wash the stains of guilt away.
Bend the stubborn heart and will;
Melt the frozen, warm the chill;
    Guide the steps that go astray.
On the faithful, who adore
And confess you, evermore
    In your sevenfold gift descend;
Give them virtue's sure reward;
Give them your salvation, Lord;
    Give them joys that never end. Amen.
    Alleluia!

Sequence for Mass during the day, Pentecost Sunday, Roman Missal

WE CARE *About Parish and Community*

The Gospel in Action

Immaculate Conception parish in Durham, North Carolina, has taken Jesus' call to be ministers of justice and peace very seriously. Its small staff of Franciscan priests does all it can to motivate the parishioners to become involved in ministries to benefit the community. Here are some examples of announcements that the pastor makes on a typical Sunday before Mass concludes.

- The youth group is leaving tomorrow for Philadelphia, where they will spend two weeks helping out a poor parish.

- The Habitat for Humanity team will begin building its next new house for a family in need this Saturday near downtown Durham.

- There will be a meeting in the parish hall on Tuesday for catechists working with migrant workers.

- It is the parish Good Samaritan team's turn to work at the homeless shelter this coming Friday.

- Those who wish to bring food for the soup kitchen this week should do so by 4:30 p.m. on Monday.

- After Mass, those interested can sign up for the AIDS Walk-Run benefit we are sponsoring with our neighboring Presbyterian church.

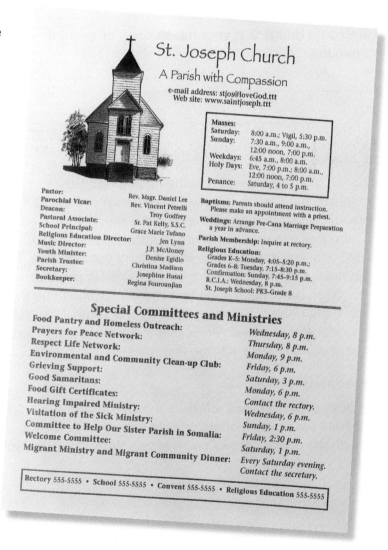

St. Joseph Church
A Parish with Compassion
e-mail address: stjos@loveGod.ttt
Web site: www.saintjoseph.ttt

Masses:
Saturday: 8:00 a.m.; Vigil, 5:30 p.m.
Sunday: 7:30 a.m., 9:00 a.m., 12:00 noon, 7:00 p.m.
Weekdays: 6:45 a.m., 8:00 a.m.
Holy Days: Eve, 7:00 p.m.; 8:00 a.m., 12:00 noon, 7:00 p.m.
Penance: Saturday, 4 to 5 p.m.

Pastor:
Parochial Vicar: Rev. Msgr. Daniel Lee
Deacon: Rev. Vincent Petrelli
Pastoral Associate: Troy Godfrey
School Principal: Sr. Pat Kelly, S.S.C.
Religious Education Director: Grace Marie Tufano
Music Director: Jen Lynn
Youth Minister: J.P. McAloney
Parish Trustee: Denise Egidio
Secretary: Christina Madison
Bookkeeper: Josephine Husni
Regina Fourounjian

Baptisms: Parents should attend instruction. Please make an appointment with a priest.

Weddings: Arrange Pre-Cana Marriage Preparation a year in advance.

Parish Membership: Inquire at rectory.

Religious Education:
Grades K-5: Monday, 4:05–5:20 p.m.;
Grades 6-8: Tuesday, 7:15–8:30 p.m.
Confirmation: Sunday, 7:45–9:15 p.m.
R.C.I.A.: Wednesday, 8 p.m.
St. Joseph School: PK3–Grade 8

Special Committees and Ministries

Food Pantry and Homeless Outreach:	
Prayers for Peace Network:	Wednesday, 8 p.m.
Respect Life Network:	Thursday, 8 p.m.
Environmental and Community Clean-up Club:	Monday, 9 p.m.
Grieving Support:	Friday, 6 p.m.
Good Samaritans:	Saturday, 3 p.m.
Food Gift Certificates:	Monday, 6 p.m.
Hearing Impaired Ministry:	Contact the rectory.
Visitation of the Sick Ministry:	Wednesday, 6 p.m.
Committee to Help Our Sister Parish in Somalia:	Sunday, 1 p.m.
Welcome Committee:	Friday, 2:30 p.m.
Migrant Ministry and Migrant Community Dinner:	Saturday, 1 p.m. Every Saturday evening. Contact the secretary.

Rectory 555-5555 • School 555-5555 • Convent 555-5555 • Religious Education 555-5555

- The staff of the local shelter for abused women and their children want to thank the parish for all the recently donated blankets and linen.

Do you know what your parish is doing to reach out to people in your community who are in need?

Think About It

As you can see, the efforts of one parish can help improve the lives of many groups of people with very different needs, if parishioners recognize their call to live the Gospel to the fullest.

How can you motivate other young people in your parish to want to help meet the needs of people in the community?

_____

_____

_____

What are some things that your parish does or could do for people in your community?

_____

_____

Learn About It

Reaching out to those in need is at the heart of the Gospel message. From its very beginning, the Church has encouraged its members to look beyond their own personal needs to those of the parish family, the local community, and the world. There was a time in the Church's history when people thought that only priests and religious communities should carry out ministries to the poor and people in need and that the role of the laity was simply to provide prayers and funds. It is clear, however, that ministries are intended to be the work of all members of the Church, including children and youth. Now that we face a serious shortage of priests and religious, it is even more important that the laity step forward to participate in these ministries.

Do Something About It

Working with others in your religious education group, compile a list of all the ministries your parish offers people in need. Then choose one parish project with which your group could assist. Write your list here, and circle the project you choose.

_____   _____

_____   _____

_____

Organizer

The titles of the chapters in Unit 4 are shown on the cross. Using the key words and phrases near each title, write a sentence that describes something you learned in the chapter.

Lazarus   chief priests and Pharisees   crucifixion

Jesus' Persecution

_____
_____
_____
_____
_____

Judas   Pilate
suffering   death
Resurrection

empty tomb
Ascension   Advocate
called to serve

Jesus' Passion

_____
_____
_____
_____
_____

The Resurrection and the Call to Discipleship

_____
_____
_____
_____
_____

Pentecost

_____
_____
_____
_____
_____

fifty days after the Resurrection   Holy Spirit
Trinity   birth of the Church

A Fill in the correct word or words to complete each sentence.

1. At the end of _____, we must give an account of how well we have _____ Christ during our lifetime.

2. Jesus Christ offers us _____, but it is up to _____ how we respond.

3. We believe that Jesus died on the _____, rose from the dead, and _____ forever.

B Find and circle the words hidden within the puzzle.

CROSS, DARKNESS, JUDAS, CROWN, PILATE, KING, NAILS, PASSION, BARABBAS, ANOINTING, SALVATION, CONFESS, EASTER, VIGIL, RESURRECTION, TRIDUUM

```
S  H  N  K  O  N  F  U  T  H  Z  y  D  W  E  G  K  G  B  R
K  A  G  B  T  W  C  T  V  Z  B  G  N  A  S  V  J  S  G  E
G  A  D  L  I  O  S  y  y  C  U  D  S  R  J  R  L  H  R  S
C  P  Q  U  S  R  S  A  Z  G  X  T  W  N  S  I  P  Q  y  U
H  M  G  M  J  C  X  S  D  F  E  H  R  K  A  V  F  Q  N  R
O  V  S  E  S  N  P  T  E  R  V  F  R  N  H  M  X  G  Z  R
N  O  I  T  A  V  L  A  S  N  K  P  Z  P  K  L  X  y  J  E
J  R  I  I  B  K  E  E  O  Z  K  A  G  K  P  I  H  J  E  C
R  Q  D  K  B  J  U  I  F  S  N  R  C  T  I  F  N  M  A  T
W  P  O  J  A  D  S  U  y  O  K  V  A  T  L  G  G  G  C  I
M  Q  O  C  R  S  D  y  I  T  E  F  E  D  A  C  L  X  y  O
P  N  W  P  A  O  Q  N  E  B  V  Q  P  Q  T  A  W  X  E  N
G  P  P  P  B  L  T  C  O  N  F  E  S  S  E  R  H  A  U  X
T  T  J  Z  B  I  P  F  L  P  D  H  S  S  O  R  C  N  W  H
H  R  H  L  N  y  E  F  G  K  Q  N  H  E  T  L  J  y  W  Z
G  y  I  G  A  N  X  I  D  M  G  B  Z  B  P  X  V  N  J  Q
Z  L  R  D  O  y  O  O  J  H  L  I  B  O  U  A  F  N  R  I
Q  N  I  R  U  W  G  Z  L  N  S  Z  S  E  J  E  Z  H  Q  O
E  R  R  G  F  U  Q  B  M  H  E  J  D  y  O  H  H  A  C  O
C  B  C  U  Z  S  M  V  I  G  I  L  D  T  C  V  R  S  U  I
```

C Circle the letter of the correct answer.

1. The man who asked for the body of Jesus was
   a. Joseph of Arimathea.
   b. Simon of Cyrene.
   c. John the Baptizer.

2. Just as the first disciples, we receive the grace of
   a. the parish pastor.
   b. the Holy Spirit.
   c. the pope.

3. We are called to bring the Gospel message to others in
   a. words and actions.
   b. penance and fasting.
   c. goods and services.

D Fill in the correct word or words to complete each sentence.

1. After the Ascension of Jesus, the disciples remained in

   _____ according to Jesus' instructions.

2. _____ days after his Resurrection, Jesus fulfilled his promise of sending the Holy Spirit to his disciples.

3. The crowds from many nations who were gathered at Pentecost were amazed that they heard the disciples speaking their own

   _____.

4. The Holy Spirit was not _____ to the disciples in the same way Jesus had been.

5. The Holy Spirit gives the Church its _____ and

   _____.

E Match the Faith Words in Column 1 with the definitions in Column 2.

Column 1

a. Passion

b. Resurrection

c. Communion of Saints

d. Holy Week

e. Paschal mystery

f. Easter Triduum

g. Ascension

h. Advocate

i. Pentecost

j. Trinity

k. life everlasting

Column 2

1. ___ the moment when Jesus, in his resurrected body, returned to his Father in heaven

2. ___ the day on which Jesus Christ's disciples received the gift of the Holy Spirit; "the day the Church was born"

3. ___ the holiest celebration of the liturgical year

4. ___ the suffering, crucifixion, and death Jesus endured for our sins

5. ___ the union of all those, both living and dead, who believe in Christ

6. ___ the week that begins on Palm Sunday of the Lord's Passion

7. ___ another name for the Holy Spirit, the Third Person of the Trinity, who helps and guides us in following Jesus

8. ___ the life that Jesus' faithful followers will share for all eternity

9. ___ Jesus' victory over death as he rose to new life

10. ___ God's plan for our salvation through the Passion, death, Resurrection, and Ascension of Jesus

11. ___ the three Persons of God: the Father, the Son, and the Holy Spirit

F What are the Stations of the Cross, and how do they help us?

_____

_____

_____

_____

_____

The Good News

The first Christians, filled with the Holy Spirit, spread the Gospel message throughout their world. The same Spirit calls us to be witnesses of the message of Christ in our world today.

Go, therefore, and make disciples of all nations, baptizing them in the name of the Father, and of the Son, and of the holy Spirit, teaching them to observe all that I have commanded you.

Matthew 28:19–20

World Religions Today

NORTH AMERICA
EUROPE
ASIA
AFRICA
SOUTH AMERICA
AUSTRALIA

Christianity
Other Religions

Saint Paul established church communities around the Mediterranean, such as the one in Corinth, Greece, shown here in ruins. Today, Christianity is the largest of the world's great religions.

Send Us Your Spirit

Words and Music by David Haas
Accompaniment by Jeanne Cotter

* May be sung in canon.

Get CONNECTED

with family and friends

The Early Church: People of Pentecost

Jesus intended his teachings and work to continue until the end of time. In this chapter, you will learn how Paul and the apostles, under the guidance of the Holy Spirit, taught the early church communities to follow Jesus. Today, all members of the Church, under the leadership of the pope and bishops, are called to spread the message of salvation.

Living as a Disciple of Jesus

My relatives come to our house on all the special holidays. We never eat dinner before six o'clock because my Aunt Ellen is always late. Most of my friends eat earlier and want me to hang out with them afterward. I always have to say no, which used to make me mad.

Then my mom told me that my Aunt Ellen volunteers at a soup kitchen on holidays, and my attitude changed. One time, my aunt even took me with her to help serve the meals. Now it doesn't bother me at all to say no to my friends. And I feel so proud telling them about my Aunt Ellen.

Activity

Do one of the following.

(1) Survey your relatives to find out how they live their faith each day. Identify ways that your family can support and help one another grow closer to God.

(2) With your family or friends, organize a charitable drive in your parish or community to collect clothing and other necessities to benefit people in need.

Check It Out

This is the flag of Vatican City. It represents the homeland of the Pope. Did you ever wonder how a pope is elected? The College of Cardinals meets in a locked room for a private meeting known as a *conclave*, which is from the Latin word for "key." The cardinals are not allowed contact with the outside world. The election continues until a two-thirds majority vote is reached. Then, white smoke rises from the Vatican chimney, signaling that a new pope has been elected.

Did you know...?

Pope John Paul II has received the most correspondence of any pope in the Catholic Church. It takes nine full-time priests to read and answer just the letters written in English.

Holy Humor!

Things Noah Would Have Said

"Strange! We haven't seen another boat for weeks."

"If only I'd brought along more rhino litter."

"Do you know where I can dock this thing?"

"How many times around this place makes a mile?"

"I never want to sleep in a waterbed again."

"An outboard motor would have made this more exciting."

"Fish for supper—again?"

"I think I need a new eye doctor. I keep seeing double."

All-Star Profile

Name: Sean Devereux
Born: 1964
Died: 1993
Occupation: teacher, coach, Salesian volunteer, and United Nations relief worker in Africa
Quote of a Lifetime: "While my heart beats, I have to do what I think I can—and that is to help those who are less fortunate."
Claims to Fame: Spent nearly five years helping the poorest of Africa's youth. Was known as an energetic leader and a loyal, dedicated, courageous, compassionate, and good-humored person. Was the first foreigner murdered in Somalia after U.S. troops arrived. Had a bridge in Somalia dedicated to him and had a youth center in Africa named after him.

Something To Do

On Sunday

At the end of Mass, pay special attention to the priest's words "Go forth to love and serve the Lord." Decide to do one thing during the day to follow this call.

Through the Week

Choose someone with whom to share your faith. For example, teach a favorite prayer to a younger sibling or discuss one of the Sunday Scripture readings with a family member or friend.

Wired

Visit Our Web Site
www.blestarewe.com

Web Site Spotlight
www.cnvs.org/vo-story.htm

On this site, Catholic lay volunteers report on how they are using their gifts in service to the Church and the world.

A Prayer for the Week

Thank you, Lord, for the leaders of our Church. Bless them with wisdom and the guidance of the Holy Spirit. Bless our family, too, so that we may lead others to you through our acts of love and kindness.
Amen.

17 The Early Church: People of Pentecost

I formed you, and set you /as a covenant of the people, /a light for the nations.

Isaiah 42:6

Share

At her teacher's request, Stephanie joined the conflict resolution team at school. She tries to help her peers find reasonable solutions to their problems relating to one another.

Chad's mother is a single parent. To help his family, Chad watches his younger sister once a week while his mother goes food shopping.

Lindsey volunteers with physically disabled children. Young people with physical limitations enjoy the friendship and assistance of volunteers such as Lindsey.

Activities

1. Together, discuss what Christian values these young people model by their actions.

2. Write about ways that you are a witness to Christ at home, at school, or in your community.

_____

_____

_____

_____

_____

_____

_____

_____

_____

_____

_____

How is the Church a witness to Christ?

Scripture A Letter from Paul to the Corinthians

I, Paul, am a slave of Christ Jesus, called to be an apostle and set apart for the Gospel of God (based on Romans 1:1).

I wrote letters to individuals, communities, and the Church as a whole. I generally included in each letter a greeting to the community, a prayer of thanksgiving, and a presentation on some Christian teaching. Then I discussed a moral teaching and provided the community with information about my upcoming travels. I concluded with some final advice.

No one can say, "Jesus is Lord," except by the holy Spirit.

There are different kinds of spiritual gifts but the same Spirit; there are different forms of service but the same Lord; there are different workings but the same God who produces all of them in everyone. To each individual the manifestation of the Spirit is given for some benefit. To one is given through the Spirit the expression of wisdom; to another the expression of knowledge according to the same Spirit; to another faith by the same Spirit; to another gifts of healing by the one Spirit; to another mighty deeds; to another prophecy; to another discernment of spirits; to another varieties of tongues. . . . But one and the same Spirit produces all of these, distributing them individually to each person as he wishes.

As a body is one though it has many parts, and all the parts of the body, though many, are one body, so also Christ. For in one Spirit we were all baptized into one body, whether Jews or Greeks, slaves or free persons, and we were all given to drink of one Spirit. Now you are Christ's body, and individually parts of it. Strive eagerly for the greatest spiritual gifts.

1 Corinthians 12:3–13, 27, 31

Guidance from Saint Paul

The Corinthians were one of the early church communities. Saint Paul would visit and write letters to the early church communities to help them live as Christians. He wrote letters to encourage people to become believers and to help believers become more united in Christ. Each letter to one of the early Christian communities is called an **epistle**.

Paul wrote the preceding epistle to explain to the Corinthians that all things of the Holy Spirit and God are equally important. The Christian community, the Church, was born on the day of Pentecost, when the disciples were filled with the Holy Spirit and began speaking in many languages. Empowered by the Spirit, they went forth and preached the good news of Jesus Christ to the people in Jerusalem, converting many of them.

The Christians at Corinth

Filled with the Holy Spirit, Saint Paul brought the good news to Corinth, a great seaport held by a community of people from different social, economic, political, and religious backgrounds. Because of this, members of the church community in Corinth began to experience division. They began to deny poor people membership into the community. Christians who prayed with great devotion in the Holy Spirit were more highly valued than those who did works of charity. People began to value certain Christian teachings over others. Paul's teachings helped the Corinthians to understand the importance of unity.

The Mission of the Church

Jesus established the Church so that his teachings and work would continue until the end of time. Jesus appointed the Twelve Apostles to be the first **missioners** of the Church. Paul, at first a persecutor of Christians, became a missioner. Filled with the Holy Spirit, the apostles and early disciples, such as Paul, joyfully spread the news of the risen Lord. The apostles and the other members of the early Christian community taught others the love of Christ by the way they lived. They shared what they had with others, particularly the poor and those in need.

Today, the Church continues the missionary work of Christ. The Holy Spirit guides the Church in preaching the good news of salvation. God loves all people and wants them to come to know his truth and be saved. The Church's mission is to preach the Gospel to people of all cultures and races throughout the world. Its message is meant for people in every age. Because no one is excluded, the Church is catholic, or universal.

We also refer to the Church as apostolic. This means that the Church passes down the teachings of the apostles, which are from Christ himself. The Church's official teaching on faith and morals is infallible, or without error. Jesus **commissioned** Peter and the other apostles and gave them the authority to continue his mission and to act in his name. Today, the pope and bishops have the same role as the apostles in proclaiming the Gospel. By remaining faithful to the teachings of the apostles, the Church preserves the truth of Christ throughout the ages.

Sharing the Missionary Work of the Church

All members of the Church are called to share in its mission. By giving Peter the "keys of the Church," Christ gave Peter the special task of leading the other apostles and being head of the newly formed Church. Peter was the first bishop of Rome. Today, the pope continues to represent Christ as the visible head of the Church. He has the full and supreme responsibility to lead the members of the Catholic Church and to care for their souls. Bishops succeed the apostles and establish unity among the churches they oversee. Priests, assisted by deacons, also teach the faith, celebrate the liturgy, and guide parish communities. People who have received Holy Orders or taken religious vows, as well as the laity, also participate in the mission of the Church. Lay people are called to holiness in their personal, familial, and social lives.

Faith Words

epistle An epistle is a letter written to a Christian community by Saint Paul or another disciple in the early Church. Such letters are included in the New Testament.

missioner A missioner is a person who shares his or her faith through preaching and charitable works. Missioners of the Church preach Christ's message of salvation to all people.

commissioned To be commissioned is to be entrusted with the power to fulfill a particular task. Christ entrusted the apostles and their successors with the task of leading and serving the Church.

What does the Church teach about the end of time?

Our Church Teaches

An essential teaching of the Church is that of the resurrection of our bodies at the end of time. Although we do not know when this will occur, we believe that we will rise on the last day, just as Jesus rose from the dead. Christ's Resurrection is the source for faith in our own resurrection. Christ lives in our hearts while we await this fulfillment.

As Christians, we believe that Christ ascended into heaven and will appear again on the last day. At that time, he will judge those who are still living as well as those who have already died. Jesus Christ, having entered heaven once and for all, intercedes constantly for us and assures us of the guidance of the Holy Spirit. At his Second Coming, Christ will judge each of us according to our works and how well we accepted God's grace in our lives. We wait for Christ in joyful hope.

> **We Believe**
> Christ established the Church. His Spirit guides the Church in spreading the Gospel to all people until he comes again.

Respond

Elizabeth Ann Seton

Elizabeth Ann Seton was born into a wealthy Episcopalian family in New York City in 1774. As a child, she enjoyed reading about historical and religious subjects. Her parents raised her to be charitable toward those who were sick or in need.

Elizabeth continued serving others after she married William Seton, a successful shipping merchant. While raising five children, Elizabeth helped found the Society for the Relief of Poor Widows with Small Children. People lovingly called her the "Protestant Sister of Charity."

When she was about twenty-nine years old, Elizabeth's life changed dramatically. Her husband's business failed and he was diagnosed with tuberculosis. Elizabeth sailed with him to the warmer climate of Italy, but he died soon after their arrival. Fortunately, Elizabeth was able to stay with the Filicchi family, longtime friends of her husband, who comforted

and supported her during this difficult time. She was moved by the strong faith of this Catholic family and became both interested in and inspired by their ways of prayer and worship.

About a year after she returned to the United States, Elizabeth joined the Catholic Church. Her family did not approve, but Elizabeth was committed to her new faith. She devoted her energy to serving the Church, and she eventually opened the first American Catholic school in Maryland. Elizabeth also formed a community of Catholic women called the Sisters of Charity. They operated many schools, orphanages, and hospitals.

Just before she died, at the age of forty-six, Elizabeth told the sisters in her community, "Be children of the Church." Elizabeth Ann Seton was the first native-born American to be canonized. Her feast day is January 4.

Activities

1. What do you think Elizabeth Seton meant by the advice "Be children of the Church"?

_____

_____

2. What challenges do young people face when trying to live their faith?

_____

_____

_____

_____

3. Explain some ways young people might overcome these challenges.

_____

_____

_____

_____

How can we celebrate our call to be disciples of Jesus?

✝ Prayer Celebration

The Commissioning of Disciples

Leader: Through Baptism, we become disciples of Christ. As members of the Church, we are called to be the light of Christ for others and to carry out his mission. We are ambassadors for Christ, invited to accept the responsibilities of discipleship with courage and to shout his name from the mountaintops for all to hear.

Reader: The eleven disciples went to Galilee, to the mountain to which Jesus had ordered them. When they saw him, they worshiped, but they doubted. Then Jesus approached and said to them, "All power in heaven and on earth has been given to me. Go, therefore, and make disciples of all nations, baptizing them in the name of the Father, and of the Son, and of the holy Spirit, teaching them to observe all that I have commanded you. And behold, I am with you always, until the end of the age."

Matthew 28:16–20

Leader: Reflect on your experiences of discipleship, such as the obstacles that you face, your challenges, and signs you have received that have helped you know and trust in God's presence.

Get Connected

with family and friends

The Church Today: Confirmed Believers

We receive the Holy Spirit at Baptism, and we are strengthened by the Holy Spirit in the sacrament of Confirmation. In the celebration of Confirmation, the laying on of hands and the anointing with chrism are signs of God's grace. In Confirmation, the Holy Spirit draws us into fuller participation in the Church, opening our hearts to God's word.

In the Spirit

Mr. Grant, our next-door neighbor, used to wait until everyone else's driveway was shoveled before he drove out in his snow blower to clear his driveway. I always thought that was selfish of him.

Mr. Grant passed away last year, and when the first snowfall came, there was no snow blower to be seen.

My mom said, "Go over and shovel the driveway for Mrs. Grant."

I wanted to mention the snow blower, but instead I just said, "Okay." I spent an hour shoveling Mrs. Grant's driveway.

Mrs. Grant came to her door and said, "Let me pay you."

Glad to have done an act of kindness, I heard myself say, "No thanks, Mrs. Grant. We're neighbors."

Activity

Do one of the following.

(1) Ask your friends to share times they felt inspired to do something good for someone without a reward.

(2) Plan to do a "random act of kindness" for someone in your family this week.

Brain Teaser

Fill in the missing letters to reveal words that are associated with the Holy Spirit.

			F		
		W			
	V		R		
P			C		T

Did you know...?

The holy oils used in Baptism, Confirmation, Holy Orders, and Anointing of the Sick are blessed by the bishop at the Chrism Mass on Holy Thursday morning. The oils are presented to each parish at Mass that evening.

SPIRIT OF FIRE

Spirit of Fire is not only the name of one of **Greg Walton's** CDs—it describes the enthusiasm of Walton himself. Walton has appeared at some of the largest Christian music festivals throughout North America and Europe, performing songs that range in style from pop to contemporary praise to alternative rock. Walton's spirited performances have been known to include heartwarming stories, humorous anecdotes, and, best of all, time for worship.

Originally from Chicago, Walton moved to Nashville in pursuit of a call to become a Christian rock artist. He felt this call as early as junior high, when, during a particularly difficult time in his family, he wanted to strengthen his relationship with God. Although Walton originally pursued a career as a teacher, he began to dedicate himself full-time to his music ministry in 1998. Walton's other albums include *I Won't Back Down* and *Stealing Moment*.

All-Star Profile

Brother Roger of Taizé

Name: Taizé Community
Begun: 1940
Purpose: working to bring about reconciliation among people, trust among nations, and peace on earth
Quote of a Lifetime: "The more a believer wishes to live the absolute call of God, the more essential it is to do so in the heart of human distress" (Brother Roger, founder of Taizé, in France).
Claims to Fame: Recognized as a sign of reconciliation among divided Christians and among separated peoples. Known for its beautiful music, style of prayer, and international conferences. Accepts no gifts or donations for itself, not even family inheritances. Has self-supporting members who share with others solely through their own work. Beginning in the 1950s, some began living outside of Taizé among the underprivileged, to be witnesses of peace alongside those who were suffering.

Wired

Visit Our Web Site
www.blestarewe.com

Web Site Spotlight
www.taize.fr

Explore the Taizé community and its international efforts for prayer and reconciliation.

Something To Do

On Sunday

Bless yourself with holy water before Mass, reminding yourself that the Holy Spirit is present to help you live as a faithful follower of Jesus.

Through the Week

Check the parish bulletin for an upcoming activity in which you can participate to learn more about your Catholic community.

A Prayer for the Week

Lord, we pray for the future of our family and the future of your Church. With the Holy Spirit as our guide, we hope to be faithful to you and to bring your good news to the world.
Amen.

Answer Key: DOVE, WIND, FIRE, PENTECOST

172

18 The Church Today: Confirmed Believers

 Under the guidance of the Holy Spirit give your lives completely in the service of all, as did Christ, who came not to be served but to serve.

Rite of Confirmation

Share

You were baptized into a faith community. The community supports you, leads you, teaches you the faith, encourages you, and provides you with the opportunity to grow as a Catholic Christian. The community helps you recognize the gifts God has given you. Your gifts should be shared with others. You can use your talents and gifts to serve your family, parish, and community. Serving others is an important part of being a Christian. In Confirmation, Catholics are invited to give more of themselves to their faith and to use their gifts in more responsible and challenging ways.

Activities

1. Consider these three questions.

How do you feel about taking responsibility for your own faith?

How do you see yourself serving as a part of your commitment to the Church?

How do you expect the Church to support and help you?

2. After reflecting on the above questions, write what you think would help prepare a person for the time he or she is invited to join the community of confirmed believers.

_____

_____

_____

_____

Why do we celebrate the sacrament of Confirmation?

Worship Rite of Confirmation

The Holy Spirit inspires us to love and serve others. The gift of the Holy Spirit is given to us in Baptism and then sealed, or strengthened, in **Confirmation**. In the Rite of Confirmation, the bishop prays that we will use the gift of the Spirit to follow Christ more closely. When Confirmation is celebrated during the Mass, the bishop may give a homily similar to the following. The homily helps explain the Scripture readings in the Mass and helps the Confirmation candidates gain deeper insight into the sacrament they are celebrating.

"On the day of Pentecost the apostles received the Holy Spirit as the Lord had promised. They also received the power of giving the Holy Spirit to others and so completing the work of baptism. This we read in the Acts of the Apostles. When Saint Paul placed his hands on those who had been baptized, the Holy Spirit came upon them, and they began to speak in other languages and in prophetic words.

"Bishops are successors of the apostles and have this power of giving the Holy Spirit to the baptized, either personally or through the priests they appoint.

"In our day the coming of the Holy Spirit in confirmation is no longer marked by the gift of tongues, but we know his coming by faith. He fills our hearts with the love of God, brings us together in one faith but in different vocations, and works within us to make the Church one and holy.

"The gift of the Holy Spirit which you are to receive will be a spiritual sign and seal to make you more like Christ and more perfect members of his Church. At his baptism by John, Christ himself was anointed by the Spirit and sent out on his public ministry to set the world on fire.

"You have already been baptized into Christ and now you will receive the power of his Spirit and the sign of the cross on your forehead. You must be witnesses before all the world to his suffering, death, and resurrection; your way of life should at all times reflect the goodness of Christ. Christ gives varied gifts to his Church, and the Spirit distributes them among the members of Christ's body to build up the holy people of God in unity and love.

"Be active members of the Church, alive in Jesus Christ. Under the guidance of the Holy Spirit give your lives completely in the service of all, as did Christ, who came not to be served but to serve."

Rite of Confirmation

Confirmed in the Spirit

Confirmation strengthens our life in Christ, which began in Baptism. Confirmation celebrates the Holy Spirit's presence in the Church and action in our lives. We relive the Pentecost experience and grow stronger in our faith so that we can do God's work in the Church.

When the Rite of Confirmation takes place during the Mass, it follows a ritual. The readings are usually ones that have been specifically chosen by the Church for use when the Church is welcoming candidates of Confirmation. After the readings, the candidates may be identified by the bishop. A homily similar to the one you just read is then given to emphasize the meaning of the sacrament. Next, the candidates renew their baptismal promises. The candidates are then invited forward, usually with a sponsor, and the bishop lays his hand on them, signifying the sending of the Holy Spirit upon the faithful, enabling them to carry out the mission of the Church.

The anointing of the forehead with the oil of chrism is an important action. As the bishop anoints the candidates, he prays, "Be sealed with the gift of the Holy Spirit." This action signifies the giving of the strength and support of the Holy Spirit, who guides us in carrying out our responsibilities as full members of the Christian community.

A Confirmation Mass then continues with the general intercessions and the Liturgy of the Eucharist. The Mass ends with a special blessing for those confirmed.

Like Baptism and Holy Orders, the sacrament of Confirmation can be received only once. The "mark of Christ" that we receive in Confirmation remains with us forever. It leads us to a life of worship and service to the Church under God's constant care and protection.

The Action of the Holy Spirit in Our Lives

The Church identifies seven particular **gifts of the Holy Spirit** received in Baptism and strengthened in Confirmation. These gifts make us aware of Christ's love and inspire us to spread his truth to others. These traditional gifts are wisdom, understanding, knowledge, right judgment, courage, reverence, and wonder and awe.

Wisdom helps us know how God wants us to live. Understanding helps us know what God teaches through Jesus, the Bible, and the Church. Knowledge helps us know and appreciate that God is more important than anything else in life. Right judgment helps us make good decisions in our everyday lives. Courage helps us be strong when we face problems. Reverence helps us love God more than anything else. Wonder and awe help us to be thankful for all God's gifts. With these gifts we can give **witness** to Jesus, who suffered, died, and rose again for our salvation. This is the good news the Holy Spirit helps us proclaim to others. This truth is essential to our Catholic faith, which is one and the same throughout the world.

 page 234 to learn more about Confirmation.

Faith Words

Confirmation Confirmation is a sacrament of initiation in which we receive the special strength of the Holy Spirit and become full members of the Church.

gifts of the Holy Spirit The gifts of the Holy Spirit are the seven special gifts or blessings that enable us to become more Christlike: wisdom, understanding, knowledge, right judgment, courage, reverence, and wonder and awe.

witness Witness is an attesting to the truth of something by words or actions. We give witness to Christ by imitating in our everyday lives what Jesus would say or do.

What is the work of the Holy Spirit in the liturgy?

Our Church Teaches

We receive the Holy Spirit in a special way in the sacrament of Confirmation. Through Confirmation our relationship with the Church deepens and we are called to spread and defend the faith by word and deed with greater commitment. The Spirit strengthens us to give witness to the Church's mission.

The Holy Spirit has a special role in the liturgy of the Church. The Holy Spirit unites us in faith and prepares the Church to be in the presence of Christ. In the Liturgy of the Word, the Holy Spirit recalls the words and deeds of Christ. Then, by the power of the Holy Spirit, the bread and wine are transformed into the Body and Blood of Christ. The Holy Spirit also transforms us into Christ's Body so that we can live as Christ lived. Both Baptism and Confirmation leave a permanent spiritual mark on our souls.

We Believe
In the sacrament of Confirmation, the Holy Spirit unites us more perfectly to Christ and to the Church.

Respond

Inspired to Serve

While attending the annual parish carnival, Heather and Carla spotted their seventh grade teacher, Mrs. DelaFuente. She was spinning a wheel at one of the game booths. They also recognized two teenagers who were helping her collect money and hand out prizes.

Heather asked, "Did you ever notice how often we bump into our teacher outside of school? She sure volunteers for a lot of different activities." Carla nodded her head in agreement, adding, "She's so enthusiastic and hard-working. I know a lot of her former students join her when she helps out in the community."

As they waited in line for one of the rides, the two girls continued their conversation about their teacher. They talked about how Mrs. DelaFuente volunteered with Habitat for Humanity, a Christian organization that brings volunteers together to build affordable housing for people in need. They remembered the party she held in school, when each of them brought in clothing to donate to poor children. Heather and Carla agreed that Mrs. DelaFuente's generosity and example of service had made them more aware of the needs of others and had helped them realize the joy that can be found in giving.

Activities

1. Think of a friend or relative who has received Confirmation. Name some ways the gifts of the Holy Spirit seem to help the person in his or her daily life.

_____

_____

2. Look at the pictures below to see how the gifts of the Holy Spirit are at work in daily life. Name some situations in which you might see yourself using the gifts of the Spirit.

Understanding helps me relate to my parents.

Right judgment helps me choose positive friendships.

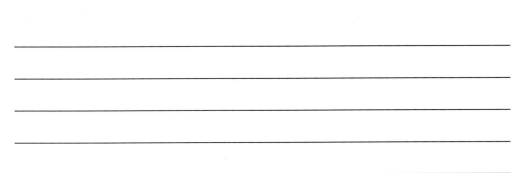

_____

_____

_____

_____

_____

_____

_____

How might we ask the Holy Spirit to empower and enlighten us?

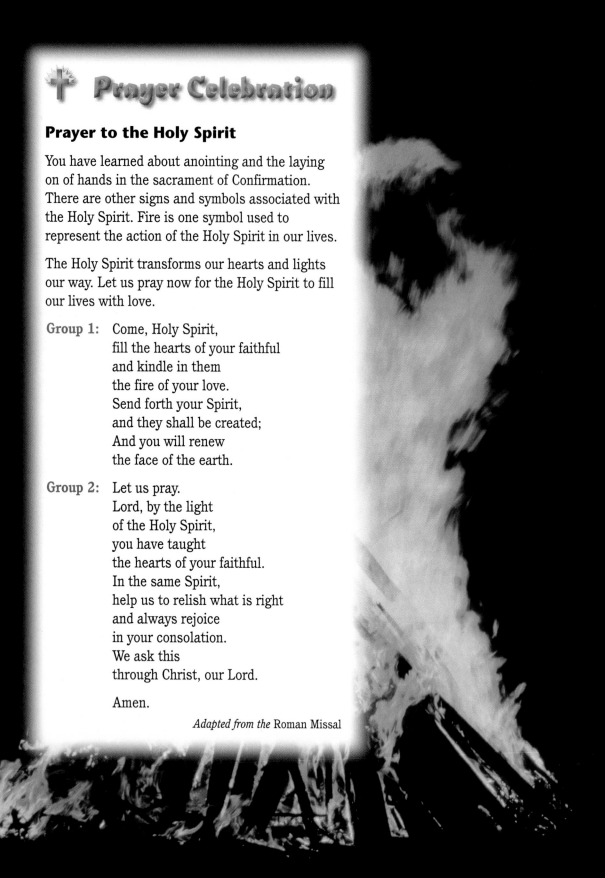

✝ Prayer Celebration

Prayer to the Holy Spirit

You have learned about anointing and the laying on of hands in the sacrament of Confirmation. There are other signs and symbols associated with the Holy Spirit. Fire is one symbol used to represent the action of the Holy Spirit in our lives.

The Holy Spirit transforms our hearts and lights our way. Let us pray now for the Holy Spirit to fill our lives with love.

Group 1: Come, Holy Spirit,
fill the hearts of your faithful
and kindle in them
the fire of your love.
Send forth your Spirit,
and they shall be created;
And you will renew
the face of the earth.

Group 2: Let us pray.
Lord, by the light
of the Holy Spirit,
you have taught
the hearts of your faithful.
In the same Spirit,
help us to relish what is right
and always rejoice
in your consolation.
We ask this
through Christ, our Lord.

Amen.

Adapted from the Roman Missal

Get Connected

with family and friends

Spreading the Gospel

"If I have all faith so as to move mountains, but do not have love, I am nothing," wrote Paul to the Corinthians (1 Corinthians 13:2). Every disciple of Jesus is called to bring the love, hope, and justice of the Gospel to the world. We spread the Gospel first at home and then in the world by the way we live. Spreading the Gospel means not only sharing our faith but acting with love toward all people.

Signs of Love

Nikki Kissane's grandfather had a series of strokes that made communication difficult. Thinking of people in the same situation as her grandfather, Kissane approached her university professor to see if she could participate in his research on sign language. Kissane invested more than 600 hours of research over several years on the project. Kissane developed a simplified 500-word sign language, called the Simplified Sign System, to give people with impaired communication skills the chance to communicate fully with others. Kissane has spread the Gospel to others through her genuine concern for people and her desire to make the world a better place for all.

Activity

Do one of the following.

(1) Visit the Web site on the next page to see the Simplified Sign System online. Together with family or friends learn the system Kissane created to help others.

(2) Pictured at right is the sign for God. You can use the Simplified Sign System to help other people communicate. Contact organizations that work with autistic children, brain-injured persons, stroke victims, and others to see if they can use your volunteer help.

F.A.Q.

Dear Mr. F.A.Q.,

I struggle to maintain a healthy weight. In my family, we eat whenever we want, and I find myself eating more than I should and "vegging out" in front of the TV. I don't like the fat comments or insults at school. I don't feel good about myself. What should I do?

Signed,
Ready for a Change in Rockville

Dear Ready,

I commend you for your honesty. Weight-related comments can be hurtful. See a doctor to check your overall health, and then make your plans for a healthier lifestyle. Drink lots of water, and choose exercises that you like (bike riding, in-line skating, and so on), and do a little each day. Remember that you were made in God's image and that you are beautiful!

God bless,
Mr. F.A.Q.

Did you know...?

Part of a Catholic's responsibility in spreading the Gospel is making decisions to support political candidates who work to protect the dignity of human life.

Holy Humor!

Sunday School Sillies

Found in religion compositions written by children:

When Mary heard that she was the mother of God's Son, she sang the Magna Carta.

When the three wise guys from the East Side arrived, they found Jesus and the manager.

The epistles were the wives of the apostles.

Adam and Eve were created from an apple tree.

Noah's wife was called Joan of Ark.

Moses went up Mount Sinus to get the Ten Amendments.

The greatest miracle in the Bible is when Joshua told his son to stand still and he obeyed.

All-Star Profile

Name: Citizens United for Rehabilitation of Errants (CURE)
Begun: 1972
Purpose: providing people in prison with all the rehabilitative opportunities they need to turn their lives around

Claims to Fame: Provides prisoners and their families with information about rehabilitative programs. Promotes the creation of additional rehabilitation programs. Supports changes to the criminal justice system, including abolition of the death penalty. Promotes For Whom the Bells Toll, a nationwide program in which religious organizations toll their church bells whenever an execution takes place. Also supports compensation for victims of crime, prisoner job training and education, handgun control, improving programs for integrating rehabilitated prisoners into society, and increasing awareness of the needs of women prisoners.

Wired

Visit Our Web Site
www.blestarewe.com

Web Site Spotlight
www.simplifiedsigns.org
This Web site displays the signs from the Simplified Sign System. Learn the word *love* in a universal language.

Something To Do

On Sunday

Participate in the hymns, allowing yourself to be moved by God's spirit and to feel God's love.

Through the Week

Choose a quote from Scripture that is meaningful for you. Write it down. Display it in your room or in another prominent place, and pray it several times during the week so that you can commit it to memory.

A Prayer for the Week

Lord, help us share your good news by treating others with love, hope, and justice so that they may see you in our actions. Make us instruments of your peace.
Amen.

19 Spreading the Gospel

You will show me the path to life, abounding joy in your presence.

Based on Psalm 16:11

Share

In the late 1800s mascots began to appear at high school and college sports events. Today, you also see them at Olympic games, theme parks, parades, and professional sports events. Dressed as special characters or animals, mascots are a fun addition to an organization or team. They represent the team's spirit. They bring energy and enthusiasm to events. Mascots help unite the team and onlookers in spirit and action.

Activity

Name a person who is like a mascot. Explain why.

_____

_____

How could a Christian act as a mascot for the Church?

_____

_____

_____

_____

What do the epistle writers say about love and the Christian community?

Hear & Believe

 Scripture The Way of Love

An **evangelist** is similar to a mascot. Evangelists **evangelize**, or proclaim the word of God to the world through their writings, word of mouth, and example. Saint Paul proclaimed the word of God by writing epistles to specific Christian communities, such as the Corinthians. He urged them to use their spiritual gifts to carry on the missionary work of the Church.

The **Catholic epistles**, which consist of three letters by John, two by Peter, and one each by James and Jude, were written to the universal Catholic community. Below is a passage from an epistle of Paul to the Corinthians and a passage from a Catholic epistle by John. These epistles were written to evangelize the early church community. Paul's letter emphasizes love—God's greatest and most precious gift. John's letter discusses love within the ideal Christian community in word and action. Read the passages below and compare their messages.

If I speak in human and angelic tongues, but do not have love, I am a resounding gong or a clashing cymbal. And if I have the gift of prophecy, and comprehend all mysteries and all knowledge; if I have all faith so as to move mountains, but do not have love, I am nothing. If I give away everything I own . . . but do not have love, I gain nothing.

Love is patient, love is kind. It is not jealous, [love] is not pompous, it is not inflated, it is not rude, it does not seek its own interests, it is not quick-tempered, it does not brood over injury, it does not rejoice over wrongdoing but rejoices with the truth. It bears all things, believes all things, hopes all things, endures all things. Love never fails. If there are prophecies, they will be brought to nothing; if tongues, they will cease; if knowledge, it will be brought to nothing. So faith, hope, love remain, these three; but the greatest of these is love.

1 Corinthians 13:1–8, 13

Beloved, let us love one another, because love is of God; everyone who loves is begotten by God and knows God. Whoever is without love does not know God, for God is love. In this way the love of God was revealed to us: God sent his only Son into the world so that we might have life through him. In this is love: not that we have loved God, but that he loved us and sent his Son as expiation for our sins. Beloved, if God so loved us, we also must love one another. No one has ever seen God. Yet, if we love one another, God remains in us, and his love is brought to perfection in us.

This is how we know that we remain in him and he in us, that he has given us of his Spirit. Moreover, we have seen and testify that the Father sent his Son as savior of the world. Whoever acknowledges that Jesus is the Son of God, God remains in him and he in God.

If anyone says, "I love God," but hates his brother, he is a liar; for whoever does not love a brother whom he has seen cannot love God whom he has not seen. This is the commandment we have from him: whoever loves God must also love his brother.

1 John 4:7–15, 20–21

Sharing the Gift of Love

We evangelize when we spread the truth of the Gospels and share the gift of God's love with others. Love is the greatest virtue and must be the motivating force behind all our words and actions. Saint Paul reminds us that despite all the gifts we might have, we are nothing without the gift of love. And in the epistle of John, we learn that our love is nothing if it does not begin with loving words and actions toward our neighbors. Both Paul's and John's epistles present us with the kind of love that is found in a perfect Christian heart, family, and community—the love of God. With the help of the Holy Spirit we can grow in this love and evangelize one another.

Evangelization in the Family

As building blocks of society, families play a key role in carrying out the Church's mission to live as a loving Christian community and evangelize the world through their example of love. In fact, the family is often called the "domestic church" because it is a community built on love.

Because a family is a sign of God's love, unity within the family is sacred. Anything that might dissolve this unity, such as adultery, divorce, polygamy, or living together outside of marriage, takes away from the dignity of marriage. Marriage is based on a lifelong commitment between a man and a woman. From their sexual union, a husband and wife become cooperators with God in creating new life. A sign of true married love is openness to children, whom the Church calls the "supreme gift" of marriage. United in love and faith, the family evangelizes one another and the world by living in God's love.

 pages 239–240 to learn more about the sacrament of Matrimony.

Evangelization in Society

The love we build in our homes and in our Church must extend to the world. It is our mission to see God in our neighbor and love our neighbor as ourselves. Our neighbor might be a person suffering from discrimination, poverty, or oppression. Social and economic inequalities go against what the Gospel proclaims. These are injustices we must work to end. When we love our neighbor in this way we begin to live in **solidarity**. Solidarity enables us to recognize the dignity of all before God. When we unite with others, we can bring God's love, justice, peace, and compassion into any situation.

A Closer Look

Paul's Evangelization

Paul journeyed to evangelize early Christian communities in places such as Italy, where he wrote to the Romans and Philemon. From various regions in Greece, Paul wrote to the Corinthians, Philippians, and Thessalonians,

and also wrote to Timothy and Titus. From areas in present-day Turkey, Paul wrote to the Galatians, Ephesians, and Colossians.

Faith Words

evangelist An evangelist is a person who proclaims God to the world by word of mouth, through writings, or as a living example. The word also refers to a writer of a Gospel. Matthew, Mark, Luke, and John are often called the four evangelists.

evangelize To evangelize is to spread the truth of the Gospels through our words and love of others.

Catholic epistles The Catholic epistles were letters written to the universal Church. These seven letters are included in the New Testament.

solidarity Solidarity is the unity we share with all our brothers and sisters, who are made in the image of God.

As citizens, how do we spread the Gospel by our actions?

Our Church Teaches

We are called to promote the dignity and equality of all people, to help eliminate the sins that cause injustice, and to make a difference where we find injustices. By living as a Christian community at home and bringing God's love to others we can make a difference. Carrying out our social, political, and economic duties can also help form a just society. We spread the Gospel when we act as responsible citizens, when we stand up for the rights of others, and when we stand up for what is morally right. God gives us the courage we need to be able to do this.

One day, it will be your civic duty to pay taxes for services others need. You will have an obligation to vote for leaders who will work for the common good. It will be up to you to support and work with civil leaders to promote truth, justice, solidarity, and freedom.

We Believe
We share in the mission of the Church when we live responsibly and stand up for our Christian ideals.

Respond

Sojourner Truth

Sojourner Truth was a powerful speaker who defended the abolition of slavery and women's rights. She couldn't read or write, so she used her gift of speech to change the injustices in society. Truth spoke from the heart because she knew what it was like to be humiliated and abused.

Truth was born into slavery in upstate New York in 1797. She never really knew her many brothers and sisters. Like her, they were taken away from the family and traded to other masters. Against her will, she married an older slave. They had five children. Truth's faith in God helped her withstand the harsh life of being a slave.

Soon after she became a free woman, Truth crusaded for a personal cause. She fought in court for her youngest son, Peter, who had been illegally sold as a slave in Alabama. Truth was a convincing speaker and won her case.

Later, she became a traveling preacher. She preached about love, equality, women's suffrage, and abolition. One observer noted that "her commanding figure and dignified manner hushed every trifler to silence."

During the Civil War, she raised food and collected clothing donations for black regiments. She met with President Abraham Lincoln at the White House in 1864. After the Civil War, she continued to support the former slaves and spoke before Congress on their behalf. Before Truth died, slavery in the United States ended.

Sojourner Truth was a woman of faith and courage who was willing to stand up for her principles.

Activities

1. How did Sojourner Truth promote the dignity and equality of people?

_____

_____

_____

2. What does the word _love_ mean to you?

_____

_____

_____

Describe what Christian love is according to the passage from the epistle of Paul that you read. Then reflect on how your ideas of love might better match the examples in Paul's letter.

_____

_____

_____

3. Living in God's love and evangelizing often mean taking risks. Think about someone you know who stood up for his or her beliefs. What questions might you ask this person to help you follow his or her example?

_____

_____

How can we praise God and celebrate those who proclaim his message?

 **Prayer Celebration**

The Blessings of God's Love

Praise is a type of prayer by which we take time to reflect on the wonder and greatness of God. We consider the blessings of God's love in our own lives and in the lives of those around us. Draw or write about a time when you experienced the greatness of God.

Let us take time to praise God and thank all those who evangelize and continue to spread God's love to the world.

All: I will praise you, my God and king;
I will bless your name forever.
Every day I will bless you;
I will praise your name forever.
Great is the Lord and worthy of high praise;
God's grandeur is beyond understanding.
One generation praises your deeds to the next
And proclaims your mighty works.
They speak of the splendor of your majestic glory,
   tell of your wonderful deeds.

Based on Psalm 145:1–5

Get Connected

with family and friends

A Prayer for the Guidance of the Holy Spirit

This chapter tells about the "Vision of Heavenly Worship" from the Book of Revelation, in which John gives an example of what the Church should be: a community of love and prayer, open to the Holy Spirit, whose purpose is to glorify God.

Symbols of Faith

At the time the Book of Revelation was written, Christians were being persecuted for their faith. The writer used symbolic language to encourage members of the Church to grow in their faith in Jesus Christ and in God's love for them. Today, the Church is a witness to the dignity of life amidst a culture that often values possessions more than human rights.

Activity

Do one of the following.

(1) Discuss with friends symbols that could be used to represent the Catholic faith.

(2) Look around your home for signs of your Catholic heritage (for example, crucifixes, palm branches, statues, and prayer plaques). Choose a Catholic symbol with which you identify, and display it in a prominent place in your room.

The Password Is

apocalypse

The word *apocalypse* comes from a Greek word, αποκαλυπσις ("apocalypsis"), meaning "to uncover or disclose." In the Book of Revelation, the author uses apocalyptic writing, revealing the meanings of symbols seen in a vision. The vision reveals the truth about God's love and mercy.

Did you know...?

The Book of Revelation uses numbers as symbols for ideas. The number seven means perfection, since it combines three (the Trinity) with four (creation).

187

The RAP on Father Stan Fortuna

Father Stan Fortuna has been playing music since he was in second grade, when his father gave him a red electric guitar for Christmas. When you first see and hear him, you don't suspect that he is a priest. Fortuna is a South Bronx rapper with shoulder-length hair and megawatts of energy. In addition to being a musician, he is also a comedian. Prior to joining the Franciscan Friars of the Renewal, he was a professional jazz musician. Since becoming a friar, Fortuna has made many recordings. His 1998 rap album *Sacro Song* remains one of the most popular Catholic and Christian contemporary recordings. Proceeds from album sales go to support the friars' hands-on work with the poor. Fortuna mixes world music and hard-core rap styles to tackle such topics as chastity, suicide, and abortion. Fortuna answers the critics of his style by saying, "There are a lot of people who say you can't make Catholic rap, but I did it and I converted critics."

All-Star Profile

Name: Jeff Johnson
Born: 1947
Died: 1991
Occupation: youth minister, trainer, author, Young Life leader
Quote of a Lifetime: "I hope our faith and lifestyle create curiosity among the young, a curiosity that leads them to track down the source of the love they experience in our presence."
Claims to Fame: Served as a youth minister in the Archdiocese of St. Paul-Minneapolis. Known for his work in bringing the Catholic Church together with Young Life, an ecumenical Christian organization. Produced videos that addressed AIDS, bringing together compassion in action with a Catholic understanding of sexuality. Trained youth ministers throughout the United States. Mentored teenagers and adults, pointing them toward Jesus to find the true meaning of happiness.

Wired

Visit Our Web Site
www.blestarewe.com

Web Site Spotlight
www.easterbrooks.com/personal/calendar

Connect with the daily Scripture readings for each feast and season of the Church year.

Something To Do

On Sunday

Look for objects in church that symbolize what the Catholic faith is about. Then look for signs that might indicate what your parish community is involved in.

Through the Week

Invite your family to pray each night before the evening meal. A simple blessing will do, but you can also try different prayers.

A Prayer for the Week

Lord, may your Holy Spirit help us grow in our ability to live as Christians and praise you with our actions. May we share the love of God in our families and bring this love to the world. Amen.

20 A Prayer for the Guidance of the Holy Spirit

 God is love, and whoever remains in love remains in God and God in him.

1 John 4:16

Share

Prayer leads us into a personal relationship with God. It is not something we do only at special moments in our lives. Prayer is a lifetime commitment in which we turn to God to share every part of our daily lives.

To pray, we must stop our busyness and slow down so that we can experience oneness with God. Spontaneous prayers should come from our hearts. As our love for God deepens through prayer, we are better able to love those around us. We pray not only for our own needs but for the needs of the church community and the world.

Activities

1. Circle the phrases that you believe best complete the following sentence.

I am most likely to talk to God in prayer when I...

am lonely.	have overcome a difficulty.	am sad.
need comfort.	am feeling loved.	feel hurt.
am happy.	want something.	am confused.
am facing a challenge.	need advice.	feel confident.

2. Can you think of times when the Church invites us to pray for it? What are some of the special needs of the Church that we pray for as a community?

_____

_____

_____

What does it mean to be part of a Christian community?

When the early Christians were being persecuted for their faith, a man named John tried to help them understand what it meant to be a part of a Christian community. He wanted them to stand up for their faith. Guided by the Holy Spirit, John wrote the Book of Revelation, the last book in the New Testament. He kept his message hidden from the enemies of the Church by using imagery and symbolism. The early Christians were familiar with this style of writing from reading the Old Testament. They understood that John was reminding them that Christ's love conquers all evil. He was telling them to trust in God's promises and continue living the Gospel.

I had a vision of an open door to heaven and I heard a voice saying, "Come up here and I will show you what must happen afterwards."

A throne was there in heaven, and on the throne sat one whose appearance sparkled like jasper and carnelian. Around the throne was a halo as brilliant as an emerald. Surrounding the throne I saw twenty-four other thrones on which twenty-four elders sat, dressed in white garments and with gold crowns on their heads. From the throne came flashes of lightning, rumblings, and peals of thunder. Seven flaming torches burned in front of the throne, which are the seven spirits of God. In front of the throne was something that resembled a sea of glass.

In the center and around the throne were four living creatures. The first creature resembled a lion, the second was like a calf, the third had a face like that of a human being, and the fourth looked like an eagle in flight. The four living creatures, each of them with six wings, were covered with eyes inside and out.

The four living creatures do not stop exclaiming, "Holy, holy, holy is the Lord God almighty, who was, and who is, and who is to come."

Whenever the living creatures give glory and honor and thanks to the one who sits on the throne, the twenty-four elders fall down and worship him, who lives forever and ever. They throw down their crowns before the throne, exclaiming, "Worthy are you, Lord our God, to receive glory and honor and power, for you created all things; because of your will they came to be and were created."

Based on Revelation 4:1–11

Vision of Heavenly Worship

The Church: A Community of Love

All Scripture is a **revelation** because it was written under the inspiration of the Holy Spirit and tells an important truth about God. To understand the truth that is being revealed in this Scripture passage we must first explore the meaning of the symbols and images used. The twenty-four elders represent the twelve tribes of Israel from the Old Testament and the Twelve Apostles from the New Testament. The four living creatures represent all creation and are covered with eyes to indicate God's concern for his creation. The use of the sparkling jewels shows the majesty of God as he sits on the throne. To describe God's presence and divine power, John uses the familiar Old Testament symbols of lightning and thunder. The seven spirits refer to the Holy Spirit who inspires and guides the Church.

The elders and the creatures represent a perfect community of faith. They are united in their love for God, who reigns over heaven and earth. Together, they praise and worship the Lord. What Christ entrusted to the apostles they, in turn, handed down by their preaching and writing, under the inspiration of the Holy Spirit. While this passage was written for the Christians of the first century, its message is relevant to the Church today. John produced an image of what the Church should be: a community of love whose purpose is to glorify God. The vision shows what happens when people allow the Holy Spirit to guide them in their faith. If we stand firm in our beliefs, we can live good Christian lives.

How Christians Live

We learn about Christian life from the apostles, who witnessed firsthand Jesus' love for God and neighbor. The apostles, commissioned to do Christ's work, were guided by the Holy Spirit in passing on Jesus' message of love. When God sends his Son, he sends the Holy Spirit. The Holy Spirit continually reveals Christ's truth in the Church and will do so until Christ returns at the end of time.

As Christians we are called to glorify God in our lives and share his love with others. We first learn to praise God in our families. Parents have a responsibility to pray with their children and guide them in following Jesus. Parents should respect and encourage their children's vocations. They should help their children grow into mature disciples.

Living as Christians means that we remain close to God. Our culture often sends messages about life that can distance us from God. We must challenge our culture when it goes against living a pure and Christian life according to God's commandments.

God's love sustains us as we live our mission as Christians. In Paul's letter to the Romans, he reminded the Christian community of God's **indomitable** love. He said, "[I] am convinced that neither death, nor life, nor angels . . . nor present things, nor future things, nor powers, nor height, nor depth, nor any other creature will be able to separate us from the love of God in Christ Jesus our Lord" (Romans 8:38–39).

 pages 239–240 to learn more about the sacraments at the service of communion.

 pages 247–248 to learn more about God's commandments.

Faith Words

revelation Revelation is God's act of revealing himself and inviting us to respond with faith. A revelation is also an important truth about God, expressed under the inspiration and guidance of the Holy Spirit.

indomitable *Indomitable* means "unable to be conquered."

How can we show that we value human life?

Our Church Teaches

John's revelation of the heavenly kingdom calls us to give glory and praise to God at all times. We must respect and love all that God has created. All life comes from God. Each person is created in God's image and shares in his divine life. We honor the sanctity of life, which begins at the moment of conception. We believe that abortion is morally wrong because it denies a growing human being the right to life.

It is important that we protect human life in all stages until natural death occurs. It is seriously wrong and against the fifth commandment to commit euthanasia, the act of ending a person's life because the person is seriously suffering or ill.

Deliberately taking away someone's life is against God's law. It is our duty to defend and protect life, whether our lives or others' lives are threatened.

Respond

Mother Catherine McAuley

When people allow themselves to be open to the Holy Spirit, amazing things can happen!

Catherine McAuley lived in Dublin, Ireland, in the late 1700s. She was pretty and had a good sense of humor. She was the first of three children. Catherine was raised as a Catholic by her father, in spite of persecution by the non-Catholics in her country. From her father, she learned compassion and service for the poor. After her father died when she was just five, Catherine continued to practice her Catholic faith, even though her Protestant mother opposed it. When her mother died fifteen years later, Catherine's brother and sister went to live with Protestant relatives of their mother. Catherine chose to live with her Catholic uncle. Unfortunately, she was unable to stay there long. She soon found herself living with her brother and sister, enduring constant mocking from her relatives for her Catholic beliefs. After a year, Catherine met a Protestant couple, the Callaghans, who welcomed her into their home. They respected her Catholic values and desire to do charitable works.

When Catherine was forty, she inherited a million dollars from the Callaghans, who had converted to Catholicism because of Catherine's example of charity and spirituality. Inspired by the Holy Spirit to use the money to help others, Catherine bought some property and had a building constructed to serve as a center where poor country girls could learn trades and also learn about God. She recruited other women to help her in this service. Soon the women under Catherine's leadership formed a religious group called the Sisters of Mercy. They took religious vows and practiced daily prayer and meditation in addition to serving poor girls in need. The "Mercys," as they were called, soon had another nickname—the "walking nuns"—because they were the first Irish nuns to leave their convent to visit and care for the poor.

Mother Catherine died in 1841. In less than 100 years, the order she founded opened 140 convents. In 1990, Pope John Paul II declared her "Venerable" Mother Catherine McAuley, the first step toward declaring her a saint.

Activities

1. How did Catherine McAuley show her commitment to her Catholic Faith?

_____

_____

2. An important way that we can bring God's love to others is to pray for their needs. We may "not know how to pray as we ought," but the Holy Spirit can inspire our prayer and join us to God. We can pray for the elderly, the sick, the homeless, and for those who are abused. We can pray for environmental, social, and political concerns. It is important to make prayer a priority in our lives and to pray always.

Centering prayer is one special way of praying that prepares us to rest in God's presence. Follow these steps to spend some quiet time with God.

1. Relax your body by shaking out the stress in your hands, arms, feet, and legs. Yawning may also help relieve you of any stress.

2. Close your eyes and sit in a comfortable position.

3. Become aware of your breathing as you inhale and exhale. Say silently, "I am breathing in, I am breathing out." Breathe in deeply and breathe out slowly.

4. As you breathe in, think of God's love within you. As you breathe out, let go of your frustrations, worries, disappointments, anger, or sadness. Give them over to God.

5. Think of God responding to you by recalling a verse from Scripture. Repeat in your thoughts how much God loves you.

6. Pray, "Here is my heart, O God; here it is with all its secrets" (based on words by Saint Augustine).

As members of the Church, we pray that the Holy Spirit will guide us in loving others as Jesus did. The good work we do daily in our vocation as students and as family members can also be our prayer to God. We also pray that the Holy Spirit will lead the Church in bringing God's love to the world.

How can we pray as a community for the needs of others?

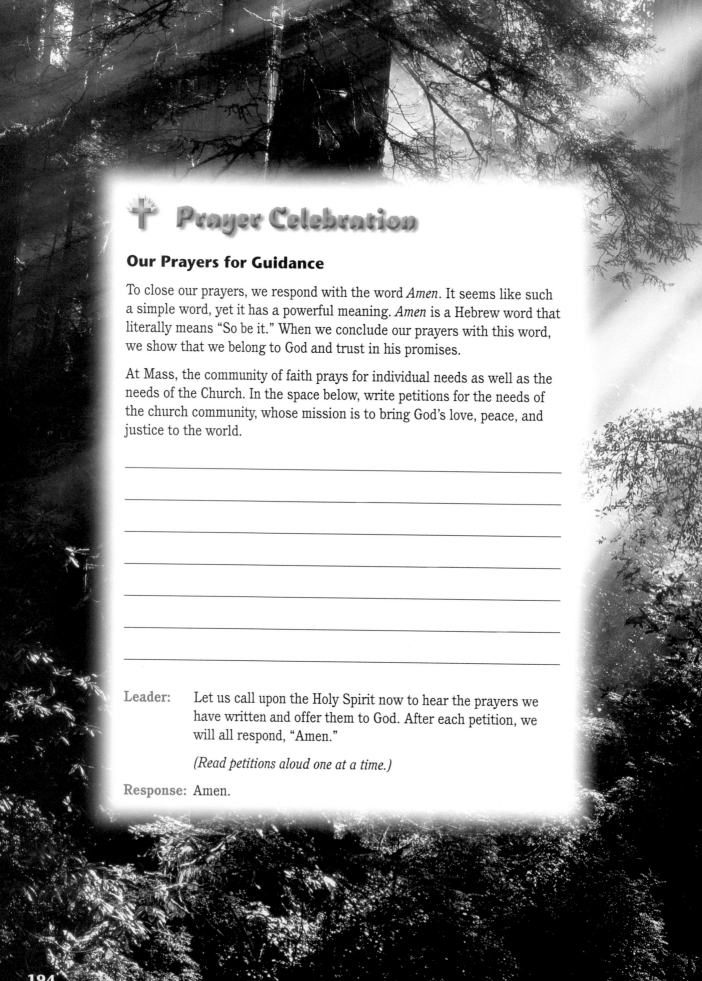

✝ Prayer Celebration

Our Prayers for Guidance

To close our prayers, we respond with the word *Amen*. It seems like such a simple word, yet it has a powerful meaning. *Amen* is a Hebrew word that literally means "So be it." When we conclude our prayers with this word, we show that we belong to God and trust in his promises.

At Mass, the community of faith prays for individual needs as well as the needs of the Church. In the space below, write petitions for the needs of the church community, whose mission is to bring God's love, peace, and justice to the world.

_____

_____

_____

_____

_____

_____

_____

Leader: Let us call upon the Holy Spirit now to hear the prayers we have written and offer them to God. After each petition, we will all respond, "Amen."

(Read petitions aloud one at a time.)

Response: Amen.

WE CARE *About the World*

Unfair Labor

An eighteen-year-old woman in China earns only 25 cents an hour to make clothes for a major department store in America. She works twelve hours a day. Her employers will not let her stop to use the restroom.

The type of factory that employs this woman is called a sweatshop. A sweatshop is a workplace where employees are mistreated. Sweatshops are unsafe places, with poor lighting and ventilation. Sweatshop employees work long hours, face hazardous conditions, and are denied basic rights. They are not paid fair wages. In El Salvador, some sweatshop workers do not even earn one-fifth of the amount of money they need to support themselves. Some sweatshops even employ young people who are much younger than you are.

Believe it or not, the clothes you wear and the products you use each day may have been made under such conditions. Some big-name stores in the United States sell clothing and other products that were manufactured in sweatshops. Because the United States has a higher minimum wage than other countries do and also has laws against sweatshops and child labor, many companies run their sweatshops in foreign countries. The big corporation owners claim that sweatshops make their products more affordable. They say that if the workers in sweatshops made more money, consumers would have to pay more for their products. But the true reason the corporations do not pay fair wages is that they are seeking bigger profits.

At a parish in Pennsylvania, a committee contacted the companies that supplied the parish with uniforms and other supplies. The committee found out where the products were manufactured and called the manufacturers to ask how the products were made. The names of companies whose products were made in sweatshops were compiled into a list. Then, using www.greenpages.org, the committee searched for area businesses that did not mistreat workers. The pastor and the school principal created buying guidelines. They urged parish buyers to boycott, or stop buying, products from the companies that ran sweatshops and to support companies who treated their workers fairly.

How can boycotting sweatshops help stop the mistreatment of workers?

Think About It

Even if we buy things from companies with unjust labor practices without realizing it, we help the injustice to continue. We must stay informed.

Would you still want your sneakers if you knew a young child who worked 12 hours a day for 13 cents an hours made them?

Yes   No   · Don't know

Which is better? (Circle one.)

being able to buy cheaper products, even if they were made in sweatshops

paying higher prices for products made by workers who were treated fairly

Learn About It

The Church teaches that every worker has a right to fair wages and safe working conditions. As human beings created by God, all workers have a right to be treated with respect. Workers in sweatshops are simply taken advantage of.

Many companies agree with the Church's teaching and try to treat workers justly. Other companies are only interested in making a profit and don't care about their employees and whether their needs are met.

Young people at universities often pressure big clothing companies to stop mistreating their workers. They hold marches and boycott the purchase of university sweatshirts and baseball caps. They write letters to the heads of companies. Their actions have had positive results. For example, many companies have revealed the names and locations of their factories or investigated reports of the abuse of their workers.

Do Something About It

The illustrations show three products that are often produced in sweatshops. Inside each one, write something you might do to help sweatshop workers.

Organizer

Draw a line to connect the beginning of each sentence to its correct ending.

1. As the bishop anoints the candidates, he prays,

2. We evangelize when we

spread the truth of the Gospels.

the disciples went forth and preached the good news of Jesus Christ to the people in Jerusalem.

to glorify God in our lives and share his love with others.

"Be sealed with the gift of the Holy Spirit."

3. Empowered by the Holy Spirit,

4. As Christians, we are called

A Fill in the remaining letters of the word or words that correctly complete each sentence.

1. The Christian community was born on the day of

   P _____, when the disciples were filled with the

   H _____ S _____ .

2. Saint P _____ brought the good news to C _____.

3. Today the p _____ and b _____ have the

   same role as the apostles in proclaiming the G _____.

4. Elizabeth Ann Seton was the first native-born American to be

   c _____ .

B Unscramble the letters and write the words on the lines. Use the clues to help you.

1. (MBTIPAS) _____, (FMICRIANOTNO)

   _____, and (LOHY DRORES) _____

   Clue: sacraments received only once

2. (MOWSID) _____

   Clue: helps us know how God wants us to live

3. (EVERRNECE) _____

   Clue: helps us love God more than anything else

4. (THRGI MUJEGNTD) _____

   Clue: helps us make good decisions

5. (TNONAI) _____

   Clue: to consecrate with holy oil

C Circle the letter of the correct answer.

1. Saint Paul proclaimed the word of God by

    a. building ships.

    b. writing letters to specific Christian communities.

    c. writing letters to the pope and bishops.

2. The family is often called the

    a. domestic church.

    b. rock of salvation.

    c. place of the heart.

3. Sojourner Truth defended the abolition of slavery and women's rights by

    a. writing to the governor of Alabama.

    b. making powerful speeches.

    c. marrying a slave.

D Complete the sentences by selecting the correct words from the box below.

Testament	glorify	share	enemies
Revelation	symbolism	Mercy	

1. Saint John wrote the Book of _____, the last book of the

    New _____.

2. Saint John kept his message hidden from the _____ of the

    Church by using imagery and _____.

3. As Christians, we are called to _____ God in our lives

    and _____ his love with others.

4. Mother Catherine McAuley formed a religious group called the Sisters

    of _____.

E Match the Faith Words in Column 1 with the definitions in Column 2.

Column 1	Column 2
a. revelation	**1.** ____ God's act of revealing himself and inviting us to respond with faith
b. epistle	**2.** ____ a person who shares his or her faith through preaching and charitable works
c. commissioned	**3.** ____ a person who proclaims God to the world by word of mouth, through writings, or as a living example
d. evangelist	**4.** ____ the unity we share with all our brothers and sisters, who are made in the image of God
e. gifts of the Holy Spirit	**5.** ____ a word meaning "unable to be conquered"
f. witness	**6.** ____ entrusted with the power to fulfill a particular task
g. evangelize	**7.** ____ a sacrament of initiation in which we receive the special strength of the Holy Spirit and become full members of the Church
h. Catholic epistles	**8.** ____ to spread the truth of the Gospels through our own words and love of others
i. indomitable	**9.** ____ a letter written to a Christian community by Saint Paul or another disciple in the early Church
j. missioner	**10.** ____ an attesting to the truth of something by words or actions
k. solidarity	**11.** ____ seven special gifts or blessings that enable us to become more Christlike
l. Confirmation	**12.** ____ letters written to the universal Church

F Name the seven gifts of the Holy Spirit.

_____

_____

_____

_____

_____

FEASTS
AND SEASONS

The Liturgical Year

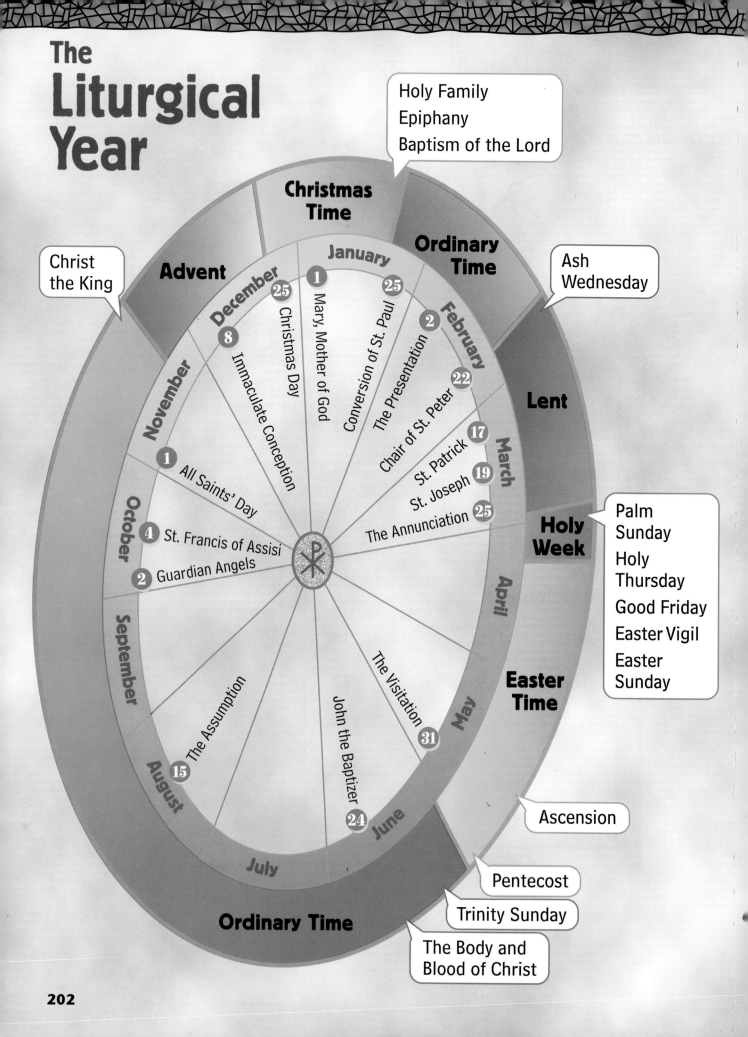

Holy Family
Epiphany
Baptism of the Lord

Christ the King

Ash Wednesday

Palm Sunday
Holy Thursday
Good Friday
Easter Vigil
Easter Sunday

Ascension

Pentecost

Trinity Sunday

The Body and Blood of Christ

Christmas Time

Ordinary Time

Advent

Lent

Holy Week

Easter Time

Ordinary Time

December
November
October
September
August
July
June
May
April
March
February
January

25 Christmas Day
8 Immaculate Conception
1 Mary, Mother of God
Conversion of St. Paul 25
The Presentation 2
Chair of St. Peter 22
St. Patrick 17
St. Joseph 19
The Annunciation 25

1 All Saints' Day
4 St. Francis of Assisi
2 Guardian Angels

The Assumption 15
John the Baptizer 24
The Visitation 31

Advent

There was no room for them in the inn.

Luke 2:7

Making Room in Our Lives for God

Let's face it: Life is busy. Who has spare time to do anything after homework, sports or club meetings, e-mailing, or meeting with friends? Sometimes when we try to fit everything in, we end up having to leave certain things out. What often goes first is prayer. We become so busy that we no longer have time for God.

During Advent, we have an opportunity to think over our priorities. What is most important in our lives? Do we stop to think about the real meaning of Christmas? For whom and what do we need to make room in our schedules? Preparing for Christmas is not about shopping, wrapping presents, going to parties, or decorating the Christmas tree. It is about making room in our lives for God through personal prayer. It is about taking time to open our minds and hearts to the true meaning of Christmas—remembering the birth of Jesus, celebrating God's presence in our lives now, and anticipating Jesus' Second Coming.

Activity

Jesus wants us to make room for him in our hearts. On each door below, write one way you can open your heart to Christ this Advent season.

Celebrating Advent

The Gospel of Luke tells us that Mary and Joseph had to travel to Bethlehem to take part in a government census. When they reached Bethlehem, Mary's time came to deliver her child. There was no room at the inn, so Mary gave birth to Jesus in a stable. She wrapped him in strips of cloth and laid him in a manger.

Many Hispanic Catholics recall this Scripture story of the journey of Mary and Joseph with a musical reenactment called *La Posada. Posada* means "inn." For nine nights, friends gather around a costumed "Mary" and "Joseph," who go from house to house, asking for a place to stay. Continually, the "innkeepers" tell them there is no room.

On Christmas Eve, the last night of La Posada, an innkeeper welcomes them. There is a fiesta, or party, for all the participants. Later, the costumed Mary and Joseph and all the people go to church to celebrate Midnight Mass. There are joyful songs and, afterwards, delicious food. Children take turns trying to break open a piñata, or hanging ornament, to get to the candies and coins inside.

There are many ways we can welcome Jesus into our hearts during Advent. We can pray each day. We can read and reflect on the Scripture readings from each Sunday's Mass. We can be patient with family members and friends. We can listen to them and love them with generous and grateful hearts.

Lord our God,
help us to prepare
for the coming of
Christ your Son.
May he find us waiting,
eager in joyful prayer.
Amen.

From the Roman Missal

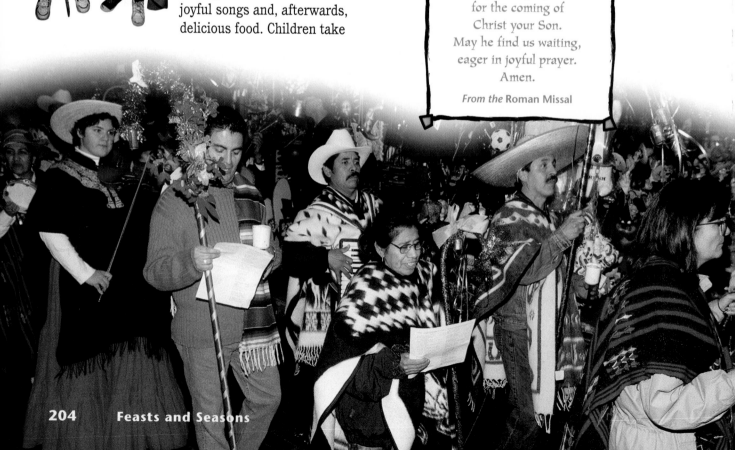

Christmas

The people who walked in darkness have seen a great light.

Isaiah 9:1

The Importance of Light

Without light, there would be no life on our earth. Light is an invaluable resource. For Christians, light symbolizes Christ. Christmas is a celebration of light. It is a celebration of the coming of Christ, our Light, into the world. He is the Light who guides us and shows us the way to eternal life.

Activity

Celebrating Christmas would not be the same without lights. Here are a few popular Christmas light traditions. Match the tradition with the correct definition.

Christmas tree lights	used by Irish immigrants to symbolically light the way for Mary and Joseph on their journey to Bethlehem
Christmas candle	the fifth candle placed in an Advent wreath to represent the birth of Jesus, the Light of the World
Window lights	candles in paper sacks filled with sand placed on sidewalks or outside churches to symbolically light the way for Mary, Joseph, and the Christ child
Luminaries	an ancient Scandinavian practice of lighting a bonfire to honor the winter solstice, which was adapted by Christians
Yule log	nineteenth-century Germans were the first to decorate fir trees with them

How has Jesus been a source of light in your life?

_____

_____

Christ, Our Light

Light represents joy, purity, beauty, festivity, and goodness. Christianity associates light with God. This association is made throughout Scripture in both the Old Testament and New Testament. The Christmas liturgy centers on the divine Light coming into the world. The Light of Christ dispels the darkness of sin and religious ignorance. At the celebration of Midnight Mass on December 24, 2000, Pope John Paul II proclaimed Christmas to be a celebration of light and a festival of life. Jesus, he said, was "born in a stable, and, coming among us, he kindles in the world the fire of God's love. This fire will not be quenched ever again." Christmas is a time of giving, a time of bringing light and hope to others. The Holy Father continued, "May this fire burn in our hearts as a flame of charity in action, showing itself in openness to and support of our many brothers and sisters sorely tried by want and suffering!"

Father, we are filled with the new light by the coming of your Word among us. May the light of faith shine in our words and actions. Amen.

From the Roman Missal

Lent

Elijah ate and drank and then strengthened by the food, he walked forty days and forty nights to the mountain of God, Horeb.

Based on 1 Kings 19:8

A Rewarding Journey

The forty days of Lent, which begins on Ash Wednesday and ends when the evening liturgy begins on Holy Thursday, have been compared to a long journey. On a spiritual level, we retrace the steps of the Israelites, who spent forty years wandering in the desert trying to escape from slavery and find a new life. We walk in the path of the prophet Elijah, who called people to change their lives by developing a personal relationship with God.

We accompany Jesus into the desert, where he fasted and was tempted for forty days. We begin our journey when we receive ashes on Ash Wednesday. The use of ashes was an ancient Hebrew penitential practice. Today, the ashes emphasize Lent as a time to turn away from sin and be faithful to the Gospel. During Lent, we prepare our hearts for the celebration of Easter, by praying more faithfully, doing more charitable acts, fasting, and abstaining from meat on Fridays. We share what we have with people in need. We sacrifice and make amends for our sins. We receive the sacrament of Reconciliation and examine our lives.

The journey of Lent may seem long, but we do not travel alone. Jesus and the Christian community walk with us, and the Feast of the Eucharist continually strengthens us. Our spiritual journey of Lent also has a reward. We travel from the slavery of sin to the freedom of being God's children.

Activity

On the lines below, write your answers to the following questions.

Where do you want to journey spiritually this Lenten season?

_____

_____

What will you have to do or change to complete this journey?

_____

_____

The Journey Toward Easter

Catechumens are people who are in the process of becoming members of the Catholic Church. Throughout Lent the Catholic community journeys with the catechumens as they prepare to receive the sacraments of initiation—Baptism, Confirmation, and Eucharist. The catechumens learn about the Catholic faith and become ready for the final phase of preparation for celebrating the sacraments at the Easter Vigil service.

During Lent the Church marks four special times in this final phase of the catechumens' journey.

• *The Rite of Election.* This ritual takes place after the homily at Mass on the first Sunday of Lent. The godparents and sponsors testify on behalf of the readiness of the catechumens to be admitted into the Church. The catechumens state their wish to become church members. Then they write their names in the *Book of Enrollment.*

St. Photini at Jacob's Well by the Holy Transfiguration Monastery

• *The First Scrutiny.* A scrutiny is like an examination of conscience. This ritual takes place on the third Sunday of Lent. The Church prays that Jesus, the Word of God, may change the catechumens' lives, just as he changed the life of the Samaritan woman at the well. (See John 4:4–42.) The catechumens reflect on how Jesus has been living water in their lives.

• *The Second Scrutiny.* This occurs on the fourth Sunday of Lent. The Church prays that God may enlighten the catechumens, just as Jesus gave sight to the man born blind. (See John 9:1–41.) The catechumens reflect on how Jesus has been the light in their darkness.

• *The Third Scrutiny.* This ritual takes place on the fifth Sunday of Lent. The Church prays that the catechumens may receive new life in Christ, just as Lazarus did when Jesus raised him from the dead. (See John 11:1–44.) The catechumens reflect on how Jesus saves them from sin and death.

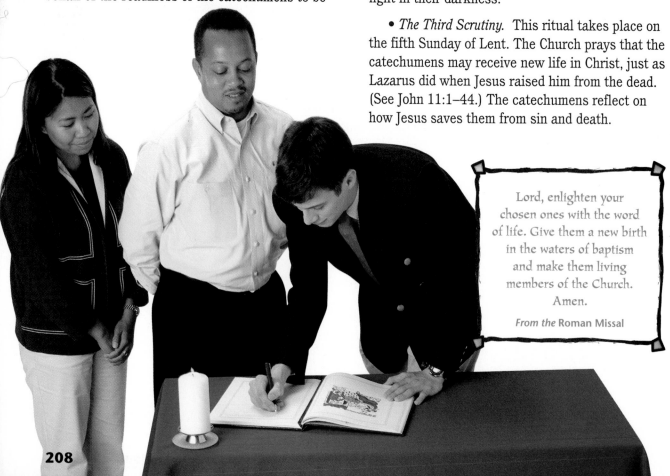

Lord, enlighten your chosen ones with the word of life. Give them a new birth in the waters of baptism and make them living members of the Church. Amen.

From the Roman Missal

Holy Week

I give you a new commandment: love one another.
As I have loved you, so you also should love one another.

John 13:34

True Love

Movies and TV shows often portray love as romantic and thrilling. They make love look as if it were easy and its sole purpose were to satisfy our own needs. Jesus' definition of love is radically different. For Jesus, love means being totally generous and unselfish. It means "going the extra mile" for others and not counting the cost of our self-sacrifice and not expecting anything in return.

Generosity, humility, and self-sacrifice are the components of Christian love. Such love is not marked by sweet words or occasional gifts. It is a day-to-day giving of oneself that does not favor one person over another but reaches out to everyone. An important form of this love is serving others.

The foot-washing ritual at the Holy Thursday liturgy reminds us that God calls all Christians to a life of service. We are to serve family members, friends, classmates, neighbors, and even strangers.

Activity

Think about someone in each of the following categories. Then write a practical way you could serve each person with generosity and humility.

Family Members _____

Friends _____

Classmates _____

Neighbors _____

Strangers _____

Holy Thursday

Although every Mass remembers and celebrates the Last Supper, the Holy Thursday liturgy celebrates the Last Supper and the institution of the Eucharist in a special way. Holy Thursday begins the Easter Triduum, the celebration of Christ's Passover from death to new life. During the Easter Triduum, the period from the sundown of one night to the sundown of the next night is considered one day. Thus, there are three days in the Easter Triduum, as follows.

Day 1: sundown on Holy Thursday to sundown on Good Friday

Day 2: sundown on Good Friday to sundown on Holy Saturday

Day 3: sundown on Holy Saturday to sundown on Easter Sunday

The liturgy of Holy Thursday, which takes place after sundown, is called "the Mass of the Lord's Supper." At this Mass we remember two events that took place at the Last Supper: Jesus' washing of the feet of his disciples (John 13:1–15) and Jesus' giving of the Eucharist (Matthew 26:26–30).

Since the fifth century, the Church has included a foot-washing ceremony in the Holy Thursday liturgy. The priest, in imitation of Jesus, washes the feet of twelve or more people chosen from the assembly. This ritual demonstrates the humility of Jesus and reminds us of our own call to serve others as he did.

On Holy Thursday, to emphasize the importance of the eucharistic liturgy in Christian life, festive colors are worn by the priest and seen in the church. Bells ring joyfully throughout the Gloria, our hymn of praise to God, which is sung for the first time since before Lent. The tabernacle, which holds the consecrated hosts, is emptied on Holy Thursday. The communion bread received by the faithful at this Mass must be consecrated during it. Enough hosts are consecrated for the Good Friday liturgy, during which there is no consecration.

Almighty God,
we receive new life from
the supper your Son
gave us in this world.
May we find full
contentment in the meal
we hope to share in
your eternal kingdom.
Amen.

From the **Roman Missal**

Easter

All you who are thirsty, /come to the water!
Come to me heedfully, /listen, that you may have life.

Isaiah 55:1, 3

Water and Life

Water is an essential ingredient for life. Did you know that the human body is 90 percent water? Without water, living things would soon wither and die. Wherever there is water, there is the potential for life.

Indeed, water is a powerful symbol of life. Throughout the Easter season the Church uses water to remind us of the new life Jesus won for us through his Resurrection. Just as Jesus died and was raised from the dead, so the Easter liturgy bids us to die to sin and rise from the waters of Baptism to new life with God.

Activity

Read or recall the following Bible stories. What does water symbolize in each story?

The Great Flood _____

_____

_____

Crossing the Red Sea _____

_____

_____

The Baptism of Jesus _____

_____

_____

Easter Holy Water

The word *Easter* means "fullness of spring." Just as nature abounds with new life each spring, so the Church celebrates spiritual rebirth during the Easter season. We rejoice in the Resurrection of Jesus, as well as our own baptism. Both events are connected; both mark a passage to new life.

We are continually reminded of our baptism throughout Easter. At Masses during the Easter season, the priest leads the people in a renewal of their baptismal vows. The assembly repeats promises to reject sin and to live as children of God. Water is blessed in an elaborate ritual at the Easter Vigil. This water is used to baptize catechumens and to fill holy water fonts at church entrances. It is also used in the sprinkling rite that replaces the Penitential Rite at Masses during this season. The priest walks throughout the church, blessing the people with the new Easter water.

They, in turn, make the Sign of the Cross. Often people bottle this holy water and use it to bless their families and homes.

Easter is a time in which we historically commemorate Christ's death and Resurrection. But more important, it is a time in which we celebrate our life in the Church, our life in Christ gained for us by his Paschal sacrifice. Easter is a celebration of Christ's Resurrection and of our redemption, and an invitation to renew our lives as children of God.

God our Father,
by raising Christ your Son
you conquered the power
of death and opened for us
the way to eternal life.
Let our celebration today
raise us up and renew
our lives by the
Spirit that is within us.
Amen.

From the Roman Missal

Holy Days

I, the Lord, am with you always, until the end of the world.

Based on Matthew 28:20

Seeing with the Eyes of Faith

You've probably heard the saying "Seeing is believing." This saying suggests that we can only trust someone's words when we see him or her putting them into action. The Feast of the Ascension calls us to another type of seeing. It calls us to see reality through the eyes of faith.

According to the Bible, the risen Jesus spent forty days on earth with his disciples. Then he was lifted up to heaven to be with God forever. We do not know exactly what happened at the Ascension, but we do know that from that point on the disciples experienced a new relationship with Jesus. They could no longer see him with human eyes, but they believed that he was always with them.

Seeing with the eyes of faith is a daily challenge. We cannot see Jesus with our eyes, but we can "see" his faithful presence in many different ways—in the Church's sacraments and liturgy, in our relationships, and in the beauty of nature.

Activity

Think about people you know who have moved or died, and how their presence is still with you. Then answer the following questions.

Imagine that a friend tells you he doesn't believe in Jesus because he can't see him. How would you respond?

_____

_____

When have you felt that Jesus was truly with you?

_____

_____

The Ascension

On the Feast of the Ascension, we celebrate our belief that the risen Jesus was raised up to God. As Saint Mark's Gospel says, "So then the Lord Jesus, after he spoke to them, was taken up into heaven and took his seat at the right hand of God" (Mark 16:19). Jesus' Ascension is central to the Paschal mystery. Through his Passion, death, Resurrection, and Ascension, Jesus destroyed our death, restored our life, and gained salvation for us.

In the early Church, the Ascension and Pentecost probably were celebrated together. In the late fourth century, the two feasts were separated. The Church began to celebrate the Ascension on the fortieth day after Easter, when the apostles were commissioned to preach the good news. Pentecost was celebrated on the fiftieth day, when the apostles actually went out and began to spread the good news. The days between the Ascension and Pentecost were known as Ascensiontide or the Pentecost Novena. They were nine days of preparation for the coming of the Holy Spirit. The Ascension is a holy day of obligation in the Church.

The Ascension of Christ took on different meaning for Jesus' followers. For John, the Ascension helped emphasize that Jesus' death and Resurrection led to our salvation. The Ascension is a reminder of all of the saving graces that came from Jesus' suffering. For Paul, the Ascension is a reminder of how humanity became united with God and was saved forever. Because Jesus was human, his Ascension meant that our human nature was raised up to God, where together with Christ we are saved. The Ascension not only marks the

The Ascension by Giotto DiBondone

moment in which Christ physically departed from the earth, but it marks the beginning of a new presence of God in the life of every believer. This new presence is the fullness of his Holy Spirit. As the disciples were commissioned to preach the good news at the Ascension, we too are reminded of Christ's presence fully alive in our hearts and our call to respond to his love.

God our Father, make us joyful in the ascension of your Son, Jesus Christ. May we follow him into the new creation, for his ascension is our glory and our hope. Amen.

From the Roman Missal

Mary

 Creation awaits with eager expectation the revelation of the children of God.

Romans 8:19

VIPs and Their Agents

In today's society, VIPs (very important persons) tend to be movie stars, rock musicians, top athletes, or best-selling authors. These people are so famous and busy that they hire agents to care for their business needs—to promote their names, to get them jobs, and to negotiate the best possible deals.

In God's eyes, each one of us is a VIP. We are God's own children. And each one of us has an agent! That agent is Mary, the mother of Jesus. Like any good mother, Mary is always ready to "promote" us and stand by our side. Mary loves us and intercedes for us before God. She asks her Son to protect us and to care for all our needs.

Activity

Think about yourself as a VIP. Then answer the following questions.

1. Explain why you are a VIP in God's eyes.

   _____

2. How can you use your talents or abilities to help others?

   _____

   _____

3. Write a prayer request for which you would like Mary to intercede.

   _____

   _____

The Mother of God

The New Testament tells us that Mary was the mother of Jesus, the wife of Joseph, and a relative of Elizabeth. The New Testament also gives us some important clues about Mary's values and relationships.

- Mary was kind and generous and a good friend. When she found out that her elderly relative Elizabeth was pregnant, she went at once to help. (See Luke 1:39–56.)

- Mary was obedient to the Jewish religious laws and customs of the day. After childbirth, she presented Jesus at the Temple and offered the prescribed sacrifice for her purification. (See Luke 2:22–39.)

- Mary was a responsible and loving mother. She traveled for three days to search for her lost son. (See Luke 2:41–52.) Mary was present at Jesus' crucifixion when others abandoned him. (See John 19:25–27.)

Filled with God's grace, Mary was conceived without original sin and remained free of sin for life. This is called the Immaculate Conception and is celebrated on December 8. Mary is the virgin mother of God, remaining a virgin in giving birth to Jesus and throughout her life. Her faith helped her to accept her unique role in God's plan for redemption. Because Mary is Jesus' mother, she can speak to him as no one else can. He listens to her, as he did at the Wedding Feast of Cana (see John 2:1–11). On January 1 the Church celebrates the Feast of Mary, Mother of God. On this day we celebrate Mary's unique role as mother of the Savior. We also celebrate her role as our mother and intercessor. We pray to Mary, asking her to talk to Jesus on our behalf. We ask Mary to help us grow as God's children.

God our Father, may we always profit by the prayers of the Virgin Mother Mary, for you bring us life and salvation through Jesus Christ her Son. Amen.

From the **Roman Missal**

This young person is placing a crown of flowers on a statue of Mary at a celebration of the May Crowning.

Saints

You have not chosen me, I have chosen you.
Go and bear fruit that will last.

Based on John 15:16

Sharing the Good News

To evangelize means to tell others the good news of Jesus Christ. The apostles were the first evangelists. They knew Christ personally, and they knew and lived his message. Because the apostles believed in Jesus and lived by his truths, they were called to go forth and evangelize the world. We too are called by God to live the Gospel message and bring Christ to all we meet.

Activity

Imagine that your parish has invited you to evangelize about Jesus and the Gospel message to your peers at school. How would you go about bringing Jesus and his message to them? Explain your strategy on the lines below and tell why you think it would be effective.

_____

_____

_____

_____

_____

_____

_____

_____

_____

The Twelve Apostles

The word *apostle* means "one sent forth on a mission." Jesus chose Twelve Apostles. Their mission was to "make disciples of all nations, baptizing them in the name of the Father, and of the Son, and of the holy Spirit" (Matthew 28:19). Jesus founded his Church with these apostles. That is why we say the Church is "apostolic."

The Gospels of Matthew and Mark list the following names of the apostles: Simon (Peter), Andrew, James, John, Philip, Bartholomew, Thomas, Matthew, James, Thaddeus, Simon, and Judas Iscariot (see Matthew 10:2–4 and Mark 3:16–19). The Gospel of Luke and the Acts of the Apostles substitute Jude for Thaddeus (see Luke 6:13–16 and Acts 1:13). After the death of Judas Iscariot, who betrayed Jesus, the apostles elected Matthias to take his place (see Acts 1:26). Later, Paul became known as an apostle too because of his work for Christ.

The Western Church officially honors the apostles on the following days:

January 25	Conversion of Paul
February 22	Chair of Peter
May 3	Philip and James
May 14	Matthias
June 29	Peter and Paul
July 3	Thomas
July 25	James
August 24	Bartholomew
September 21	Matthew
October 28	Simon and Jude
November 30	Andrew
December 27	John

The apostles were not perfect, but they did show great courage and persistence in sharing the good news of Jesus Christ with the world. According to tradition, all of the apostles except John were martyred for their faith in Jesus.

Christ Washing the Disciples' Feet by Adrian Kupman

Lord,
give your Church the constant joy of honoring the holy apostles. May we continue to be guided and governed by those leaders whose teaching and example have been our inspiration.
Amen.

From the Roman Missal

Holy People

Let the children come to me; do not prevent them, for the kingdom of God belongs to such as these. Amen, I say to you, whoever does not accept the kingdom of God like a child will not enter it.

Mark 10:14–15

What Is Really Important?

Much of today's society is based on survival of the fittest. We see people compete against one another to be the best, the richest, the smartest, or the most powerful. Making money, wearing designer clothes, buying fancy cars and big houses—our culture counts these as important.

The Gospel tells us something very different. Jesus tells us that to enter his kingdom, we must become like children. If we want to spend eternity with God, we must have the qualities of a little child. When we observe little children, we see that they are full of love, playful, trusting, and gentle. When we exhibit these and other childlike qualities, we show God's goodness to others and point the way to God's kingdom.

Activity

Choose a childlike quality that you would like to develop. Then, on the lines below, write a letter to Jesus asking for his help in developing this quality.

_____

_____

_____

_____

Jean Vanier

This Roman Catholic layman never married or had children. Yet he probably knows more about childlike qualities than most people in today's society. Jean Vanier learned the value of these qualities, not through higher education or worldly financial success, but from day-to-day living with developmentally disabled people.

Jean Vanier is the son of General Georges P. Vanier, who was Canada's first French-Canadian governor general (1959–1967). Jean Vanier served both the British navy and the Canadian navy during World War II. After resigning his commission in 1950, Jean Vanier returned to school and earned a doctorate in philosophy. He began teaching at St. Michael's College at the University of Toronto, but he felt that something was still missing from his life.

In 1964, at the age of 35, Vanier moved to Trosly-Breuil, a small village outside Paris, France. There he joined his spiritual mentor, Father Thomas Philippe, a chaplain at a residence for men with developmental disabilities. Vanier soon bought a house, which he named L'Arche (The Ark), and invited two men with disabilities to live with him.

"I began to find the child in myself," he later wrote. "I was never so happy as when I was living with them in a little house, working together, having fun together, praying together." With these developmentally disabled men, Vanier discovered his mission in life—he would focus on sweeping away barriers between disabled people and the rest of the world.

To date, Vanier has founded more than 117 L'Arche communities in 30 countries, including 25 in Canada and 13 in the United States. These communities are rooted in Roman Catholic tradition but have become interfaith "families" made up of developmentally disabled people, their caretakers, and staff members.

In 1989, Vanier was received into the Order of Canada for his work with developmentally disabled people. In 1997 he won the Vatican's Paul VI International Prize and used the $168,000 award to expand L'Arche into Eastern Europe. Despite his fame, Vanier remains a simple and humble man. He is an example to everyone of the importance of finding the "child within."

> Father,
> keep before us the
> wisdom and love you have
> revealed in your Son.
> Help us to be like him
> in word and deed.
> Amen.
>
> *From the* Roman Missal

OUR CATHOLIC TEACHINGS

What Catholics Believe

We share a common faith based on Sacred Scripture and on the Tradition of the Church founded on the teachings of the apostles. Guided by the Holy Spirit, the Church teaches the authentic message of Jesus Christ.

How Catholics Worship

We celebrate our faith in worship when we give honor and praise to God. Worship is so important for us that the Church calls it the first "work" of God's people. The official public worship of the Church is called liturgy.

How Catholics Live

Living as Jesus taught us is not easy, but God gives us lots of help. Our conscience and other special gifts help us. When we turn away from sin and make good choices, we live as children of God.

How Catholics Pray

When we pray, we express our faith in God. We can pray privately. We can also pray with others in the church community when we gather for worship.

Doctrine Review

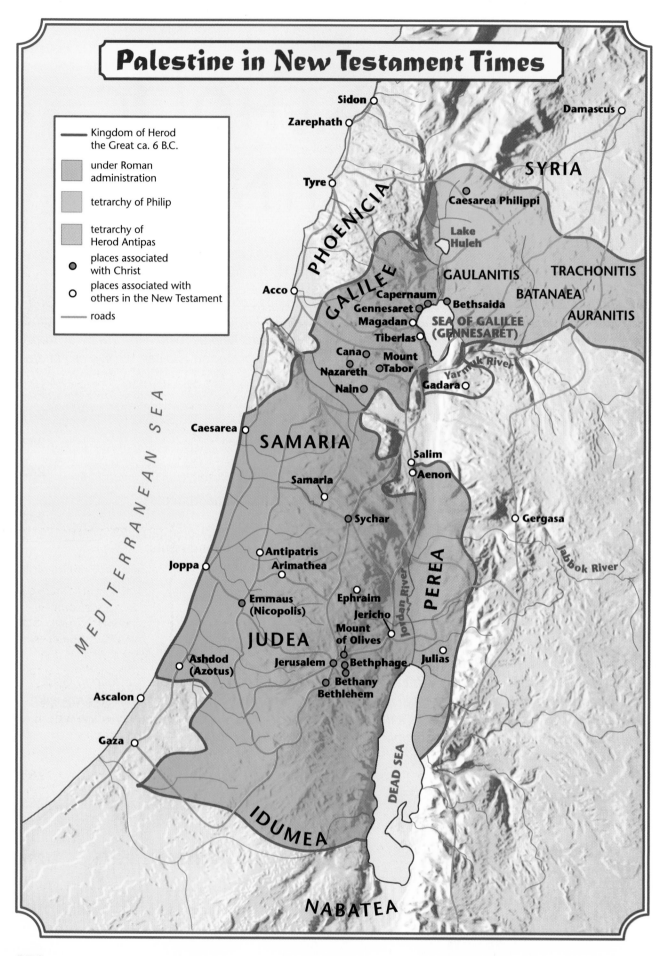

Palestine in New Testament Times

Kingdom of Herod the Great ca. 6 B.C.

under Roman administration

tetrarchy of Philip

tetrarchy of Herod Antipas

● places associated with Christ

○ places associated with others in the New Testament

roads

Sidon

Zarephath

Damascus

SYRIA

Tyre

PHOENICIA

Caesarea Philippi

Lake Huleh

Acco

GALILEE

GAULANITIS

TRACHONITIS

Capernaum

Bethsaida

BATANAEA

Gennesaret

Magadan

SEA OF GALILEE (GENNESARET)

AURANITIS

Tiberias

Cana

Mount Tabor

Yarmuk River

Nazareth

Nain

Gadara

Caesarea

SAMARIA

Salim

Aenon

Samaria

Gergasa

Sychar

Jabbok River

Antipatris

Arimathea

PEREA

Joppa

MEDITERRANEAN SEA

Emmaus (Nicopolis)

Ephraim

Jericho

Jordan River

JUDEA

Mount of Olives

Ashdod (Azotus)

Jerusalem

Bethphage

Julias

Bethany

Bethlehem

Ascalon

DEAD SEA

Gaza

IDUMEA

NABATEA

Revelation

Whoever has seen me has seen the Father.

John 14:9

We believe that God created human beings so that we might live in communion with him. All human beings have a natural desire for a relationship with God. We will be fully happy only when we achieve the communion with God that he intends for us. Our experience of the wonders of creation around us and the inner voice of our own conscience help us arrive at the certainty that God in fact exists. In other words, human reason alone should be enough to convince us that God exists. By using our human reason to reflect on ourselves and the wonders of creation, we gain some knowledge of God's nature.

The Gift of Revelation

We believe that God reveals himself to us because of his love for us. Through his revelation to humanity, we are able to more fully understand who God is, who we are, and how God seeks communion with us. We get some sense of God's desire to reveal himself to us and to be with us in the Book of Genesis, where we find the story

of how God "walked" with our first parents in the Garden of Eden before they fell from grace and sought to hide themselves from him. Despite their sin, God promises to remain with and offer salvation to their descendants. Throughout the Old Testament we find the stories of how God continued to take the initiative and reveal himself to humanity through the special relationships he formed with holy people whose stories we find recorded there. God also revealed himself, his love for humanity, his mercy, and his saving power through the great events associated with the rescue of Abraham's descendants from slavery in Egypt. In a special way, God continued to reveal himself through the teachings of the great Hebrew prophets he raised up to instruct the people.

The Fullness of Revelation Resides in Jesus

We believe that it is finally in the person of Jesus that God is fully revealed. Jesus is the Son of God, who became human for us. For this reason, he is able to say to his apostle, Philip, at the Last Supper, "Whoever has seen me has seen the Father. How can you say, 'Show us the Father'? Do you not believe that I am in the Father and the Father is in me? The words that I speak to you I do not speak on my own. The Father who dwells in me is doing his works" (John 14:9–10). So, it is in the words and deeds of Jesus that we find the fullness of God's self-revelation to us.

Faith Words

Tradition Tradition is the body of official teachings, rituals, customs, and practices of the Church that have developed under the guidance of the Holy Spirit and are handed down from the apostles.

Sacred Scriptures The term *Sacred Scriptures* refers to the Old and New Testaments of the Bible, which have been accepted by the Catholic Church as the word of God written under the inspiration of the Holy Spirit.

Jesus' Revelation Entrusted to the Apostles and Church

During his life on earth, Jesus chose and specially trained those who would become his apostles. Jesus entrusted to them the mission of preserving and sharing all that he had taught about God and God's plan for humanity. The Church believes that the apostles, under the guidance of the Holy Spirit, faithfully fulfilled this mission through their preaching and inspired writings, which have come to be known as the New Testament.

To this day, the Church has had the same mission to preserve and share the truth revealed to us in and through Jesus. This truth entrusted to the Church can be found in what is called the Church's **Tradition** as well as in the **Sacred Scriptures**: the Old Testament and the New Testament. The Church's Tradition (the official teachings, rituals, customs, and practices that have developed over the centuries under the guidance of the Holy Spirit) helps us better understand the meaning of the truths found in the Sacred Scriptures. The Sacred Scriptures, on the other hand, provide the doctrinal framework within which the Church's teaching and practices develop.

That is why we rely on both Scripture and Tradition to know and understand what Jesus has revealed to us.

Sacred Scripture

The Church venerates the forty-six books of the Old Testament and the twenty-seven books of the New Testament as inspired writings, that is, as having been written under the guidance of the Holy Spirit. Though it is true that the Bible was written by human beings using their own language and experiences, it nevertheless reveals to us what God intends. It is the responsibility of the Church to determine the meaning of the truths revealed in the books of the Bible.

Of all the sacred writings, the four Gospels have a certain special place because their focus is Jesus in whom we find the fullness of God's revelation.

Activity

If you had a friend who was an atheist (a person who does not believe in the existence of God), how would you explain to that friend why you believe in God's existence? Could you do this *without making use of the Bible?*

The Trinity

Go, therefore, and make disciples of all nations, baptizing them in the name of the Father, and of the Son, and of the holy Spirit.

Matthew 28:19

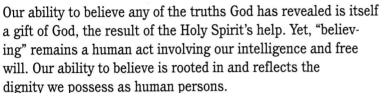

Our ability to believe any of the truths God has revealed is itself a gift of God, the result of the Holy Spirit's help. Yet, "believing" remains a human act involving our intelligence and free will. Our ability to believe is rooted in and reflects the dignity we possess as human persons.

"Believing" is also an ecclesial act, that is, an act of the Church. The Church's belief precedes our own act of believing. We depend upon the faith of the Church to call forth, support, and nourish our own personal faith.

The ultimate result of the gift of faith is that it enables us to recognize and accept God as the source and goal of our life, preferring God to all else and never treating any creatures as if they were more important to us than God.

The Mystery of the Trinity

We believe that God reveals himself to be three distinct Persons—Father, Son, and Holy Spirit—all sharing equally the divine nature. So, whatever divine qualities we can say belong to one of the divine Persons belong equally to all three divine Persons. Yet each Person remains totally distinct from the other.

We also speak of distinct relationships each of the divine Persons has with creation in general and us as human beings in particular. We speak of God the Father as our Creator (though all three divine Persons participate in creation). We speak of God the Son, having become incarnate for us, as our Savior (though all three Persons participate in our salvation). We speak of God the Holy Spirit as our Guide and Sanctifier (though all three divine Persons participate in guiding and sanctifying creation).

Creation and God the Father

In creating the universe, God acted freely, directly, and without any help. In other words, we believe that God created **ex nihilo** (from nothing). The act of creation is the Father's first revelation of his love and wisdom and of his ultimate goal, which is to establish a new creation in Christ. The many diverse creatures that God has created are each good in their own way and together are destined for the good of the human race. Human beings are ultimately destined for the glory of God by imitating Jesus, God's Son made human. God created each person with both a physical body and a spiritual soul. We believe that each person's immortal soul is created directly and personally by God.

Faith Words

ex nihilo *Ex nihilo* is a Latin phrase meaning "from nothing." It is used to describe how God created the universe.

original sin Original sin is the sin of the first man and woman, which has been passed on to all human beings. Because of it, we are weakened in our ability to resist sin and do good.

Salvation and God the Son

Our first parents originally enjoyed a state of holiness, justice, and intimate friendship with God and consequently an experience of the perfect happiness of paradise. All this was lost when, enticed by the evil one, our first parents, at the very start of history, chose to abuse their freedom and look for happiness apart from God. As a consequence of this **original sin**, human nature has been weakened. The result can be seen all around us and within us in the form of ignorance, suffering, sinful behavior, and ultimately death itself. Each of us personally inherits original sin and its consequences by being born into the human race.

Our Christian faith is based on the belief that Jesus Christ, the Second Person of the Blessed Trinity, came to rescue us from the consequences of original sin and our own personal sinfulness. Through his life, death, and Resurrection, Jesus overcame the power that sin and death held over humanity. By faith and union with Jesus, we are restored as the obedient and loving children our merciful and loving Father intended us to be. Though we cannot fully understand why physical and moral evil remains in the world, we do know that because of Christ's victory on the cross, all suffering and death will ultimately be conquered.

Sanctification and the Holy Spirit

The Holy Spirit, the Third Person of the Blessed Trinity, was sent by the Father and the Son to bring about the renewal and sanctification of humanity that was won through Jesus' death and Resurrection. The Church teaches that the Holy Spirit has been poured out upon the Body of Christ, to build it up and strengthen it. Thus, the Holy Spirit is adored as the ever-present guide and inspiration of the Church, protecting it from error and animating it to a life of ever greater unity, love, and justice.

Activity

List some of the ways other members of the Church have helped you grow in faith through their words and actions.

The Church

And so I say to you, you are Peter, and upon this rock I will build my church, and the gates of the netherworld shall not prevail against it.

Matthew 16:18

The word *church* means "convocation" or a "calling together." The Church is the assembly of people that God calls together to be nourished with the Eucharist and to become the Body of Christ. Because Christ is the head of this Body, the Church lives from him, in him, and for him.

The Church by nature has both a visible dimension and a spiritual dimension. It is formed of both a human component and a divine component, yet remains one Church. The Church is a mystery which requires the gift of faith to fully accept.

Because the Church is by its nature "one body," it reflects the unity of the Blessed Trinity: Father, Son, and Holy Spirit. The Holy Spirit, who is the soul of the the Church, is the source of its unity, as well as the source of its many gifts. For that reason the Church is often described as the Temple of the Holy Spirit.

God's Plan for the Church

Since God intends the Church to be the means for fulfilling his plan for humanity, all people are called to membership in the Church, the "new People of God." At the same time, the Church is a sacrament, or sign, of the goal of God's plan of salvation, namely the communion of God with humanity. It is God's intention that all people form one family and one People of God.

One enters the Church by means of faith and by Baptism. For that reason, we believe that non-Catholics who believe in Christ and have been baptized properly according to the tradition of the apostles also enjoy a certain although imperfect communion with the Catholic Church.

While it is true that Christ is at the center of God's plan for salvation, Catholics also believe that those who through no fault of their own have not come to know Jesus and the Church can also achieve everlasting salvation. They do this by seeking God with a sincere heart and striving to do God's will as it is revealed to them through their conscience.

Catholics believe that the Catholic Church has been given the fullness of revelation and is the fullest expression of the Church established by Jesus through the apostles. There are, nevertheless, many elements of sanctification and truth that can be found outside the structures of the Church.

Faith Words

papal infallibility
Papal infallibility is the doctrine that when the pope speaks officially for the Church on a matter of faith or morals, he is guided by the Holy Spirit and what he says is free from error.

diocese A diocese is a region or district whose parishes a bishop serves and oversees.

Overview of the Church's Organizational Structure

The Church requires organization to function and carry out its mission to the world. Jesus provided the basis for its organization by first choosing and training the Twelve Apostles and by appointing Peter as their head. Thus, the pope, the successor of Peter, is the rightful head of the visible Church and the vicar, or representative, of Jesus on earth. It is the pope's responsibility to preserve and proclaim the truth entrusted to the Church by Jesus, to preserve the unity of the Church, and to shepherd the People of God in their journey of faith and the pursuit of justice. To ensure that the pope can fulfill these important responsibilities, he is assisted by the Holy Spirit through the gift of **papal infallibility**. This means that through the Holy Spirit's guidance the pope will always be protected from error when he is called upon to officially proclaim what the Church teaches in matters of faith and morals.

As the pope provides leadership and guidance to the universal Church, the bishops, the successors of the apostles, have similar leadership responsibilities. A bishop is the chief pastor and teacher of the faith in his own **diocese**. In union with the pope, they have the duty to preserve the truth Jesus has entrusted to the Church and to provide moral guidance. Bishops are assisted in carrying out these responsibilities by the priests, who serve as the pastors of the local parishes.

Through their leadership and pastoral service, the pope and the bishops nourish and teach the People of God throughout the world. The People of God have the vocation and duty to participate in the overall mission of the Church. In this same way, the People of God, through the ministry of the pope and the bishops, are able to remain in communion with one another throughout the world despite their great diversity in terms of culture, ethnicity, and nationality.

Activity

Review the description of how the Church is organized. Draw a large circle on a sheet of paper. Using the outside of the circle as the boundary of the visible Church, show how the Church is organized.

The Church's Mission

There are different kinds of spiritual gifts but the same Spirit; there are different forms of service but the same Lord.

1 Corinthians 12:4–5

"Go, therefore, and make disciples of all nations, baptizing them in the name of the Father, and of the Son, and of the holy Spirit, teaching them to observe all that I have commanded you. And behold, I am with you always, until the end of the age" (Matthew 28:19–20). These words of Jesus, found at the end of Matthew's Gospel, present to us both the purpose and the scope of the Church's mission. The Church is sent to all the nations, since God desires to offer the salvation won by Jesus to the entire human race. All people are to be invited to believe in Jesus and to become his disciples, accepting Baptism in the name of the Father, Son, and Holy Spirit. The Church is to teach each new disciple to live as Jesus taught the first disciples to live.

The Church's Nature Describes Its Mission

In the Nicene Creed we proclaim that we believe the Church is "one, holy, catholic, and apostolic." Those qualities, or "marks" of the Church as they are called, indicate what the Church is to achieve through its mission.

One

Because the Church is *one*, it calls all people to unity through belief in one Lord, Jesus Christ; through celebrating one Baptism; through receiving one life in the Spirit; through sharing in the one Body of Christ in the Eucharist; and through sharing one hope in the final victory over sin and death.

Holy

In the same way, because the Church is *holy*, it is sent to lead all people to the source of its holiness: the Father who has called the Church into being, Jesus who sanctified the Church with his blood, and the Holy Spirit who gives life to the Church.

Catholic

The Church is **catholic**, that is, it enjoys the fullness of faith and administers the totality of salvation. It is this same fullness of faith and saving grace that the Church is sent by Jesus to share with *all* people through *all* time.

Faith Words

catholic The word *catholic* means "universal." With a capital *C*, it describes the Church founded by Christ's apostles. Because it welcomes all people who believe in Jesus Christ, the Catholic Church is universal.

charism A charism is a talent or gift from the Holy Spirit that an individual uses to serve the Church, live a Christian life, and work for the good of all people.

Apostolic

Finally, the Church is *apostolic* because it traces its origins back to Peter and the other apostles whom Jesus had chosen and entrusted the truth he came to reveal. The Church is sent to bring this same teaching of Peter and the apostles to all who will listen. Those who accept the teaching of the apostles thus become united to one another and to the very source of the teaching, Jesus Christ, the incarnate Word of God.

One Mission, Many Ministries

To achieve its goal of bringing the salvation won by Jesus to all people, the Church engages in a wide variety of ministries. These include first of all evangelization, which is most basic to the Church's mission. Evangelization is the task of proclaiming by word and example the Good News to those who have never heard it. Jesus prepared the apostles in a special way for this ministry.

There are many other ministries that various members of the Church carry out, each according to his or her own **charism**, or gift, he or she has received from the Holy Spirit. These ministries each contribute to the Church's mission of salvation. For example, the Church has a prophetic ministry, a preaching ministry, a teaching ministry, a healing ministry, a liturgical ministry, and a pastoral ministry on behalf of the poor and unjustly oppressed.

Some ministries of the Church require Holy Orders and are proper to bishops, priests, and deacons. However, all of the faithful by virtue of their baptism share the responsibility of carrying out the mission of the Church.

Mary and the Mission of the Church

Mary is the model for all who seek to participate in the mission of the Church. In a real sense, the birth of the Church and its mission to bring salvation to all people can be traced back to Mary's acceptance of God's invitation to become the mother of Jesus. It is that same kind of courage and willingness to cooperate with God's grace that is required for anyone to be effective in carrying out the Church's mission.

Activity

Make a list of as many church ministries you can think of in which a person can participate without first having to be ordained. Now circle all those you think you personally could do.

Life Everlasting

 Jesus told her, "I am the resurrection and the life; whoever believes in me, even if he dies, will live..."

John 11:25

The Church believes that each human being is endowed with an immortal soul by God at the moment of his or her creation. Through Scripture, God reveals that people, because they possess immortal souls, are destined for everlasting life. This revelation is most clear in the teaching and life of Jesus. The Church teaches that Jesus' Resurrection points to the fact that all people will experience a resurrection at the end of time.

Our Just Reward

Because of the gifts of intelligence and free will, each person is given the choice of following God's will. God reveals his will to us through the teaching of the Church and our conscience. At the moment of death, each person experiences a **particular judgment** by Christ, who has been appointed by the Father to be the Judge of the living and the dead. Whether each of us is judged worthy of the eternal happiness of heaven or the eternal punishment of hell is determined by the free choices each of us make while on earth.

Fortunately, in God's mercy and wisdom, he has given the Church the power to forgive any sins we have made after Baptism. This power is entrusted to the bishops and the priests appointed by them and is normally exercised in the sacrament of Reconciliation, or Penance.

The Church understands heaven as the supreme happiness of enjoying the presence of God "face to face" for all eternity. The Church views hell, on the other hand, as a state of eternal separation from the presence of God for whom we have been created and from whom our happiness ultimately comes.

Faith Words

particular judgment At the end of our lives, Jesus Christ judges how well we have followed him. Particular judgment is the judgment each individual receives from Christ at his or her death.

purgatory Purgatory is a final purification from sin after death.

indulgence An indulgence is the removal of all or some of the punishments that we must suffer in purgatory for the effects of our sins on earth.

Period of Purification

It is possible to die in God's grace and friendship and be judged by Christ to be worthy of heaven and nevertheless still bear some of the effects of our sinful choices. In that case we still lack the complete purity of soul needed to enter fully into God's presence. For this reason, the Church teaches that after death some of us may have to undergo a period or process of final purification to remove remaining effects of sin before entering heaven. Traditionally this period or process of purification has been called **purgatory**. It has long been a custom in the Church to pray for the dead so that we might help them pass through this purification if it has been required of them. We may offer such prayers for ourselves, too. Through prayers or good actions offered for souls in purgatory an **indulgence** may be obtained.

The Communion of Saints

The Church believes that we are united to all those who believe in Jesus Christ, in every time and place. Thus, we are united as a communion of saints not just to the living but to those who have gone to heaven, as well as with those undergoing purification after death. We pray for those needing purification, and we also pray to the saints in heaven for their help and guidance in our own journey of faith. From its earliest days the Church has taught its members the value and importance of praying to the men and women of faith who have gone before us. Our whole tradition of various devotions to the saints has its roots in the Church's belief that all the faithful, both living and dead, are united in Christ in one communion.

Statues of saints on Gemona Cathedral, Italy

The Kingdom of God

A major theme in Jesus' teaching is that at the end of time God will establish his kingdom of justice and peace in all its perfection. The Church believes that all human beings will experience a resurrection and transformation of their earthly bodies. There will be a final judgment, and then the just will reign with Christ forever, having been glorified in both body and soul. Even the universe will undergo a transformation, the nature of which has not been fully revealed. God will then be "all in all" for all eternity.

Activity

Do you remember when you first heard about heaven? How old were you then? List some of the things you imagined heaven would be like back then. Now that you are older describe what you now think heaven might be like. Do you think your ideas will change again as you grow older? Why or why not?

Sacraments of Initiation

Amen, amen, I say to you, no one can enter the kingdom of God without being born of water and Spirit.

John 3:5

The Church's liturgy, in all its forms, is intended first and foremost to praise and adore God. The Holy Spirit guides the Church in its celebration of the liturgy in several important ways: by preparing the assembly to encounter Christ, by recalling Christ's presence in our midst, by making present the saving action of Christ, and by making the communion we experience with Christ bear fruit. Even though throughout history various diverse liturgical traditions have developed within the Church, unity is preserved because all legitimate traditions can be traced back to the teaching and practice of the apostles. As Catholics, we believe that because the Church is the Body of Christ, the Church is a sign and instrument through which we experience the saving presence and action of Jesus.

A **sacramental** is a sacred sign (an object, prayer, blessing, or action) instituted by the Church to help prepare us to receive the grace of the sacraments. Genuflecting and blessing one's self with holy water are examples of sacramentals.

Baptism

People are initiated into the Church through three distinct but related sacramental celebrations: Baptism, Confirmation, and First Eucharist. Baptism marks the beginning of the person's new life in Christ and membership in the Church. According to Scripture and the Tradition of our Church, Baptism is necessary for salvation. The Church teaches that people who do not receive Baptism through no fault of their own can achieve salvation by sincerely seeking God and striving to do his will. (Catechumens, people preparing to receive the sacraments of initiation in order to become Catholics, can also be saved if they die for the faith before being baptized.)

Baptism has the special effect of imprinting a permanent spiritual sign upon the soul, thereby consecrating the baptized person for participation in Christian worship. It has been the Church's custom from earliest times to baptize children, since Baptism is a gift and grace from God that does not presuppose any human merit. The faith of the Church provides what infants and children may lack at the time of their baptism. In the case of children who die without baptism, the Church invites us to trust in God's mercy and to pray for their salvation.

Faith Words

sacramental A sacramental is a symbolic prayer, blessing, object, or action instituted by the Church that can lead us to a fuller participation in the grace of the sacraments.

candidate A candidate is a person who pursues and prepares for a certain role. A person who is preparing to receive the sacrament of Confirmation is called a candidate.

chrism Chrism is the perfumed oil that has been blessed by a bishop and is used for anointing in the sacraments of Baptism, Confirmation, and Holy Orders. Being anointed with chrism is a sign of receiving the Holy Spirit.

Confirmation

At the celebration of Confirmation, the bishop (or priest acting on the bishop's behalf) anoints the forehead of the **candidate** with sacred **chrism**. The bishop prays, "Be sealed with the gift of the Holy Spirit." Though the ritual is rather simple, the results are quite significant. Through the work of the Holy Spirit, the newly confirmed person is rooted more deeply and firmly in Christ and his or her bond with the Church is strengthened. The person is also empowered to help carry out the Church's mission and bear witness to the Christian faith.

Ordinarily, to receive Confirmation, the candidate must first be baptized and have reached the age of reason (age seven). He or she must profess faith in Christ and the Church, be in a state of grace, and have the clear intention of receiving the sacrament. Finally, he or she must be prepared to assume the role of a disciple and give witness to Christ in word and deed, both within the Church and in society.

Eucharist

The Eucharist is both the heart and summit of the Church's sacramental life. A person's initiation into the fullness of the life of the Church is achieved when he or she has received Baptism, Confirmation, and the Eucharist. This marks the completion of the initiation process and the beginning of the person's full participation in the life and worship of the faith community. Regular reception of the Eucharist continues to both deepen our union with Jesus and the Church and also provides ongoing strength for carrying out the mission of the Church.

Activity

See if you can recall New Testament passages that mention Baptism, Confirmation, and Eucharist. (If you have a Bible, look at the end of Matthew's Gospel, the beginning of the Book of Acts, and the end of Mark's Gospel.) List Scripture stories in which you find mention of these sacraments.

The Mass

...Do this in memory of me.

Luke 22:19

Each time we celebrate the Eucharist, we both remember and make present again the Passover of Christ, that is, the work of salvation accomplished by Jesus through his life, death, and Resurrection. Because the Mass makes present in this way the entire mystery of Jesus' saving action on our behalf, the Church considers the Eucharist to be at the very heart of our sacramental life. The Church teaches that the other sacraments all lead to and flow from the Eucharist, which is the center and highest point of the Church's liturgical life.

Essential Elements of the Mass

In keeping with the Church's Tradition, each Mass should always include the following actions: (1) the proclamation of the word of God, which can include passages from either (or both) the Old Testament and New Testament and must always include a reading from one of the four Gospels; (2) prayers of thanksgiving to God the Father for all the gifts he continually bestows on us, especially the gift of his Son; (3) the consecration of bread and wine through which it becomes the very Body and Blood of Jesus; and (4) communion through which we receive the Body and Blood of Jesus under the appearances of bread and wine. All these distinct elements constitute a single unity, a single act of worship.

Transubstantiation

At the heart of the Eucharist is the mystery of the transubstantiation of the bread and wine into the Body and Blood of Christ, which takes place at that part of the Mass called the consecration. We cannot hope to fully understand how it happens. But the Church from the time of the apostles has always believed and taught that at the consecration, the risen Christ himself, living and glorious, becomes present even though the appearances of bread and wine remain. The Church teaches that Jesus is present to us under those appearances of bread and wine in a true, real, and substantial manner, that is, the very Body and Blood, Soul and Divinity of Jesus are present. In memory of Jesus' own action at the Last Supper, the Church requires that only wheat bread and grape wine be used in the celebration of the Mass.

Faith Words

Lord's Day The Lord's Day is another name for our Sabbath, or day of rest in honor of God. We celebrate Mass on the Lord's Day.

liturgical cycle The liturgical cycle is the recurring calendar of church celebrations and seasons honoring the Paschal mystery throughout the year.

Jesus, Our High Priest

The worship we offer God through the celebration of the Mass is a perfect act of worship because in reality it is our high priest Jesus himself, acting through the ministry of our ordained priests, who offers this sacrifice. It is also Jesus, present on the altar under the appearances of bread and wine, who is being offered in worship to the Father. In this way each Mass makes present again the one perfect priestly sacrifice Jesus made when he first offered himself on our behalf to his Father on the cross at Calvary. For this reason, the Church allows only ordained priests to preside at the eucharistic celebration.

The Mass, the Lord's Day, and the Liturgical Cycle

Although in many places the Mass is celebrated daily, the Church has set aside Sunday as the **Lord's Day**, the principal day for the faithful to participate in the eucharistic celebration. In memory of the fact that Jesus' Resurrection occurred on a Sunday, it has been chosen by the Church as the preeminent day for the faithful to assemble and offer worship and thanks to God and to enjoy a day of rest.

While the main elements of the Mass, such as the words of consecration, do not change, various prayers and Scripture readings used in the Mass do change throughout the liturgical year. Each year the Church leads us through a **liturgical cycle** of specially chosen prayers and Scripture readings to help us recall and enter more deeply into the various mysteries of Jesus. The Church has also identified various feast days throughout the year on which prayers and readings at Mass help us recall the event or the saint whose feast is being celebrated.

Activity

What details about the Last Supper do you recall from Scripture stories you have heard or from the prayers the priest says at Mass?

Sacraments of Healing

Come to me, all you who labor and are burdened, and I will give you rest.

Matthew 11:28

While he was on earth, Jesus went about healing the spiritual and physical illnesses of the people. Through the sacraments of healing, the Church continues the healing ministry of Jesus. The two sacraments of healing are Reconciliation and Anointing of the Sick. The sacrament of Reconciliation is also known as the sacrament of confession, the sacrament of conversion, the sacrament of forgiveness, and the sacrament of Penance.

Reconciliation

Reconciliation is the sacrament through which we celebrate God's forgiveness. When we receive this sacrament, sins we have committed after Baptism are forgiven, thus healing our relationship with God and the Church. The sacrament of Reconciliation is administered by a priest who has received authority from the Church to absolve sins in the name of Christ.

There are three actions the penitent must carry out in the sacrament of Reconciliation. The penitent must express contrition or sorrow for the sins he or she committed, confess these sins to the priest, and intend to make reparation and do works of reparation to correct any harm the sins may have caused.

Celebrating the Sacrament

The first step in celebrating the sacrament of Reconciliation is to call upon the Holy Spirit to help us examine our conscience. We seek to recall any sins we may have committed since our last confession. Having done this, we then approach the priest, who welcomes us in the name of Christ. The priest then helps us reflect on a story or Scripture passage intended to nurture a spirit of contrition or sorrow for having offended God. We are also allowed to suggest an appropriate reading for this reflection. Then we confess our sins to the priest, who offers words of advice and encouragement in our struggle to avoid sin in the future. Next the priest "gives a penance," asking us to say some particular prayers or perform some act of service to make reparation for the harm our sins may have caused. After accepting the penance, we express sorrow for our sins, usually by praying some form of the Act of Contrition. At this point the priest, acting in the name of God and on behalf of the Church, prays these words of absolution: "I absolve you from your sins in the name of the Father, and of the Son, and of the Holy Spirit." You are now free to go, knowing with certainty that God has forgiven your sins.

Faith Words

Extreme Unction
Extreme Unction, or "last anointing," is another term for the sacrament of the Anointing of the Sick.

viaticum Viaticum, which means "provision for the journey" in Latin, is Holy Communion that is given to a dying person.

Anointing of the Sick

Through the sacrament of Anointing of the Sick, the Church celebrates God's love and healing for the sick and elderly of the Church. The purpose of this sacrament is to provide special grace for those experiencing the difficulties that accompany serious illness or old age. Though a person need not be in imminent danger of death to receive the sacrament, the Church does seek to make the sacrament available especially when death is clearly near because of serious illness or old age. For this reason there was a time when the sacrament was called **Extreme Unction**, meaning "last anointing." However, a person may receive the sacrament whenever his or her health is seriously impaired. For example, it is now the custom in some parishes to have a communal celebration of the sacrament of Anointing of the Sick each year. All the elderly and all those with serious or chronic physical or emotional illnesses are invited to participate.

Effects of the Sacrament

The special grace or effects of the sacrament of Anointing of the Sick include the following: The sick person is united in his or her suffering to Jesus, who suffered on the cross for us; the sick person receives strength, peace, and courage to endure in a Christlike way the sufferings related to the illness or old age; the sick person's sins are forgiven if he or she has been unable to celebrate the sacrament of Reconciliation. Although the primary effects of the sacrament are spiritual in nature, it is not unusual for the person to also experience a degree of physical healing.

The Rite of Anointing of the Sick

The sacrament of Anointing of the Sick is always administered by a bishop or priest. Using the oil specially blessed for this purpose by the bishop of the diocese, the minister anoints the forehead and hands of the sick or elderly person while praying these words: "Through this holy anointing may the Lord in his love and mercy help you with the grace of the Holy Spirit. May the Lord who frees you from sin save you and raise you up" (Rite of Anointing).

In the case of people who are clearly about to die, it is also the custom of the Church to offer Holy Communion. The Eucharist such people receive is called **viaticum**, meaning "food for the journey of God."

Activity

The Church uses specially blessed oil in the sacrament of Anointing of the Sick because oil symbolizes healing. Make a list of all the ways we use oil in some form today to improve or maintain our health.

Sacraments at the Service of Communion

This is my commandment: love one another as I love you.

John 15:12

The sacraments at the service of communion are Holy Orders and Matrimony. Each sacrament nourishes and maintains the life of the church community in its own special way.

Holy Orders

In the sacrament of Holy Orders, men are ordained deacons, priests, or bishops. They serve the Church in a special way by carrying out the mission that Christ entrusted to his apostles. Bishops are the rightful successors of the apostles and possess the fullness of the priesthood. A priest, or **presbyter**, has the role of assisting the bishop in ministering to the Church by celebrating the sacraments, proclaiming God's word, and guiding the parish community. Deacons also assist in the work of the parish by carrying out important priestly duties, such as baptizing, preaching, presiding at weddings, and administering the parish.

Only bishops, as the successors of the apostles, may ordain other bishops, as well as priests and deacons. As successors of the apostles, the bishops assist the pope, the successor of Saint Peter, in guiding and governing the Church. They carry out this responsibility by serving as pastoral leaders of the various dioceses, or geographical areas into which the Church is divided. Bishops are also the ordinary ministers of Confirmation, although priests may confirm in the name of the bishop in special circumstances.

Faith Words

presbyter In the Church today, the term *presbyter* means "priest." In the early Church, presbyters were the appointed religious leaders, or elders, of the early Christian communities.

polygamy Polygamy is the state of having several marriage partners at the same time.

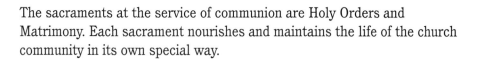

Bishops and Priests

As the bishops serve in unity with the pope and under the pope's leadership, priests are united to their bishop in the diocese in which they serve. Sharing in the priestly dignity of their bishop, priests are called to be the bishop's prudent co-workers. As such, they depend upon their bishop in the exercise of their pastoral functions in the local churches.

It should be noted that the Church confers Holy Orders only on baptized men. Church authority alone has the right to call men to Holy Orders. It is the practice of the Church to call to the priesthood only men who have first been found suitable for exercising the priestly ministry.

The Rite of Holy Orders

In this rite the bishop lays hands upon the man to be ordained and offers a solemn prayer of consecration that asks God to grant the graces required for his ministry. Like Baptism and Confirmation, Holy Orders imprints a permanent spiritual mark upon the soul, making the man a priest forever.

Matrimony

The sacrament of Marriage, which signifies the union of Christ and the Church, gives the spouses special grace to perfect love for each other, strengthen their unity, and help them grow together in holiness. By mutually consenting to give themselves entirely to each other, the couple establishes a covenant of faithful and fruitful love. Because the Church views marriage as a sacrament, the couple are asked to celebrate their marriage in public, before a priest and in the presence of witnesses and the assembly of the faithful.

The Church considers the union formed by sacramental marriage to be indissoluble and teaches that divorce separates what God has joined together. It is the teaching of the Church that divorced persons cannot remarry as long as their spouses remain alive. Should divorced persons remarry anyway, they are not separated from the Church but cannot receive the Eucharist. The Church also opposes **polygamy**.

Because it is in the home that Christian children first hear the Gospel proclaimed, the Church considers the family to be the "domestic church," a community of grace and prayer. Also because the Church considers that having children is one of the primary purposes of marriage as ordained by God, it opposes the practice of artificially preventing the conception of children.

Activity

In some parts of the world today, the Church is experiencing a serious priest shortage. List some of the consequences that can occur when there are not enough priests available to serve the people.

Conscience

For the law of the spirit of life in Christ Jesus has freed you from the law of sin and death.

Romans 8:2

God created us in his own image, with a spiritual soul having both an intellect and a free will. We are by nature destined to find everlasting happiness in God. To achieve that destiny, however, we are obliged to "do good and avoid evil," which is the fundamental moral law. The role of our conscience is to help us recognize and then choose good over evil. However, it is not always that easy because, having been wounded in our nature by original sin, we are subject to errors of judgment and are inclined to seek evil when exercising our freedom. On the positive side, the Holy Spirit guides us toward moral maturity, a maturity that finally reaches its fulfillment in heaven.

Conscience and the Moral Act

Our conscience is our capacity as human beings to judge whether a particular act is good or evil. There are three things we must consider in making such a judgment. First, we must consider the nature of the act itself. Second, we need to consider our intention or the end we hope to achieve by doing the act. Third, we need to consider the important circumstances that surround the act. All three of these elements together become the source for determining the morality of a given act.

Some wrong acts are by nature more serious or harmful than others. The more evil you know an act to be, the more morally responsible you are if you choose to do it. One's intention is also critical in determining the morality of an act. To fully intend to do an act one knows is wrong is clearly a more serious moral evil than doing the same act without fully intending to do it. Finally, circumstances affect the morality of our acts. In some cases we may not be as free to choose what is good as we are in others.

Faith Words

prudence Prudence, a moral virtue, is the habit of making good judgments and decisions.

justice Justice, a moral virtue, is the practice of treating others fairly.

fortitude Fortitude, a moral virtue, is the courage to do what is right.

temperance Temperance, a moral virtue, is the habit of living in moderation and controlling our desires.

The Importance of Conscience Formation

Even good people with the best of intentions are still capable of making wrong judgments of conscience. The Church reminds us that we have to find ways to better inform our conscience regarding the true nature of the choices we face. The Church points out that to nurture a well-formed conscience we need to turn to prayer, the guidance of the Holy Spirit, the wisdom of the Church's **Magisterium** or teaching, and the advice and good example the faith community provides for us. This is all the more important because the Church also teaches that in the last analysis we are obligated to obey what our conscience tells us is the right moral choice.

Conscience and Virtue

Virtue can be described as a habitual and firm disposition to do good and avoid evil. A virtue is a good moral habit. It is acquired with the help of God's grace by repeatedly choosing what our conscience judges to be the good and by rejecting those choices our conscience judges to be evil. Through the strength of virtue (*virtue* comes from the Latin word for *strength*), we are better able to govern our actions and guide our overall conduct in accord with reason and faith.

Having been baptized into Christ, we are graced by the Holy Spirit with the four **moral virtues** of **prudence**, **justice**, **fortitude**, and **temperance**. These are sometimes called the cardinal virtues (from the Latin word for *hinge*) because our moral life hinges upon these four virtues. Prudence helps us make good judgments and decisions in complicated matters. Justice helps us treat others fairly. Fortitude helps to habitually resist evil courageously. Temperance helps us live in moderation and control our natural desires for self-gratification.

Activity

Write a prayer to the Holy Spirit that you can say before making difficult moral decisions.

Sin and Mercy

Blessed are the merciful,
for they will be shown mercy.

Matthew 5:7

Sin is any choice that we make that is contrary to God's law and his plan for creation. Sin is by nature an offense against God in which we rise up in disobedience. To sin is also to act contrary to human reason and as such it always has the effect of harming our human nature and injuring the solidarity we are intended to enjoy with all human beings. Because sin always involves a free choice, the one who sins bears personal responsibility for the harmful consequences that may result from the sinful choice. On the positive side, Jesus teaches that God is all-merciful and is always ready and eager to forgive and welcome back all those who seek his forgiveness. This love and mercy of God is revealed in an especially powerful way in the parables of Jesus, especially through the Parable of the Prodigal Son (Luke 15:11–32).

The Prodigal Son
by Albrecht Durer

Elements and Forms of Sin

The Church distinguishes between two kinds of sin: grave (or mortal) sin and venial sin. To deliberately choose to do something that is seriously harmful and contrary to the ultimate end for which we were created is by nature a grave, or mortal, sin. It is called mortal because it destroys charity in us. It separates us from God's grace and damages our friendship with our neighbor. Remaining in mortal sin, we cannot experience heaven, which is dwelling in the presence and love of God.

The Church teaches that three conditions must be present for an act to be judged a grave, or mortal, sin: (1) the act itself must be such that it seriously violates the eternal law, for example, murder, perjury, unjust treatment of the poor, hatred of another, and so on; (2) the person doing the act must fully know and understand at the time of the act the serious nature of the offense; (3) the person must freely choose to commit the offense. If any of these conditions is missing, the person doing the act is not judged to have committed a mortal sin even if the act itself is by nature seriously wrong.

Venial sin is a less serious offense against the law of God and does not separate us from God's grace nor destroy charity. While it is virtually impossible to avoid venial sin all the time, this does not mean that venial sin should be taken lightly. Having become members of Christ's Body through Baptism, our goal as Christians should go beyond simply avoiding sin. We are called to "put on the mind of Christ," who sought in all things to do his Father's will.

Faith Words

justification
Justification is God's act of freely forgiving our sins and giving us the grace we need to become holy and Christlike.

God's Mercy

Throughout the entire Old Testament and New Testament, God is revealed to us above all else as a merciful God. God's merciful love forgives us for the sins we have committed, heals the wounds our sins have brought upon us, and welcomes us as his beloved children and as heirs of his kingdom. This great mercy is ultimately revealed and these saving works of mercy are ultimately brought about through the life, death, and Resurrection of Jesus Christ. The Church uses the term **justification** to describe the effects of God's merciful and saving love. We do not earn or merit this justification. It is a grace, that is, a free gift of God that Christ's Passion, death, and Resurrection merited on our behalf. It is through Baptism, which unites us to Christ, that we have access to this grace of justification. God continually bestows his grace upon us so that we may respond to this call to grow in holiness.

The Holy Spirit is sent by God to infuse our souls with the very life of God. This gift of God's life within is what the Church calls sanctifying grace. Thus, "to be in a state of grace" means that we are indeed sharing in this free gift of God's life and are intimately united to God.

The sacrament of Reconciliation, or Penance, entrusted to the Church is a special sign of God's merciful love for us. Even if we should reject God's grace and sin mortally after our baptism, we have direct access to God's mercy and forgiveness in the sacrament of Reconciliation. Through our repentance, the confession of our sins, and our willingness to make amends, we can receive absolution for our sins and be restored to sanctifying grace. No matter how often we might fall back into sin through human weakness, we can receive God's merciful forgiveness in the sacrament of Reconciliation. In fact, God's mercy always goes before us since it is God's grace that urges and prompts and guides us to repent and seek his mercy.

Activity

Try to recall parables in the Gospels besides the Parable of the Prodigal Son that teach about God's mercy. (If you have a Bible, see Luke's Gospel.) Explain in your own words what you think these stories teach us about God's mercy.

The Beatitudes

When he saw the crowds, he went up the mountain, and after he had sat down, his disciples came to him. He began to teach them....

Matthew 5:1–2

◇　◇　◇

God has created in us a fundamental desire for happiness, a happiness that ultimately can be experienced only through union with God. In the Old Testament God revealed to the Israelites that the path to union with him and to fullness of life and happiness lies in following the **Mosaic Law** or Law of Moses. The Law provides us a blueprint for living in union with God, in loving community with one another, and in harmony with all creation.

The Beatitudes as Revolutionary Ideas

We find the most complete expression of the Beatitudes presented in Matthew's Gospel at the beginning of the Sermon on the Mount (Matthew 5:3–12). Over the centuries, Christians have become very familiar with the Beatitudes, since they lie at the heart of all that Jesus taught us about how to achieve true happiness. When the first disciples heard the Beatitudes, they thought they were revolutionary. As "rules" for achieving happiness, the Beatitudes completely went against what the people of Jesus' time believed would give them happiness. In fact, the very things that Jesus seemed to be saying would bring happiness (being poor, being hungry and thirsty, being meek rather than standing up for one's rights, and so forth) were the things the people felt were causes for unhappiness. The same can be said for virtually all that Jesus taught in the Sermon on the Mount.

The Beatitudes and the Kingdom of God

The Beatitudes describe life in the kingdom as it will exist at the end of time, when it is fully realized. They tell us the virtues of those who will inhabit the kingdom. Further, we are taught that the kingdom that Jesus describes will not be the result of the efforts of people but will be brought about by the will of the Father.

The kingdom is also present on earth today, especially in the witness given to it by the members of Christ's Body, the Church. Jesus came to announce and usher in the kingdom of God, where we are called to rely on God's love and mercy to provide all that we need. This does not mean we are to sit idly by allowing God to do everything for us. It does mean that by embracing the Beatitudes through the gift and inspiration of the Holy Spirit, we will be cooperating with God, who is establishing a society whose members live together in mutual love, justice, and peace.

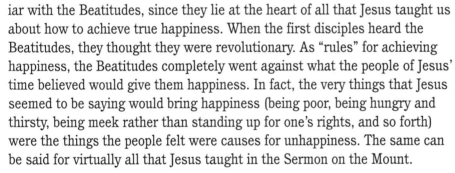

Faith Words

Mosaic Law The Mosaic Law, or Law of Moses, sets forth rules and practices that Jewish people have followed from the time of Moses, for whom the Law is named. The Ten Commandments, the basis of Mosaic Law, are found in the Bible, in Exodus 20 and Deuteronomy 5:6–21. The Book of Leviticus contains further details of the Law.

Beatitudes: A Summary

Beatitude	Our Challenge
Blessed are the poor in spirit, for theirs is the kingdom of heaven.	Learn to put all our trust in God rather than in material possessions.
Blessed are they who mourn, for they will be comforted.	Learn not to expect perfect happiness on earth. Grow in hope and confidence that God can and will provide us with perfect happiness in his kingdom.
Blessed are the meek, for they will inherit the land.	Learn that happiness does not come from self-promotion and gaining control over others. It comes from treating one another with gentleness and patience.
Blessed are they who hunger and thirst for righteousness, for they will be satisfied.	Learn that being upset with the injustice and evil we see around us is a result of God's grace and an invitation to strive to promote a just society.
Blessed are the merciful, for they will be shown mercy.	Learn that the very foundation of God's kingdom rests on our being willing to forgive those who wrong us. Refusing to forgive and seeking vengeance only continues the cycle of hatred and violence.
Blessed are the clean of heart, for they will see God.	Learn that growing in friendship with God is our single most important task on earth.
Blessed are the peacemakers, for they will be called children of God.	Learn that as children of God one of our most fundamental tasks is to help others forgive each other and live in peace together.
Blessed are they who are persecuted for the sake of righteousness, for theirs is the kingdom of heaven.	Learn that persecution is inevitable whenever we are truly working to promote God's kingdom. Rather than being surprised and discouraged, we should be reassured that we are on the right track.

Activity

First, decide which of the Beatitudes you personally consider the most difficult to follow. Next, choose the one you feel is the easiest for you to follow. Be prepared to discuss the reasons for your choices.

The Ten Commandments:
Love of God

 I, the LORD, am your God, who brought you out of the land of Egypt, that place of slavery.

Exodus 20:2

The Ten Commandments are a set of instructions that God our loving Father has revealed to us to guide us to true happiness and help us avoid harming ourselves and others. They reflect the natural law that God established from the beginning of time to order creation. It is this same natural law, available to us through our reason, that provides the foundation for all moral rules and civil laws.

The first three commandments focus on our relationship with God. The remaining seven focus on our relationship with one another and with all creation. Each commandment imposes a grave moral obligation on us.

As Christians we believe the Ten Commandments prepare the way for the new law of Christ, which fulfills and perfects what God has revealed to us in the Ten Commandments. Finally, it is important to recall that God in his mercy and love always provides the grace we need to do what he has commanded of us.

I am the Lord, your God. You shall not have other gods besides me.

The first commandment provides the foundation for the others. It tells us never to regard any person or thing as more important than God. It calls us to believe in, hope in, and love God above all else. To raise any creature above God in any way is a form of idolatry. The first commandment also forbids us to make "gods" of money, power, and fame by looking to them rather than God to give us happiness and fulfillment.

Many people do not realize that the first commandment also warns against superstition, that is, relying on various human actions or creatures rather than on God to protect us and provide for our needs. Superstition is a form of idolatry, as is belief in divination (fortune telling, horoscopes, palm reading, astrology) and magic (such as satanism and witchcraft). We are called to avoid any practices that deny God's grace.

Because of our belief in the Incarnation, the Church allows and encourages the veneration of sacred images (statues, crucifixes, pictures of saints, and so on) in its prayer and worship. These are not the same as the "gods" the first commandment forbids. They are not objects of worship nor are they considered to have any magical powers. Sacred images are intended as aids for helping us better focus our hearts on God.

Faith Words

blasphemy Blasphemy is the act of showing contempt for God or sacred things through one's words or actions.

perjury Perjury is the act of lying after having made an oath to tell the truth, with God as one's witness.

You shall not take the name of the Lord, your God, in vain.

The second commandment obliges us to show proper respect to God in keeping with his holiness and his nature as our Creator. Actions such as **blasphemy** or the desecration of a church are forbidden by this commandment. The second commandment also forbids us from using God's holy name disrespectfully and from committing **perjury**, or making false oaths. When we call upon God to witness to a lie, we commit perjury.

By extension the second commandment forbids us to treat disrespectfully any person or object that has been consecrated to God for the purpose of honoring him. Being disrespectful of priests and religious brothers and sisters, making fun of sacred objects and rituals, and being unruly and disruptive during Mass are all examples of ways people might—often unknowingly—violate the second commandment. If a person consciously intends to show disrespect to God when doing such things, he or she commits a very serious offense against the commandment.

Remember to keep holy the Sabbath day.

The third commandment obliges us to set aside one day each week to focus in a special way on giving honor to God and on nurturing our relationship with him. In the Jewish tradition the last day of the week is set aside for that purpose. In the Christian tradition, Sunday, the first day of the week, is set aside in memory of Jesus' Resurrection, which happened on the first day of the week.

The Church teaches that all Catholics throughout the world are obligated to "keep holy the Sabbath" by participating in the Mass each Sunday and on holy days of obligation. The Mass, of course, is the highest form of honor and worship we can offer to God.

In obedience to the third commandment, the Church also teaches that in addition to participating in Mass, Catholics are to refrain from all unnecessary work or business activities that would prevent them from giving proper worship to God. Sunday is intended in God's plan for humanity as a day of rest for the body as well as a day for the nourishment of the soul. Likewise, Christians are not supposed to make demands of others that might prevent them from offering worship to God.

Activity

List some objects and activities in our society today that you think some people tend to turn into "idols" by regarding them as more important for their happiness than God.

The Ten Commandments:
Love of Neighbor

For life is more than food and the body more than clothing.

Luke 12:23

The last seven commandments show us how we are to respect and relate to one another in the human family. The moral principles they present are well known, since, besides being revealed to us by our loving God, they can also be discovered through the use of reason and by reflecting on the natural law.

Honor your father and mother.

The fourth commandment deals with how we are to relate to those in authority over us. It is God's will that children honor, respect, and obey their parents in much the same way as they honor God their heavenly Father. All those who exercise legitimate authority over us derive this authority from God. So we should honor and obey them as God's representatives.

You shall not kill.

The Church teaches that the fifth commandment includes other serious obligations beside the obvious one, that we are forbidden to kill others. Every human life is sacred from the moment of conception until natural death, because each human being has been called into existence by God and bears God's image and likeness. For that reason, the Church forbids abortion and the practice of euthanasia, or "mercy killing," of the elderly or the physically or developmentally disabled. The Church also teaches that suicide is forbidden by the fifth commandment, as well as any other deliberate acts that unnecessarily threaten the life or health of ourselves or others.

You shall not commit adultery. You shall not covet your neighbor's wife.

The sixth and ninth commandments call us to respect our bodies and the gift of sexuality with which God has blessed us. It is important to nurture the virtues of chastity and temperance. The Church teaches that, besides adultery, other acts to be considered serious sins against the sixth commandment include masturbation, sexual intimacy outside of marriage, pornography, homosexual practices, and rape and incest. The gift of human sexuality includes our capacity to procreate. One of the purposes of marriage is to bring forth children. Although the Church encourages the responsible planning of pregnancies, the Church considers it wrong for a couple to use artificial means to prevent a pregnancy, no matter how good their intentions might be.

Faith Words

plagiarism Plagiarism is the use of someone's ideas or works as if they were one's own.

covet To covet means to have an excessive desire for what rightfully belongs to someone else.

You shall not steal.

The Church teaches that stealing can take many forms. Not paying a worker a just wage is a form of stealing. Charging a customer an unfair price or not giving the employer a fair day's work for one's wages are forms of stealing. **Plagiarism**, or claiming another's creative work as one's own, is a form of stealing. Wasting the earth's resources also violates the seventh commandment, since it is in effect stealing from others and from future generations. Stealing in any form is an offense against the seventh commandment, but stealing from or defrauding the poor and needy of their goods or services is an especially grave offense.

You shall not bear false witness against your neighbor.

Lying consists in saying what is false with the conscious intention of deceiving one's neighbor. The eighth commandment forbids all lying regardless of how we communicate the lie: orally, in writing, or through means of objects, gestures, or actions. The more a person or group needs and has the right to a particular truth, the more grave is the sinfulness of the lie that prevents the person or group from obtaining it. For example, intentionally lying to a jury regarding the innocence of a person suspected of a crime is a grave sin.

You shall not covet your neighbor's goods.

The tenth commandment forbids us from coveting our neighbors' possessions. To **covet** means to have an excessive desire for what rightfully belongs to another. The commandment also forbids envy, which makes us sad to see another's wealth and creates an immoderate desire in us to acquire it for ourselves.

Precepts of the Church

There are certain specific duties we have as Catholics in addition to obeying the commandments. They are called the Precepts of the Church and include the following duties.

(1) Participate in Mass on all Sundays and holy days of obligation. (2) Confess serious sins once a year. (3) Receive the Eucharist at least once during the Easter season. (4) Fast and abstain on days appointed by the Church. (5) Contribute to the Church's support.

Activity

On a separate sheet of paper, try to rewrite the fifth through tenth commandments, using "You shall" statements rather than "You shall not" statements.

Social Justice

Amen, I say to you, whatever you did for one of these least brothers of mine, you did for me.

Matthew 25:40

Jesus Christ came to "bring glad tidings to the poor, liberty to captives, and recovery of sight to the blind" (based on Luke 4:18–19). *Social justice* is the term used to describe the Church's mission to continue Jesus' service to the poor and the oppressed.

Underlying Moral Principles

There are certain moral principles that serve as the foundation for the Church's teaching on social justice. The most basic of these is recognition of the rights and dignity of each human being as a child of God, created in God's own image and likeness and destined to enjoy everlasting happiness in communion with God. Whatever individuals or societies do that lessens the dignity or takes away the legitimate rights of individuals or groups can be considered unjust, contrary to God's law and the spirit of the Gospel.

In fact, the goal of all legitimate government and social organizations should be to promote the dignity and rights of human beings. To maintain good order, political communities must use only those means that are considered morally acceptable. Just as it is wrong for one person to try to control another through deception, fear, or physical force, it is unjust for government to use immoral means to control and dominate its citizens. It is the duty of legitimate government to promote rather than obstruct the exercise of virtue in its citizens, using a just hierarchy of values as the basis for its laws. In this way it defends and promotes the common good of all its citizens, which is the fundamental role of all government. At the same time government needs to provide legitimate processes such as a court of appeal, through which individuals and associations can obtain their legitimate rights.

Faith Words

war crimes War crimes are acts of violence against innocent people during wartime.

preferential option for the poor The preferential option for the poor is an understanding that we must give priority to the needs of the poor and vulnerable in society.

Governments and Organizations

The Church also teaches that, because all people throughout the world make up one human family, there is a need to establish an organization for ordering society at the international level to promote peace and good order and to protect the rights of small nations against unjust treatment by more powerful ones.

The Church stresses that the seventh commandment, which forbids stealing, applies to governments and organizations as well as to individuals. God intends the goods of the earth to be available to all people. It is therefore unjust for governments or organizations to act in such a way that some people do not have access to the world's goods while others amass great wealth. The right to private property does not abolish the obligation to ensure that the earth's goods are distributed fairly. Slavery, of course, in any form, is a gross injustice. No political or commercial purpose can ever justify the enslavement of human beings.

War and Peace

Because all wars result in terrible evils and injustices inflicted on human beings, especially the innocent and helpless, the Church teaches that we need to always take every reasonable means to avoid all armed conflict. The Church also opposes what is called the "arms race," the practice of governments to build up large arsenals of weapons, even though they are not at war. This not only creates a spirit of mistrust between governments that can lead to war, it also causes wealth and natural resources to be diverted from peaceful uses.

Given the very nature of war, some take the attitude that a government or individuals are allowed to use any means available to obtain victory, no matter how immoral society considers those means to be in times of peace. The Church, however, maintains that even in times of war we must conduct ourselves according to sound moral principles. Individuals or governments that act contrary to the established law of nations during times of war are to be considered guilty of what has come to be called **war crimes**.

Social Concerns

Since a Christian's fundamental duty is to promote social justice, most parishes have established *social concerns* committees. Their purpose is to help parishioners identify and pursue activities intended to bring about a more just and peaceful community. Typical activities include sponsoring food pantries, supporting homeless shelters, and extending help to the elderly and the poor. Part of social justice is supporting the **preferential option for the poor**.

Activity

Name some of the social concerns activities your parish sponsors during the year. In which of these activities can young people your age participate?

Prayer

And I tell you, ask and you will receive; seek and you will find; knock and the door will be opened to you.

Luke 11:9

Prayer and the Christian life are inseparable. Prayer has always been an integral part of the Church's life. Aided by the Holy Spirit, the Church teaches each new generation of Christians to pray because prayer is deeply rooted in the Church's living Tradition. It is the Church's wish that the Christian family, through the guidance and example of the parents, be the first place children come in contact with this Tradition and receive instruction in prayer. The word of God, the liturgy of the Church, and the theological virtues of faith, hope, and charity are sources God provides to inspire and shape Christian prayer.

Some Principles of Prayer

Prayer is essentially talking to and listening to God. This "conversation" revolves around four basic topics: praise, thanksgiving, petition, and contrition. In prayer we praise the goodness and love of God and thank God for his many gifts and his ongoing care for us. We tell God of our needs and those of others, asking his help in meeting them. We ask God for forgiveness for our own sins and the sins of others.

In keeping with the Church's tradition of prayer, we are encouraged to appeal to the saints who have gone before us, asking them to join us in offering our prayers to God. Throughout history Mary, the Mother of Jesus, has always been given a preeminent place in the prayer life of Christians. The Church teaches that God always hears our prayers and always answers them, always providing what is best for us.

It is not uncommon, however, to experience difficulties when we strive to pray. We can become distracted by the events around us or by various tasks we need to do. We may experience periods of "dryness" during which God seems to be absent from us. In reality, God is always present with us in prayer no matter what feeling we may be experiencing.

Faith Words

novena A novena is a Catholic devotion in which specific prayers are said on nine consecutive days.

pilgrimage A pilgrimage is a journey to a holy place or sacred site for spiritual or devotional reasons.

Quiet Prayer

We do not need to use words to pray. When we are quiet and simply focusing our attention on God, we are praying. This is a very good way to pray, because it is especially during those times when we are silent that the Holy Spirit speaks to our hearts. Simply reflecting on a Scripture passage or a story from the Gospels can be a form of prayer. When the beauty of nature moves us to become aware of the beauty and wisdom and power of God, we are praying even if we do not say a word.

Vocal Prayer

The Church has a rich source of formal prayers that it has developed over the centuries. These include prayers such as the Sign of the Cross, the Hail Mary, the Rosary, acts of faith, hope, love, and contrition, prayers to the Holy Spirit, and so forth. When we pray by using one of these traditional prayers, it is called "vocal prayer," even though we may not be praying aloud. This can be a very good way to pray, provided we strive to reflect on the meaning of the words we are using as we pray.

Liturgical Prayer

Liturgical prayer is the official prayer of the Church. In liturgical prayer the Church is inspired by the Holy Spirit, praying with and in Christ who himself presents our prayers to the Father. For that reason liturgical prayer is the highest and most perfect form of prayer we can offer to God. Besides the Mass, the chief forms of liturgical prayer include the celebration of the other sacraments and the Liturgy of the Hours.

The Liturgy of the Hours involves reciting certain psalms, Scripture passages, hymns, and prayers at set times throughout the day. Many religious, especially those living in monasteries, gather for morning, daytime, evening, and nighttime prayer.

Private Devotions

Besides participation in liturgy, the Church encourages the faithful to participate in private devotions, provided people do not regard them as a substitute for their obligation to participate in liturgical prayer. Some of the more common private devotions include praying the Rosary, the Stations of the Cross, or a **novena** to a saint; adoration of the Blessed Sacrament; and making a **pilgrimage** to a holy place or shrine.

Activity

List all the occasions you can think of when you prayed this past week. Now, on a scale of one to ten, how strong do you think your prayer life is? If you feel you need improvement in your prayer life, what are some things you might do?

The Lord's Prayer

Your Father knows what you need before you ask him.

Matthew 6:8

The Lord's Prayer holds a preeminent place in the Church's life of prayer for several reasons. First of all, it is the prayer Jesus personally taught his disciples—and through them the whole Church—to pray. Second, in the Lord's Prayer, we find summarized all that Jesus reveals to us about how we should relate to God and treat each other. The Lord's Prayer has often been referred to by the Church as "the little Gospel." In the opening words, we address the Father, and each of the things we pray for in the Lord's Prayer is a form of a **petition**.

Our Father Who Art in Heaven

By teaching us to address God as *our* Father, Jesus is teaching us that we are not to view our relationship with God as a private matter. No one has a special, private claim on God. God is the Father of all people. In approaching God, we are to remember that we are members of a family. All people are our brothers and sisters. Perhaps the most important lesson Jesus teaches us through these opening words is that we should approach God as a loving, caring Father. We are to approach this loving Father as a little child approaches a parent, fully confident that he loves us and is eager to receive us. Through the words, "who art in heaven," Jesus reminds us that we are to balance this sense of intimacy with deep respect and reverence for the Father, who is Lord of heaven and earth.

Hallowed Be Thy Name

By making this the first petition of the prayer and using the word *hallow*, Jesus is teaching us that above all else we should desire and seek the Father's glory and praise. With all our hearts, we pray that every people in every time may come to know, honor, and praise our loving God.

Thy Kingdom Come

By his words and deeds, Jesus revealed to us that the Father promised to one day establish his kingdom of perfect justice, peace, unity, and happiness. Likewise, in words and deeds, Jesus gave us certain "previews" of what this kingdom is like. In this second petition of the Lord's Prayer, he teaches us that we have a special duty to pray continually, asking the Father to hasten the arrival of that kingdom.

Faith Words

petition A petition is a solemn prayer of request.

hallow To hallow is to venerate, honor, or treat as holy.

Thy Will Be Done on Earth As It Is in Heaven

Jesus taught by word and example that human happiness is the result of obedience to the Father's will. Disobedience to the Father's will, on the other hand, is the source of human misery and evil. Jesus teaches us that we are to pray that the human family learn to obey the Father's will perfectly, just as it is obeyed in heaven. Such obedience has the effect of hastening the day when God's kingdom will arrive.

Give Us This Day Our Daily Bread

In this petition, Jesus teaches us to turn to our loving Father each new day in trust and confidence, convinced that God knows and will provide what we need this day. Jesus teaches us that we are doomed to failure if we refuse to trust in God and rely instead solely on ourselves by striving to amass earthly wealth and power. Also by asking for *our* daily bread, Jesus is reminding us that the earth's goods are intended to be shared with all people. There is more than enough for everyone if we share.

Forgive Us Our Trespasses As We Forgive Those Who Trespass Against Us

This petition is quite unusual. Jesus teaches us to ask the Father's forgiveness for our sins, which seems normal enough. However, Jesus has included a condition in our request. Jesus tells us we are to ask the Father to forgive us *only if and to the same degree that we forgive those who trespass against us.* In this way, Jesus is emphasizing how important it is that we be willing to forgive one another if we are to expect the Father to forgive us. The forgiveness of our sins depends not so much on God's willingness to forgive us as it does on *our willingness* to forgive one another.

Lead Us Not into Temptation but Deliver Us From Evil

In these final petitions, Jesus teaches us to ask the Father's continuing help and protection from falling prey to evil and from becoming victims of the effects of the evil of others.

When we say the Lord's Prayer, we are reminded of all the central truths of the Gospel and at the same time we ask the Father for all that is really important for human happiness.

Activity

Print the Lord's Prayer on an index card, using your best printing. When you go home, tape it to your bathroom or bedroom mirror as a reminder to say it each day.

Doctrine Review

What Catholics Believe

Word Power

Circle the letter before the word or phrase that best completes each sentence.

1. Sacred Scripture is a term we use to indicate **a.** statues. **b.** the Bible. **c.** the Ten Commandments. **d.** the time of Jesus.

2. The official teachings, rituals, customs, and practices of the Church are called **a.** sacraments. **b.** Tradition. **c.** Sacred Scripture. **d.** revelation.

3. We call original sin **a.** the sin of the first man and woman. **b.** the sin of Judas. **c.** the sin of Lucifer. **d.** the first sin a person commits.

4. The gift that ensures the pope's teaching on faith and morals is free from error is called **a.** charism. **b.** papal infallibility. **c.** chrism. **d.** sacramental.

5. A diocese is **a.** a region or district whose parishes are served by a bishop. **b.** a region administered by a priest. **c.** the boundaries of a parish. **d.** the bishop's residence.

6. A charism is **a.** the power to celebrate Mass. **b.** holy oil. **c.** a group of Christians. **d.** a talent or gift from the Holy Spirit.

7. The word *catholic* means **a.** orthodox. **b.** true. **c.** universal. **d.** holy.

8. Purgatory is **a.** a section of a church. **b.** a confession of sins. **c.** a final purification from sin. **d.** a period of happiness.

9. Particular judgment takes place **a.** at the end of one's life. **b.** at the end of the world. **c.** before Confirmation. **d.** in the bishop's presence.

10. To be a member of the Communion of Saints, one must be **a.** alive. **b.** dead. **c.** in purgatory. **d.** a believer in Jesus Christ.

What Do You Think?

Turn to page (265) and read the Nicene Creed. Which parts of the Creed are the easiest for you to understand? Which parts do you feel that you need to know more about? Give reasons for your answers.

Doctrine Review

How Catholics Worship

Word Power

Circle the letter before the word or phrase that best completes each sentence.

1. Chrism is   **a.** a gift or talent.   **b.** holy oil.   **c.** a baptismal candle.
   d. a bishop's staff.

2. Symbolic prayers, blessings, objects, or actions that can lead us to a fuller
   participation in the grace of the sacraments are   **a.** candidates.   **b.** liturgy.
   c. sacramentals.   **d.** commandments.

3. The Lord's Day is   **a.** Sunday.   **b.** Easter.   **c.** Christmas.   **d.** Pentecost.

4. The word *liturgical cycle* refers to   **a.** sacred readings.   **b.** the recurring
   calendar of church celebrations and seasons.   **c.** private prayer.
   d. moral laws.

5. The sacraments of healing include   **a.** Marriage and Holy Orders.
   b. Reconciliation and Anointing of the Sick.   **c.** Baptism and Confirmation.
   d. all of the above.

6. Viaticum is   **a.** a visit to a holy place.   **b.** another name for confession.
   c. where the pope lives.   **d.** Holy Communion given to a dying person.

7. *Presbyter* is another word for   **a.** bishop.   **b.** priest.   **c.** deacon.   **d.** pope.

8. Polygamy refers to   **a.** divorce.   **b.** multiple births.   **c.** multiple
   marriage partners.   **d.** a lack of belief in God.

9. Extreme Unction is another term for   **a.** Reconciliation.
   b. Anointing of the Sick.   **c.** Holy Orders.   **d.** viaticum.

10. A person who prepares to receive Confirmation is called a   **a.** presbyter.
    b. presider.   **c.** candidate.   **d.** minister.

What Do You Think?

Imagine that you are planning a program to prepare people your age for
Confirmation. What requirements would you ask of the candidates?
What kind of instruction would you plan?

Doctrine Review

How Catholics Live

Word Power

Circle the letter before the word or phrase that best completes each sentence.

1. The teaching authority of the Church is **a.** the city of Rome.
   b. the sacraments.   **c.** the bishop's residence.   **d.** the Magisterium.

2. The moral virtues include **a.** faith, hope, and charity.
   b. prudence and temperance.   **c.** faith and justice.   **d.** charity and justice.

3. The basis of the Mosaic Law is **a.** the Ten Commandments.
   b. the eight Beatitudes.   **c.** the seven sacraments.   **d.** the Twelve Apostles.

4. Blasphemy shows **a.** thanksgiving to God.   **b.** contempt for God.
   c. respect for the clergy.   **d.** repentance for sin.

5. Perjury is **a.** a time of purification after death.   **b.** disrespect for God.
   c. lying under oath.   **d.** a sin against the sixth commandment.

6. *Covet* means to **a.** desire.   **b.** obscure.   **c.** disregard.   **d.** gather.

7. Plagiarism is the use of **a.** God's name in vain.   **b.** Jesus' name in vain.
   c. someone else's work as your own.   **d.** other people's money.

8. The precepts of the Church do not say that we must **a.** participate at Mass
   on Sundays and holy days.   **b.** say the Rosary each week.   **c.** contribute to
   the Church's support.   **d.** confess serious sins once a year.

9. The Church teaches that all human life is sacred **a.** from the moment
   of birth.   **b.** from the moment of Baptism.   **c.** from the moment
   of conception.   **d.** from the moment a baby can breathe on his or her own.

10. The commandment that forbids stealing of any kind is the **a.** first.   **b.** third.
    c. fifth.   **d.** seventh.

What Do You Think?

What is the most difficult moral problem for young people today? How would you advise young people your age to deal with it? To whom would you go for help?

Doctrine Review

How Catholics Pray

Word Power

Match the words in Column A with the phrases in Column B.

A	B
1. prayer	**a.** the Church's official prayer
2. saints	**b.** a journey to a holy place
3. quiet prayer	**c.** talking and listening to God
4. Liturgy of the Hours	**d.** to treat as holy
5. liturgical prayer	**e.** pray with us to the Father
6. hallow	**f.** "the little Gospel"
7. petition	**g.** meditating on Scripture
8. novena	**h.** solemn prayer of request
9. pilgrimage	**i.** prayed throughout the day
10. the Lord's Prayer	**j.** prayed for nine days

What Do You Think?

Imagine that you are getting ready to publish a prayer book for young people. Which prayers would you include? What intentions would you pray for? At what times during the day would you suggest people pray?

Glossary

Abba *Abba* is the word that Jesus used to teach people to call God "Father" in prayer. The word meant "Daddy" to the Jewish people. *(page 71)*

adoration Adoration is the act of worshiping or honoring God as divine. *(page 95)*

Advocate The Advocate is another name for the Holy Spirit, the Third Person of the Trinity, who helps and guides us in following Jesus. *(page 143)*

almsgiving Almsgiving is the act of giving time, money, or goods to people who are poor or in need. *(page 87)*

Ascension The Ascension was the moment when Jesus, in his resurrected body, returned to his Father in heaven. He will come again at the end of time. *(page 143)*

baptismal grace Baptismal grace is the gift of sharing in God's divine life that we receive at Baptism, which frees us from sin. *(page 15)*

Beatitudes The Beatitudes are Jesus' teachings about how to live and find real happiness in God's kingdom. They teach us to love God, love each other, seek justice, and spread peace. *(page 71)*

blasphemy Blasphemy is the act of showing contempt for God or sacred things through one's words or actions. *(page 247)*

candidate A candidate is a person who pursues and prepares for a certain role. A person who is preparing to receive the sacrament of Confirmation is called a candidate. *(page 233)*

catholic The word *catholic* means "universal." With a capital *C*, it describes the Church founded by Christ's apostles. Because it welcomes all people who believe in Jesus Christ, the Catholic Church is universal. *(page 229)*

Catholic epistles The Catholic epistles were letters written to the universal Church. These seven letters are included in the New Testament. *(page 183)*

charism A charism is a talent or gift from the Holy Spirit that an individual uses to serve the Church, live a Christian life, and work for the good of all people. *(page 229)*

chastity Chastity is a virtue that helps us express our sexuality in a mature and unselfish manner. The word *chastity* describes a state of being morally pure in thought and conduct. *(page 103)*

chrism Chrism is the perfumed oil that has been blessed by a bishop and is used for anointing in the sacraments of Baptism, Confirmation, and Holy Orders. Being anointed with chrism is a sign of receiving the Holy Spirit. *(page 233)*

commissioned To be commissioned is to be entrusted with the power to fulfill a particular task. Christ entrusted the apostles and their successors with the task of leading and serving the Church. *(page 167)*

Communion of Saints The Communion of Saints is the union of all those, both living and dead, who believe in Christ. *(page 127)*

Confirmation Confirmation is a sacrament of initiation in which we receive the special strength of the Holy Spirit and become full members of the Church. *(page 175)*

conscience A conscience is an ability to know what is right and what is wrong. *(page 23)*

consecrate To consecrate is to make sacred. The priest calls upon the Holy Spirit to consecrate the bread and wine, or change them into the Body and Blood of Christ. *(page 55)*

contemplation Contemplation is prayer without the need for images, words, or thoughts; it is resting in God's presence. *(page 31)*

covet To covet means to have an excessive desire for what rightfully belongs to someone else. *(page 249)*

diocese A diocese is a region or district whose parishes a bishop serves and oversees. *(page 227)*

disciple A disciple is a follower of Christ who carries on Christ's mission by showing others the love of God. *(page 55)*

Easter Triduum The Easter Triduum is the holiest celebration of the liturgical year. It begins on Holy Thursday evening and concludes with the evening prayer on Easter Sunday. The Triduum includes the Mass of the Lord's Supper on Holy Thursday, the remembrance of Jesus' crucifixion on Good Friday, and the celebration of Jesus' Resurrection at the Easter Vigil. *(page 135)*

epistle An epistle is a letter written to a Christian community by Saint Paul or another disciple in the early Church. Such letters are included in the New Testament. *(page 167)*

evangelist An evangelist is a person who proclaims God to the world by word of mouth, through writings, or as a living example. The word also refers to a writer of a Gospel. Matthew, Mark, Luke, and John are often called the four evangelists. *(page 183)*

evangelize To evangelize is to spread the truth of the Gospels through our words and love of others. *(page 183)*

ex nihilo *Ex nihilo* is a Latin phrase meaning "from nothing." It is used to describe how God created the universe. *(page 225)*

exposition Exposition is a manner of honoring the Blessed Sacrament by placing it in view of worshipers for adoration. *(page 95)*

Extreme Unction *Extreme Unction*, or "last anointing," is another term for the sacrament of the Anointing of the Sick. *(page 237)*

fortitude Fortitude, a moral virtue, is the courage to do what is right. *(pages 87 and 241)*

gifts of the Holy Spirit The gifts of the Holy Spirit are the seven special gifts or blessings that enable us to become more Christlike: wisdom, understanding, knowledge, right judgment, courage, reverence, and wonder and awe. *(page 175)*

grace Grace, a gift that God freely gives us, is God's life within us, which fills us with his love and enables us to live according to his will. *(page 63)*

hallow To hallow is to venerate, honor, or treat as holy. *(page 255)*

holy oil Holy oil is oil blessed by the bishop and used in the Anointing of the Sick and other sacraments. *(page 111)*

Holy Week Holy Week is the week that begins on Palm Sunday of the Lord's Passion. It includes the final days of Lent, as well as Holy Thursday, Good Friday, and Holy Saturday. During this week, we remember in a special way the events that are at the center of our lives as Christians: the Passion, death, and Resurrection of Christ. *(page 135)*

Incarnation The Incarnation is God's Son becoming man, one like us, Jesus Christ, who is both human and divine. *(page 7)*

indomitable *Indomitable* means "unable to be conquered." *(page 191)*

indulgence An indulgence is the removal of all or some of the punishments that we must suffer in purgatory for the effects of our sins on earth. *(page 231)*

intercession An intercession is a prayer that we say on behalf of others in need of God's help. *(page 111)*

justice Justice, a moral virtue, is the practice of treating others fairly. *(pages 87 and 241)*

justification Justification is God's act of freely forgiving our sins and giving us the grace we need to become holy and Christlike. *(page 243)*

kingdom of God The kingdom of God is God's reign of peace, justice, and love, initiated on earth by Jesus and reaching perfect fulfillment at the end of time. *(page 47)*

life everlasting Life everlasting is the life that Jesus' faithful followers will share for all eternity. *(page 127)*

liturgical cycle The liturgical cycle is the recurring calendar of church celebrations and seasons honoring the Paschal mystery throughout the year. *(page 235)*

Lord's Day The Lord's Day is another name for our Sabbath, or day of rest in honor of God. We celebrate Mass on the Lord's Day. *(page 235)*

Magisterium The pope, in communion with the bishops, is the teaching authority, or Magisterium, of the Church. *(page 103)*

meditation Meditation is a type of prayer in which we are silent and concentrate on listening to God through our feelings, imagination, and thoughts. Meditation is thinking about God's presence in our lives. *(page 31)*

Messiah *Messiah* means "God's anointed one" or "savior." A messiah is a person chosen to save people from a particular fate. Jesus is the Messiah, the One promised to deliver all people from sin. *(page 7)*

miracle A miracle is a wondrous sign or event that can only have happened through the power of God. *(page 111)*

missioner A missioner is a person who shares his or her faith through preaching and charitable works. Missioners of the Church preach Christ's message of salvation to all people. *(page 167)*

monstrance A monstrance is a special container in which the Eucharist is placed for adoration. *(page 95)*

morality Morality is a system of rules for good conduct based on our beliefs. Christian morality includes keeping the commandments in response to God's love. *(page 103)*

moral virtues The moral virtues are four spiritual qualities—temperance, prudence, justice, and fortitude—that we receive through the Holy Spirit. They help us avoid sin. *(page 87)*

mortal sin A mortal sin is a serious act against God's law, done purposely. It separates us from God's grace. It normally requires the sacrament of Reconciliation to be forgiven. *(page 23)*

Mosaic Law The Mosaic Law, or Law of Moses, sets forth rules and practices that Jewish people have followed from the time of Moses, for whom the Law is named. The Ten Commandments, the basis of Mosaic Law, are found in the Bible, in Exodus 20 and Deuteronomy 5:6–21. The Book of Leviticus contains further details of the Law. *(pages 152 and 245)*

novena A novena is a Catholic devotion in which specific prayers are said on nine consecutive days. *(page 253)*

oral tradition Oral tradition is a body of stories that has been passed down by word of mouth. In ancient Israel, before the Gospels were written, people told stories about God and all he did for them. *(page 7)*

original sin Original sin is the sin of the first man and woman, which has been passed on to all human beings. Because of it, we are weakened in our ability to resist sin and do good. *(page 225)*

papal infallibility Papal infallibility is the doctrine that when the pope speaks officially for the Church on a matter of faith or morals, he is guided by the Holy Spirit and what he says is free from error. *(page 227)*

parable A parable is a story that teaches a moral or religious lesson. Parables often use everyday events and objects to explain important truths. *(page 47)*

particular judgment At the end of our lives, Jesus Christ judges how well we have followed him. Particular judgment is the judgment each individual receives from Christ at his or her death. *(page 231)*

Paschal mystery The Paschal mystery is God's plan for our salvation through the Passion, death, Resurrection, and Ascension of Jesus. The Church celebrates the Paschal mystery in the liturgy throughout the year, but in a special way during the Easter Triduum. *(page 135)*

Passion Jesus' Passion is the suffering, crucifixion, and death he endured for our sins. *(page 127)*

Penance Penance is another name for the sacrament of Reconciliation. With a lowercase *p*, it refers to a prayer or kind act that we do as an expression of sorrow for our sins. *(page 55)*

Pentecost Pentecost is the day on which Jesus Christ's disciples received the gift of the Holy Spirit, which empowered them to proclaim the good news. Pentecost is often referred to as "the day the Church was born." *(page 151)*

perjury Perjury is the act of lying after having made an oath to tell the truth, with God as one's witness. *(page 247)*

petition A petition is a solemn prayer of request. *(page 255)*

Pharisees Pharisees were Jewish people who accepted the written laws of the Old Testament and tradition (the spoken teachings of religious leaders). *(page 63)*

pilgrimage A pilgrimage is a journey to a holy place or sacred site for spiritual or devotional reasons. *(page 253)*

plagiarism Plagiarism is the use of someone's ideas or works as if they were one's own. *(page 249)*

polygamy Polygamy is the state of having several marriage partners at the same time. *(page 239)*

preferential option for the poor The preferential option for the poor is an understanding that we must give priority to the needs of the poor and vulnerable in society. *(page 251)*

presbyter In the Church today, the term *presbyter* means "priest." In the early Church, presbyters were the appointed religious leaders, or elders, of the early Christian communities. *(page 239)*

prudence Prudence, a moral virtue, is the habit of making good judgments and decisions. *(pages 87 and 241)*

purgatory Purgatory is a final purification from sin after death. *(page 231)*

Resurrection The Resurrection is Jesus' victory over death as he rose to new life. On the last day there will be a resurrection of our bodies as we rise to new life with Christ. *(page 127)*

revelation Revelation is God's act of revealing himself and inviting us to respond with faith. A revelation is also an important truth about God, expressed under the inspiration and guidance of the Holy Spirit. *(page 71)*

sacramental A sacramental is a symbolic prayer, blessing, object, or action instituted by the Church that can lead us to a fuller participation in the grace of the sacraments. *(page 233)*

Sacred Scriptures The term *Sacred Scriptures* refers to the Old and New Testaments of the Bible, which have been accepted by the Catholic Church as the word of God written under the inspiration of the Holy Spirit. *(page 223)*

salvation Salvation is freedom from the pain of sin and assurance of permanent union with God. *(page 15)*

sanctification Sanctification is the act of making or of being made holy. *(page 63)*

solidarity Solidarity is the unity we share with all our brothers and sisters, who are made in the image of God. *(page 183)*

temperance Temperance, a moral virtue, is the habit of living in moderation and controlling our desires. *(pages 87 and 241)*

temptation Temptation is an enticement or a pressure to turn away from God through sinful thoughts, words, or actions. *(page 31)*

theological virtues The theological virtues are three spiritual qualities—faith, hope, and charity—that come from God and help us become more holy. *(page 87)*

Tradition Tradition is the body of official teachings, rituals, customs, and practices of the Church that have developed under the guidance of the Holy Spirit and are handed down from the apostles. *(page 223)*

trespass *Trespass* means "to commit a sin." *(page 71)*

Trinity The Trinity is the three Persons of God: the Father, the Son, and the Holy Spirit. We believe that there is only one God, who is revealed to us in these three divine Persons. *(page 151)*

venial sin A venial sin is less serious than a mortal sin. Venial sins weaken our relationship with God and the church community. *(page 23)*

viaticum *Viaticum*, which means "provision for the journey" in Latin, is Holy Communion that is given to a dying person. *(page 237)*

virtue A virtue is an ability to make morally good decisions that lead to the habit of doing good. Christian virtues are considered gifts from God that we can develop into habits of Christian living. *(page 87)*

war crimes War crimes are acts of violence against innocent people during wartime. *(page 251)*

witness Witness is an attesting to the truth of something by words or actions. We give witness to Christ by imitating in our everyday lives what Jesus would say or do. *(page 175)*

CATHOLIC PRAYERS

The Lord's Prayer

Our Father, who art in heaven,
    hallowed be thy name;
thy kingdom come;
thy will be done on earth
    as it is in heaven.
Give us this day our daily bread;
and forgive us our trespasses
    as we forgive those
    who trespass against us;
and lead us not into temptation,
    but deliver us from evil.
              Amen.

Act of Contrition

My God,
I am sorry for my sins with all my heart.
In choosing to do wrong
and failing to do good,
I have sinned against you
whom I should love above all things.
I firmly intend, with your help,
to do penance,
to sin no more,
and to avoid whatever leads me to sin.
Our Savior Jesus Christ
suffered and died for us.
In his name, my God, have mercy.

Rite of Penance

Hail Mary

Hail Mary, full of grace,
    the Lord is with you.
Blessed are you among women,
    and blessed is the fruit
    of your womb, Jesus.
Holy Mary, Mother of God,
    pray for us sinners, now,
    and at the hour of our death.
              Amen.

Glory Be to the Father

Glory be to the Father,
    and to the Son,
    and to the Holy Spirit.
As it was in the beginning,
is now, and will be forever.
              Amen.

Nicene Creed

We believe in one God,
    the Father, the Almighty,
    maker of heaven and earth,
    of all that is seen and unseen.

We believe in one Lord, Jesus Christ,
    the only Son of God,
    eternally begotten of the Father,
    God from God, Light from Light,
    true God from true God,
    begotten, not made, one in Being with the Father.
    Through him all things were made.
    For us men and for our salvation
        he came down from heaven:

By the power of the Holy Spirit
    he was born of the Virgin Mary, and became man.

For our sake he was crucified under Pontius Pilate;
    he suffered, died, and was buried.
    On the third day he rose again
        in fulfillment of the Scriptures;
    he ascended into heaven
        and is seated at the right hand of the Father.

He will come again in glory to judge the living and the dead,
    and his kingdom will have no end.

We believe in the Holy Spirit, the Lord, the giver of life,
    who proceeds from the Father and the Son.
    With the Father and the Son he is worshiped and glorified.
    He has spoken through the Prophets.
    We believe in one holy catholic and apostolic Church.
    We acknowledge one baptism for the forgiveness of sins.
    We look for the resurrection of the dead,
        and the life of the world to come.

Amen.

Prayer to the Holy Spirit

Come, Holy Spirit,
    fill the hearts of your faithful
    and kindle in them
    the fire of your love.
Send forth your Spirit,
    and they shall be created;
    and you will renew
    the face of the earth.
                        Amen.

Hail Holy Queen

Hail Holy Queen,
    Mother of Mercy;
our life, our sweetness, and our hope!
To you do we cry,
poor banished children of Eve;
to you do we send up our sighs,
mourning and weeping
    in this vale of tears.
    Turn, then, most gracious advocate,
your eyes of mercy toward us;
and after this exile,
show to us
    the blessed fruit of your womb, Jesus.
O clement, O loving, O sweet Virgin Mary!
                        Amen.

Saint Patrick's Breastplate

Christ, be with me, Christ before me,
    Christ behind me, Christ within me,
Christ beneath me, Christ above me,
    Christ on my right, Christ on my left,
Christ where I lie, Christ where I sit,
    Christ where I arise.
Christ in the heart of everyone who thinks of me,
    Christ in the mouth of everyone who
        speaks to me,
Christ in the eye of everyone who sees me,
    Christ in the ear of everyone who hears me.
                        Amen.

Vocation Prayer

Lord, show me how to be of service,
    in your Church and in the world.
Help me see what you want me to do.
Give me vision, courage, and friends
    who encourage me to do your work.
                        Amen.

Grace Before Meals

Bless us, O Lord, and these your gifts,
    which we are about to receive
    from your goodness,
    through Christ our Lord.
                        Amen.

Index

overcoming difficulties in, 31
principles of, 253
quiet, 254
of Saint Francis, 90, 130
vocal, 254
Precepts of the Church, 250
Preferential option for the poor, 251, 252
Presbyter, 239
Priests, 54, 167, 228, 239, 240
responsibility of, in hearing confession, 55, 144
role of, in Church, 55
Private devotions, 254
Prudence, 87, 241, 242
Psalm 23, 34
Purgatory, 136, 231, 232

Q

Quiet prayer, 254

R

Reconciliation, 55, 135, 231, 238. *See also* Penance.
sacrament of, 55, 135, 136, 144, 231, 238, 244
Religious vows, 167
Resurrection, 127, 168, 232
of Jesus Christ, x, xii, xiii, 127, 128, 135, 142–143, 168, 212, 231
Revelation, xvii, 191, 192, 223–224
Book of, xiii, xvii, xviii, 190, 191
Rite of Election, 208
Romans, in Jesus' time, xv
Rosary, 254

S

Sabbath, 248
Sacramental, 233
Sacraments, 14–15, 54–56, 173–176, 177, 178, 208, 233–234, 237–238, 239–240
of healing, 237–238. *See also* Anointing of the Sick, Reconciliation.
of initiation 233–234. *See also* Baptism, Confirmation, Eucharist.
at the service of communion, 54–56, 239–240. *See also* Holy Orders, Matrimony.
Sacred Scriptures, 223, 224. *See also* Bible.
Saint Patrick's Breastplate, 266

Saint
Elizabeth Ann Seton, 168
Francis of Assisi, 88, 130
Joan of Arc, 128
John the Apostle, 136
John the Baptizer, 6, 7
Josephine Bakhita, 16
Paul, 96, 174
Paul Miki, 144
Peter the Apostle, xv, 66, 72, 136, 167, 218, 239
Pio of Pietrelcina, 112, 113
Stephen (martyr), 96
Salvation, 14, 15, 127, 128, 130, 133–136, 226, 233
Samaritans, 63
Sanctification, 63, 226
Saul. *See* Paul.
Scribes, in Jesus' time, xiv
Scriptures. *See* Sacred Scriptures.
Scrutinies, for catechumens, 208
Sea of Galilee, xv
Second Coming, xiii, 168
Second Scrutiny, 208
Self-sacrifice, 209
Sermon on the Mount, 70–71, 76, 245
Shepherds, 7
Sign of the Cross, 254
Simeon, 15
Sin, 7, 243
mortal, 23, 135, 243
original, 144, 225, 226
venial, 23, 243
Snyder, Makenzie, 85
Social justice, 35–36, 75–76, 115–116, 155–156, 195–196, 251–252
Solidarity, 183
Stations of the Cross, 130
Stealing, 104, 250
Stephen, Saint (martyr), 96
Sweatshops, 195–196

T

Temperance, 87, 241, 242
Temple, 81
Temptation, 30, 31, 71, 256
of Jesus, 30, 31
Ten Commandments, 63, 103, 104, 152, 247–250
eighth of, 250
fifth of, 249
first and second of, 24, 247
fourth of, 248
ninth of, 250

seventh of, 104, 249
sixth of, 249
tenth of, 250
third of, 248
Theological virtues, 87. *See also* Charity, Faith, Hope.
Tradition, vi, x, 223, 224, 253
Transfiguration, 72
Transubstantiation, 235
Trespass, 71
Trinity, 7, 21–25, 87, 151, 225–226, 227
Trust, 109
Truth, Sojourner, 184

U

Unfair labor, 195, 196

V

Vanier, Jean, 220
Veni Sancte Spiritus ("Come, Holy Spirit"), 154
Venial sin, 23, 243
Viaticum, 237, 238
Virtues, 87, 242. *See also* Moral virtues, Theological virtues.
Vocal prayer, 112, 254
Vocation, 47, 53, 54, 55, 56
Vocation Prayer, 266

W

War, 252
War crimes, 251, 252
Washing of feet, on Holy Thursday, 209
Water, 101
in Baptism, 14, 211
in Bible, 14
in Jesus' time, xiv
as symbol, 211
Way of the Cross. *See* Stations of the Cross.
Wedding feast at Cana, 216
Weddings, in Jesus' time, xiv
Western Wall, 81
White garment, in Baptism, 14
Witness, 175
Women,
in Bible, 8
in Jesus' time, xiv, xv

Z

Zechariah, 6